PSALMS AND THE TRANSFORMATION OF STRESS

Louvain Theological and Pastoral Monographs is a publishing venture whose purpose is to provide those involved in pastoral ministry throughout the world with studies inspired by Louvain's long tradition of theological excellence within the Roman Catholic tradition. The volumes selected for publication in the series are expected to express some of today's finest reflection on current theology and pastoral practice.

LOUVAIN THEOLOGICAL & PASTORAL MONOGRAPHS
16

PSALMS AND THE TRANSFORMATION OF STRESS

POETIC-COMMUNAL INTERPRETATION AND THE FAMILY

by Dennis Sylva

PEETERS PRESS
LOUVAIN
W.B. EERDMANS

On Cover: *Quiet Talk* by Dennis Smith. Photograph by Gary Kabrick.

ISBN 90-6831-634-6
D. 1993/0602/96

TABLE OF CONTENTS

PART I

THE PERSPECTIVES AND THE METHODS

Chapter

PART II

TRUST, SECURITY AND RELATIONSHIPS

PART III

THE BASIS OF TRUST

PSALMS OF GOD'S STEADFAST LOVE (ḤESEḎ) AND FAITHFULNESS ('ĔMEṮ)

PART IV

SUSTAINING HEALTHY RELATIONSHIPS

ABBREVIATIONS

AB	Anchor Bible
AJSL	*American Journal of Semitic Languages and Literatures*
ASTI	*Annual Swedish Theological Institute*
BAGD	W. Bauer, W.F. Arndt, F.W. Gingrich and F.W. Danker, *A Greek-English Lexicon of the New Testament and Other Early Christian Literature*. 2nd ed., rev. and enl. Chicago: U. of Chicago, 1979.
BDB	F. Brown, S.R. Driver, C.A. Briggs, *A Hebrew and English Lexicon of the Old Testament*. Oxford: Clarendon, 1978.
BHK[3]	*Biblia Hebraica*
BHS	*Biblia Hebraica Stuttgartensia*
Bib	*Biblica*
BKAT	Biblischer Kommentar zum Altes Testament
BN	*Biblische Notizen*
BT	Bible Translator
BVC	*Bible et Vie Chrétienne*
BWANT	Beiträge zur Wissenschaft vom Alten und Neuen Testament
BWAT	Beiträge zur Wissenschaft vom Alten Testament
BZAW	Beihefte Zeitschrift für die alttestamentliche Wissenschaft
CBQ	*Catholic Biblical Quarterly*
CBQMS	Catholic Biblical Quarterly Monograph Series
CD	*Child Development*
FOTL	Forms of Old Testament Literature
FRLANT	Forschungen zur Religion und Literatur des Alten und Neuen Testaments
FZTP	*Freiburger Zeitschrift für Philosophie und Theologie*
GKC	E. Kautzsch and A. Cowley, *Gesenius' Hebrew Grammar*. 2nd English ed. Oxford: Clarendon, 1910.
GNS	Good News Studies
HAL	W.L. Holladay, *A Concise Hebrew and Aramaic Lexicon of the Old Testament*. Leiden: E.J. Brill, 1988.
HJ	*Heythrop Journal*
HSM	Harvard Semitic Monographs
ICC	International Critical Commentary
Int	*Intrepretation*
JB	Jerusalem Bible
JBL	*Journal of Biblical Literature*
JCP	*Journal of Communal Psychology*

JNSL	*Journal of the Northwest Semitic Languages*
JQR	*Jewish Quarterly Review*
JR	*Journal of Religion*
JSOT	*Journal for the Study of the Old Testament*
JSOTSS	Journal for the Study of the Old Testament Supplement Series
KB	L. Koehler and W. Baumgartner, *Lexicon in Veteris Testamenti Libros*. Leiden: Brill, 1958.
LCBI	*Literary Currents in Biblical Interpretation*
LS	*Louvain Studies*
LXX	The Septuagint
MT	Massoretic Text
NAB	New American Bible
NCB	New Century Bible
NCL	Nouveau classiques Larousse
NIGTC	*New International Greek Testament Commentaries*
NT	New Testament
NTM	New Testament Message
OBT	Overtures to Biblical Theology
OT	Old Testament
OTL	Old Testament Library
OTM	Old Testament Message
PC	Proclamation Commentaries
PR	*Psychological Reports*
RNS	Recherches nouveaux ser
RSV	Revised Standard Version
SBLDS	Society of Biblical Literature Dissertation Series
SBLMS	Society of Biblical Literature Monograph Series
SBT	Studies in Biblical Theology
UF	*Ugarit Forschungen*
VT	*Vetus Testamentum*
WBC	Word Biblical Commentary
WMANT	Wissenschaftliche Monographien zum Alten und Neuen Testament
ZAW	*Zeitschrift für die alttestamentliche Wissenschaft*
ZTK	*Zeitschrift für Theologie und Kirche*

A TABLE OF TRANSLITERATED HEBREW

Consonants

ʾ is pronounced like the h in the word "honest." It is often not pronounced because of the difficulty of pronouncing it.
b = b as in "bed"
ḇ = v as in "vat"
g = g as in "go"
g̱ = g as in "go"
d = d as in "day"
ḏ = a hard th as in the word "the"
h = h as in "he"
w = w as in "wet"
z = z as in "zoo"
ḥ = ch as in the name "Bach"
ṭ = t as in "time"
y = y as in "yes"
k = k as in "king"
ḵ = ch as in the Scottish word, "loch"
l = l as in "let"
m = m as in "moon"
n = n as in "now"
s = s as in "sing"
ʿ = do not pronounce
p = p as in "pet"
p̱ = f as in "fog"
ṣ = ts as in "kits"
q = ch as in the Scottish word, "loch"
r = r as in "red"
ś = s as in "set"
š = s as in "she"
t = t as in "time"
ṯ = t as in "think"

Vowels

a = a as in "that"
ā = a as in "father"
î = i as in "machine"
i = i as in "fit"
ê or ē = ey as in "they"
e = e as in "get"
û = oo as in "cool"
u = u as in "bull"
ô or ō = o as in "bone"
o = o as in "hop"
ĕ = the quick sound like the first e in the word "because"
ă = a rapid short a sound

PREFACE

This is a critical, biblical study; I have attempted, however, to write this book in such a way that pastoral theologians, pastors and parents may benefit from it. Scholarly jargon has been reduced to a minimum and, where used, it is explained. Most of the technical minutiae have been placed in discrete sections on textual considerations (in the individual chapters) or in footnotes. These parts may be skipped without missing the central line of thought. References to the Massoretic Text are followed by the word "Hebrew" in parentheses to clearly indicate that I am referring to a type of Hebrew text of the Psalms.

This study is not about meter in biblical poetry, although in chapter two this issue will be treated as it pertains to my methods of interpretation. It is about the larger rhythms of tensions which the psalmists experienced and about God's care which they discerned. It is also about how these stresses are experienced in the family today and how the psalmists' discoveries can strengthen the family's response to them.

At the beginning of the book there is a table which shows one how to pronounce the letters which are used to transliterate the Hebrew letters. This enables the reader to correctly pronounce key Hebrew words which are found in the psalms.

The verse numbers of the New Revised Standard Version (NRSV) and the Hebrew text of the psalms often differ because in the Hebrew text the superscriptions to the psalms are considered to be either the first verse or part of the first verse of the psalms. This is not the case in the NRSV. I use the verse numbers as they appear in the NRSV.

I am very grateful for the assistance provided by a number of friends. John Schmitt, Bishop Richard Sklba and Sr. Mary Roy McDonald read the manuscript carefully. Their suggestions have resulted in a number of improvements. I also appreciate the work of the following colleagues and students who read a draft of this manuscript and commented on matters of consistency and style: Myrna Schultz, Agnes Rosenau, Kevin Kowalske, Stephen Price, Lucille Contorno, Marmion Walsh, Cathy Labinski, Martha Van Duser, Sibyl Grandeck, Stephen Lampe, Barbara Turner, David Sanders, Mary Utzerath and Alice Jerskey.

Gregory Greiten and Paul Hudec were very generous in providing me with computer assistance, as was Debbie Janczak who also helped both in formatting this manuscript and in typing large segments of it with carefulness, industry and persistence. Cari Rutkowski, Fran Wilson and Marelene Groff also ably aided me in typing or copying as the project progressed.

The librarians at Saint Francis Seminary and those of the Memorial Library at Marquette University provided bibliographical assistance, and Noel McFerran, Colleen Koll and Pat Schweizer always managed to obtain the book or article which I needed.

Conversations with Terrance Merrigan, Daryl Olszewski, Mary Kay Balchunas, Kevin Kowalske and Michael Savio helped refine my ideas for the title of this book. Marmion Walsh, Michael Witczak, Anne Reissner and Arthur G. Heinze provided encouragement as the project progressed.

Robert Wild, S.J., Frederick Schlatter, S.J., Bernard Tyrrell, S.J., Richard Edwards, J. Coert Rylaarsdam and Thomas Caldwell, S.J. have helped and challenged me through the years. I owe much to their sage counsel and criticism, and this book could undoubtedly have been improved by more attention to their instruction and example.

I am very grateful to the Reverend Raymond Collins for his acceptance of this manuscript for the Louvain Theological and Pastoral Monographs series, for his skillful editing, and for his encouragement. I have appreciated this opportunity to work with a scholar who has made many significant contributions to the field of biblical studies.

Professor Terrence Merrigan inherited the editing responsibilities of this work. Industriously and graciously, he guided the manuscript to publication. Mr. Paul Peeters and his expert staff were helpful and thorough in their work.

I owe the greatest expression of thanks to my wife and son. The concreteness of this book is the result of our shared life: one that has been nurtured by my wife, Mary Ann. It is to her that this book is dedicated.

To Mary Ann
with love

PART I

THE PERSPECTIVES AND THE METHODS

CHAPTER 1

INTRODUCTION

Communal Interpretation

This book explores the topic of what types of family relations foster children's emotional and social health and growth. It does so by correlating behavioral science and literary perspectives on the needs of children with psalmic insights which empower parents to meet these needs.[1] This type of correlation is not only a good way to do pastoral theology, but it is also a way to sensitize interpreters to important dimensions of the biblical message.

A common thread running through the various oral and written strands that went into the composition of the Old Testament is the concern for the religious life of the community. The ways in which different biblical traditions present this religious life may be

[1] For a similar type of correlation of insights from psychoanalytic psychology with Christian theology see D. Martyn, *The Man in the Yellow Hat: Theology and Psychoanalysis in Child Therapy* (Decatur: Scholars, 1992). By way of contrast, the dominant model of correlating these two disciplines has been to view psychic needs as giving rise to religious concepts and correspondingly to look at a religious text from the perspective of a psychological or psychosocial phenomenon to which it witnesses. See, e.g., R. Carroll, *When Prophecy Failed* (New York: Seabury, 1979).

In the final analysis it is up to the reader to determine if the model does justice to his or her experience, or, more precisely, to what degree it is illuminative of it. A model is useful only to a certain degree. While the judgment does rest with the reader it is incumbent on the one who proffers such contemporary understandings to choose responsibly from the plethora of theories that exist in a given discipline. One should do a wide-ranging search of the writings of the exponents of a theory, as well as, to a reasonable degree, its reception among other scholars in the same discipline. These measures can guard against the acceptance of schema which have not commanded respect from experts in the discipline.

disputed, but the pastoral concern to nurture it is a strong impetus to these writings and one which is reflected in them. To discern how the texts function to exhort and admonish is to appropriate critical aspects of our biblical heritage.

Put another way, the OT traditions do not systematize or uncover the past for its own sake; rather, they explore the traditions of the past in the light of God's activity in the present. Their function is to help people participate in the God-filled present. Thus, the relation between pastoral theology and biblical studies is not that of debtor to creditor. The fund of information between the two flows both ways and enriches both disciplines.

In seeking to understand meanings of the biblical texts,[2] a biblical scholar will utilize the critical methods and language skills in which he or she has been trained. In the process, the interpreter does well to remember that faith is never formulated, tried or refined in a vacuum, but rather in the trials, struggles and joys of day to day living. Thus, the biblical scholar does well to be immersed both in the ancient text and in the present experience of ecclesial communities. This will sensitize the exegete to the realities behind the Scriptures: the realities to which the Scriptures respond.[3]

The contemporary focus of this study is the family, and more specifically the problem of how stress vitiates parenting. The textual focus is a group of seven psalms which, in one way or another, function as stress relievers. The perception of the dynamics of each discloses dimensions of the text and opens up family experience to the possibility of textual and existential transformation: change effected by the text and in the experience of the family.

[2] Just precisely where such meaning is located – in the author, the text, the reader, in between them or in a combination of them – is moot.

[3] This is not to say that, at any time, one's community is experiencing precisely the same needs which a biblical community experienced. Communities confront, however, the same types of problems from generation to generation and from culture to culture. The basic human needs remain the same; what changes is the ways these needs are expressed and the ways in which different generations or cultures seek to respond to these needs.

Robert Alter has noted correctly that "a particular poetics may encourage or reinforce a particular orientation toward reality. For all the untold reams of commentary on the Bible, this remains a sadly neglected question."[4] Similarly, Harold Fisch has argued that biblical poetry is designed to establish the relationship between God and the people.[5] I contend that the poetics of the seven psalms which I treat both encourage and strengthen trust and peace in situations which evoke stress and anxiety. This study is a step in considering psalmic poetics and the life-orientations which they call forth and support.

In this context, I should note that I take seriously the rhetorical-critical concern to pay attention to the literary artistry of the text. Often it seems like a number of different parts of the Scriptures are conveying the same message. We must be sensitive to the way in which different sections articulate their message for at least two reasons. First, different types of expression nuance an idea in different ways. The "message" of a section is inextricably bound up with the literary medium from which it receives hues and tones which may not be found in some other passages which deal with the same basic idea.

Second, different types of expression affect people in different ways. Someone may not respond to a certain person's advice to do something, but will respond to another's recommendation to do the same thing. While there are many reasons why this may be the case, at times part of the reason is the different way in which the advice was expressed. Thus, to ignore the rich, literary artistry of different sections of Scripture which are supposedly saying the same thing is to run the risk of not broadcasting the type of formulation that may be helpful to someone.[6]

[4] R. Alter, *The World of Biblical Literature* (New York: Basic, 1992) 185.

[5] H. Fisch, *Poetry with a Purpose: Biblical Literature and Interpretation* (ISBL; Bloomington, IN: Indiana U., 1990).

[6] In *Beyond the Written Word: Oral Aspects of Scripture in the History of Religion* (New York: Cambridge University Press, 1987) 110-115, 163-165, W. Graham suggested the study of "the sensual meaning" of religions, "the affective role of texts in everyday life" as essential to understanding any religion's scriptures or

This is what I call the exhortatory function of Scripture. These writings were intended to be faith statements shared with the community. They were meant to motivate and to encourage. Attention to the specific way in which each text is formulated opens up a world of exhortation in diverse aspects of the life of faith. At times people are unable to appreciate the significance of a certain formulation, and therefore it does not become helpful to them. Attention to the literary artistry shows dimensions of the passage's formulation which may have been unclear or which may have been overlooked.[7] The rhetorical critic should stand at the service of an appreciative and an incorporative meeting between the reader/listener and the Scriptural passage. By an "incorporative meeting" I mean one in which the person can appropriate into his/her perspective the nuanced ideas offered by the passage.[8]

traditions. I have independently come to the same conclusion with regard to the Judeo-Christian scriptures for reasons which I will presently articulate.

[7] Pastoral theologians such as D. Capps, *Biblical Approaches to Pastoral Counseling* (Philadelphia: Westminster, 1981), and W. Oglesby, Jr., *Biblical Themes for Pastoral Care* (Nashville, TN: Abingdon, 1980), have looked respectively at biblical forms and biblical themes to inform their reflections on pastoral care. Such approaches attempt to discern what certain biblical passages have in common with other biblical passages. This is a study of what is unique about seven psalms: the literary art of each psalm.

D. Capps, *The Poet's Gift: Toward the Renewal of Pastoral Care* (Philadelphia: Westminster/John Knox, 1993), has looked at the poetry of William Stafford and Adrienne Rich to inform pastoral care.

[8] Scholars such as W. Brueggemann and P. Miller, among others, should be noted as exhibiting a concern to appreciate the psalms in the original matrices of their formation and in their significance for people today. See, e.g., W. Brueggemann, *Israel's Praise: Doxology against Idolatry and Ideology* (Philadelphia: Fortress, 1988); Idem, "From Hurt to Joy, From Death to Life," *Int* 28 (1974) 3-19; Idem, "Psalms and the Life of Faith: A Suggested Typology of Function," *JSOT* 17 (1980) 3-32; P. Miller, *Interpreting the Psalms* (Philadelphia: Fortress, 1986).

Brueggemann, *Israel's Praise* notes that literature is a world-making production. The focus of this study is on the worlds of meaning created in the psalms and on how they can help us with the worlds of meaning which we create in our families. The goal is to encounter these "classic texts" in such a way as to be open to the possibility of personal and familial transformation.

A New Metalanguage for Biblical Poetics

A metalanguage is a language used to attempt to explain another language. Literary criticism is a metalanguage for literature. The 1980's witnessed the development of a new metalanguage for Biblical poetry. While parallelism is still recognized as a crucial feature in this corpus, it is seen increasingly as the constant, structuring element in larger patterns of sameness and difference by which biblical poetry is formed. The new organizing principle is this larger pattern, itself.

This new poetics is discussed in the following chapter. The perspectives from this investigation – as well as the concern of a still larger metapoetics encompassing what Alter has called the "orientation toward reality"[9] – guide the interpretation of selected psalms in subsequent chapters.[10]

Stress and the Family

Stress, "the bodily or mental tension resulting from factors that tend to alter an existent equilibrium,"[11] is frequently the underlying source of dysfunction in families. It can be caused by unresolved difficulties from the past, by taxing situations in the present or by anxieties about the future, but no matter what the cause its

[9] *The World of Biblical Literature*, 185.

[10] The goal, in the words of Frederic Jameson, is to respect "the specificity and radical difference of the social and cultural past while disclosing the solidarity of its polemics and passions, its forms, structures, experiences, and struggles, with those of the present day." See *The Political Unconscious: Narrative as a Socially Symbolic Act* (Ithaca, NY: Cornell University Press, 1981) 18. Contrary to Jameson, however, it is not only a Marxist philosophy of history that offers the basis for such an endeavor (pp. 18-19). A sensitivity both to the biblical poetics and to the experiences of present day communities which were formed within the biblical interpretive matrix sensitizes one to the specificity of the psalmic texts and to the solidarity between them and the present day experiences of ecclesial communities.

[11] *Webster's Ninth New Collegiate Dictionary* (Springfield, MA: Merriam-Webster, 1991) 1166.

effects on the family are often invasive and invidious. It is catching: stress experienced by one member of the family is easily passed to others in the family by means of the new type of relationship which stress establishes. It is transferred from word to word, from look to look.

There is no insulation from the numerous events that can cause stress, but there are ways to manage it so that it does not overwhelm the family. The purpose of this book is to provide resources from our biblical heritage to help parents cope with stress. This accomplishment would improve the quality of the relationship between husband and wife. It would also help them to provide a nurturing home environment for their children because stress lessens parents' ability to attend to the emotional requirements of children. Emotional strength is a foundation for engaging in responsible, vivific relationships with others: only if children's emotional needs are met will they develop the capacity and the propensity for engaging in healthy relationships.

How can we live faithfully and well when there are so many events that can cause debilitating stress? In a world filled with tensions how can we make the home into a haven of emotional rest and by so doing aid the growth of children into caring, sociable members of a community? These are the types of questions which this book addresses.

As we will see, the point at which a number of psychological studies and the psalms intersect is the necessity of faith for healthy relations. Psychologists have said that both parents and children must believe that certain types of care will be given to them when they need it in order for them to enter into authentic relations with others. It is this trust that alleviates the stress which hinders parents from attending to their children's needs, and this trust which gives children the confidence to enter into relationships and to continue seeking relationships when they are rebuffed. The psalms present God as the one who gives us the care which we need. They do so in ways that can strengthen the faith which allows the parent to respond wholly to the child so as to promote the child's healthy psychic and social growth.

The manner in which parents relate to their children will necessarily change as the children grow from youth to adolescence to young adulthood; there are, however, basic needs of children that cut across these stages. It is these psycho-social constants of children and the psalmic resources for loving parental responses to them that is the subject of this book.

The Psalms and Theotherapy

The composers of the psalms brought the difficulties which they encountered and the anguish which they experienced into the light cast by their religious traditions. They found in these correlations of tradition and experience the means to live trustingly and confidently rather than giving in to anxiety and despair. Their problems, if not exactly the same as ours, were the types which we too experience in numerous ways. The perspectives which they discovered are relevant and applicable to situations which we face. These perspectives are healing viewpoints of our faith heritage which constitute guidelines for a theotherapy.

The psalms are well-suited both for relieving the stress that hinders the care of children and for promoting emotional health because the psalms are literature in which the emotions of a people come to expression. What enters into the psalm is raw emotion. What emerges from the psalm is emotion guided by faith in God.[12] Christianity must reclaim the realm of the emotions as a sphere to which its message has relevance. This is so not only because of the importance of the emotions in all vital and committed living, but also because we need to be healing communities.[13]

[12] J.G. Herder, *The Spirit of Hebrew Poetry* (Burlington, VT: Edward Smith, 1933) 2:10, claimed that the images in biblical poetry were created to express emotions. A more nuanced view is given by D. Petersen & K. Richards, *Interpreting Hebrew Poetry* (GBS; Minneapolis: Fortress, 1992) 9, that such emotive theories may adequately explain certain types of Hebrew poetry. I agree, and I claim that the Psalms are one such type.

[13] A number of people working in various areas dealing with the "psychobiological constitution" of people have argued that there is often a connection between

Jesus healed the sick, and the use of *sōzein* ("to save") and *sōtēria* ("salvation") to describe Jesus' healings[14] shows the importance of healing activities for Christians.

The poetry of the psalms is particularly well-suited to touching and healing people's emotions because the psalms are primarily the expressions of human emotions guided by faith. This is important because while the psalms move in the sphere of human emotions and never leave that sphere, they bring to these emotions the underpinnings that are necessary to sustain healthful emotions over the long haul. These underpinnings are the implications of faith in God.[15]

emotional health and one's physical health or disease. See, e.g., H. Benson, *The Mind/Body Effect* (New York: Simon & Schuster, 1979); Idem, *The Relaxation Response* (New York: Morrow, 1975); R. Bergland, *The Fabric of Mind* (New York: Viking, 1986); N. Cousins, *The Healing Heart* (New York: W. Norton, 1983); Idem, *Anatomy of an Illness* (New York: W. Norton, 1979); Idem, *Head First: The Biology of Hope* (New York: Dutton, 1989); E. & K. Green, *Beyond Biofeedback* (New York: Delacorte, 1977); R. Eliot, *Stress and the Major Cardiovascular Disorders* (Mount Kisco, NY: Futura, 1979); K. Pelletier, *Mind as Healer, Mind as Slayer* (New York: Delacorte, 1977).

N. Cousins has written of the "biochemistry of the emotions," claiming that faith, hope, love, confidence, humor, creativity, great expectations and the will to live are beneficial to one's health, and that panic, stress or tension are harmful to it. See N. Cousins, *The Healing Heart*, 36, 37, 234, 235. While the various theses relating to the mind-body connection in relation to physical health are still being tested, there has been an impressive array of evidence which has led many to consider them more fully. Be this as it may, the bible has much to contribute to the emotional health of people.

[14] For example, Mark 5:34; 10:52; Luke 7:50; 8:36; 48, 50; 17:19; 18:42. See B. Throckmorton, "*Sozein*, *Soteria* in Luke-Acts," *Studia Evangelica* 1973, 517-518; N. Flanagan, "The What and How of Salvation in Luke-Acts," *Sin, Salvation and the Spirit*, ed., D. Durkin (Collegeville, MN: Liturgical Press, 1979) 204, 205.

[15] H. Fisch, *Poetry with a Purpose*, 106, 110-11, 118, 126, claimed that, in the psalms, the inner lives of people are revealed more than in any other book in the bible; however, he also said the psalmists are not content to remain in the sphere of the emotions, as are many romantic poets, but move back and forth between it and outer events. This interplay of the subjective and the intersubjective in psalmic poetry is designated "covenantal discourse" by Fisch. The psalms do not simply talk about the relationship between God and the psalmist; they do so in ways that establish this relationship.

I concur that psalmic poetry may establish and strengthen faith links to God. By saying that the psalms never leave the sphere of the emotions, I mean that it is the

This Study in the Context of the Epidemiology of Religion

This exegetical study may undergird ministry to families. How it can function in such a way can be understood more clearly by explaining my work in terms of the science which has been called the "Epidemiology of Religion."

Epidemiology is the study of the "distribution and determinants" of health, sickness and death. Social and psychosocial epidemiology are the studies of how social and social-psychological factors influence these aspects of a person or group. Jeffrey Levin and Harold Vanderpool have proposed that the words "Epidemiology of Religion" be used to designate a subdiscipline of social epidemiology which deals with how religion influences people's health status.[16]

There has been a good deal of research on how religion affects health. The results have been mixed. In part this is due to the difficulty in measuring both religiousness and well-being. The inconsistent results are also due to the lack of distinction, in many studies, among the many ways in which one's religious commitment is nourished and expressed. Precision in determining the effects of religion on health, morbidity and mortality can only be approached by determining which aspects of one's health are influenced by which aspects of one's religious life. In the process, researchers must "control for the effects of numerous social and psychological causes, including social class, marital status, resilience and life stress" which could account for differences in health status.[17]

emotional life of the psalmist that is integrated with the psalmist's faith. This integration requires the treatment of "outer events" so that a healthier correspondence between feelings and circumstances ensues.

[16] J. Levin & H. Vanderpool, "Is Frequent Religious Attendance *Really* Conducive to Better Health? Toward an Epidemiology of Religion," *Social Science and Medicine* 24 (1987) 589-600; Idem, "Religious Factors in Physical Health and the Prevention of Illness," *Religion and Prevention in Mental Health: Conceptual and Empirical Foundations*, ed. K. Pargament & K. Maton (Prevention in Human Services, 9; N.Y.: Haworth, 1991) 51.

[17] J. Levin & H. Vanderpool, "Religious Factors in Physical Health," 46-48, 51; I. Payne, A. Bergin, K. Bielema & P. Jenkins, "Review of Religion and Mental Health: Prevention and Enhancement of Psychosocial Functioning," *Religion and Prevention in Mental Health*, 11, 14.

Levin and Vanderpool have distinguished six functional components of religion.

1. Religious rules which promote healthy habits regarding tobacco, alcohol, drugs, exercise, hygiene, sex and diet.
2. Psychological effects of religious involvement.
3. Psychodynamics of religious belief systems.
4. Psychodynamics of religious rites.
5. Psychodynamics of religious faith.
6. Superempirical or supernatural influences.

My concern is with the third category: the psychodynamics of religious belief systems. By this Levin and Vanderpool mean that belief systems may encourage such qualities as "peacefulness, self-confidence, autonomy and a sense of purpose on the one hand, and guilt, depression, self-doubt and co-dependency on the other."[18]

The specific health concern which this study may benefit is the ability of people to cope with stress. Coping is the means by which "people try to understand and deal with significant personal or situational demands in their lives."[19] There are a number of distinct elements in the coping process. The first is the situations in which people find themselves. They do not only happen by chance; people also place themselves in certain situations by means of the choices which they make. These situations, however, are not good indicators of how one will cope with them. Numerous studies have shown that people cope with the same situation in different ways.

There are three other elements of the coping process. The second is one's appraisal of the situation. This includes estimations of how the situation will affect one and what resources and options are available for dealing with the situation. The third and fourth elements are the activities which one takes to cope and then the

[18] J. Levin & H. Vanderpool, "Is Religion Therapeutically Significant for Hypertension?" *Social Science and Medicine* 29 (1989) 69-78; Idem, "Religious Factors in Physical Health," 48.

[19] W. Hathaway & K. Pargament, "The Religious Dimension of Coping: Implications for Prevention and Promotion," *Religion and Prevention in Mental Health*, 67.

actual outcome of the coping process. This outcome can be looked at in terms of the physical, psychological and social results of coping.[20]

Many social factors affect the coping process by preconditioning one both to choose to live in a certain situation and to appraise and act on the situation in a particular way. Religion can be one such factor and the possibility of it exerting a strong epidemiologic influence in certain populations should not be downplayed. Just as with numerous other studies on the effects of religion on health, the results of studies on religion and coping have been mixed. Hathaway and Pargament theorize that this is the result of not distinguishing which characteristics of religion or which ways of being religious help or hinder different aspects of the coping process.[21]

This study demonstrates some of the contributions which the psychodynamics of the Christian belief system (Levin and Vanderpool's third functional component of religion) can make to the appraisal element (the second component) of the coping process. The focus is on seven psalms as part of the multifaceted and rich Christian heritage. They help us to estimate God's actions for us in diverse, difficult situations and by so doing they provide us with effective resources to deal with these problems. Hathaway and Pargament have said that faith traditions have ways of "conceptualizing stressful situations." These can function as "cognitive stress inoculations" which "mitigate the effects of potentially stressful situations."[22] The seven psalms which I treat are especially effective in this way.

The psalm which each chapter treats should be read at the beginning and at the end of my treatment of it. Hopefully, the

[20] Ibid., 67-70; See also L. Cohen, "Measurement of Coping in Stress and Health," *Issues in Research Methodology*, ed. S. Kasl & C. Cooper (New York: J. Wiley, 1987) 283-305; R. Lazarus & S. Folkman, *Stress, Appraisal and Coping* (New York: Springer, 1984).
[21] "The Religious Dimensions of Coping," 72, 73.
[22] Ibid., 83, 84. See also D. Meichenbaum & M. Jaremko, *Stress Reduction and Prevention* (New York: Plenum, 1983).

interpretation found in these chapters will help one to appreciate the theopoetics of the psalms: their symbolic and imaginative constructions which are "the essential dynamics of the heart and soul."[23] Analysis fragments the poem into a number of constituent parts and relations. The poem needs to be read again to be experienced as a whole. Scripture readings should never end with interpretation; rather, interpretation should be part of a bridge from a first reading in which much may be missed to a second reading in which the passage can be appreciated and newly experienced.[24].

[23] A. N. Wilder, *Theopoetic* (Philadelphia: Fortress, 1976) 2; Idem, *Grace Confounding: Poems* (Philadelphia: Fortress, 1972) ix.
[24] Cf. C. Broyles, *The Conflict of Faith and Experience in the Psalms: A Form-Critical and Theological Study* (JSOTSS, 52; Sheffield: JSOT, 1989) 33, 34.

Robert Frost once said "Poetry is that which is lost in translation." It is hoped that the combination of interpretation and rereading of the psalms will invalidate, or at least vitiate, the subsequent remark by Frost: "It is also what is lost in interpretation." See L. Untermeyer, *Robert Frost* (Washington, DC: Reference Department of the Library of Congress, 1964) 18.

CHAPTER 2

DEVELOPING A SENSITIVITY TO BIBLICAL POETRY

> Words – so innocent and
> powerless as they are, as
> standing in a dictionary,
> how potent for good or ill
> they become, in the hands of
> one who knows how to combine
> them!
>
> Nathaniel Hawthorne,
> *American Notebooks*

Parallelism: The Traditional View of Biblical Poetry

In 1753 Robert Lowth, in Lecture 19 of *De Sacra poesi Hebraeorum*, wrote that Hebrew poetry is characterized by three types of parallelism: synonymous, antithetical and synthetic. He claimed that synonymous and antithetical parallelism are repetitions of the same idea in different lines or half-lines. Synonymous parallelism does this by saying the same thing in a different way.

> The wicked go astray from the womb,
> they err from their birth speaking of lies
> (Ps 58:3).

Antithetical parallelism conveys the same idea by combining a positive statement and a negative statement. Prov 3:5 is an example of antithetical parallelism:

> Trust in the Lord with all your heart,
> on your own intelligence rely not.

Synthetic parallelism is found where the second line or half-line completes the thought found in the first. This has often been called a catch-all category.[1] A number of scholars do not think that the designation "parallelism" can be applied to these passages because there are clearly elements in the second part which are not paralleled in the first.[2] Although other types of parallelism have been recognized, the history of scholarship has shown a remarkable acceptance of Lowth's categories.

Parallelism and Beyond: A New View of Biblical Poetry

Three studies have called into question the static conception of much of Hebrew poetry that is implied in the synonymous and antithetical categories, that is, the idea that the same idea is expressed in two different ways in successive half-lines or lines.[3]

The first is a monograph by James Kugel. According to Kugel, the basic feature of biblical poetry is that each line has usually two and sometimes three clauses. Often clauses within a line have a common element, be it a word, phrase, "the same syntactic structure, or commonly paired concepts ('by day.../ by night...//'), or some similarity in the ideas expressed." Thus, "parallelism" is the basic feature of biblical poetry. The term "parallelism" may be misleading, however, because it may lead the reader to overlook the differences between the clauses. According to Kugel, a majority of parallelistic clauses or lines are such that the second clause or line (B) does not simply repeat the idea expressed in the first one (A) in other terms, but it also goes beyond the first clause or line to particularize, define or expand the meaning. It is this "what's more" aspect of Hebrew poetry that scholars have failed to appreciate.[4]

[1] R. Lowth, *De Sacra poesi Hebraeorum* (Oxford: Clarendon, 1753).
[2] See, e.g., D. Freedman, *Pottery, Poetry and Prophecy: Studies in Early Hebrew Poetry* (Winona Lake, IN: Eisenbrauns, 1980) 32.
[3] According to R. Alter, *The World of Biblical Literature*, 178, such restatements occur in less than a quarter of the lines of biblical poetry.
[4] J. Kugel, *The Idea of Biblical Poetry* (New Haven: Yale University, 1981) 1, 2, 7-10, 23, 29. Some of Kugel's examples are from Ps 145:10; Isa 1:3; Eccl 7:1; Prov 26:9.

As an example, let us look at Kugel's interpretation of Isa 1:3.

> An ox knows its owner;
>   and an ass its master's trough.
> Israel does not know;
>   my people do not understand.

Kugel argues for the following type of progression in this verse. An ox, though hardly "the most praiseworthy of beasts," is considered superior to an ass. An ox knows its owner, and even an ass "at least knows where to stand to be fed," but Israel does not know. There is a rhetoric of descent: moving from an ox to an ass and from knowing an owner to knowing only where to be fed. This places Israel's lack of knowledge of God at the bottom of the descent and by so doing stresses Israel's sorry state.[5]

The basic feature of biblical poetry, according to Kugel, is not parallelism or symmetry. Rather, it is the form in which clause A is followed by clause B and in which clause B is connected to but goes beyond clause A.[6] Symmetry was not the primary point for the psalmist but was present only to establish the relations between the clauses and the "what's moreness" of the B clause.[7]

While there is a connection between the two clauses, there is a "relative disjunction" between the second clause in a line and the following line. Kugel writes about instances of disjunction between lines in psalms, but notes that there is a symmetry between many lines.[8] An obvious corollary (not made by Kugel) is that there may be a "what's more" dimension not only between the clauses but also between the lines and strophes of Hebrew poetry.

[5] Ibid., 9.

[6] Actually, Kugel sees this feature in much of biblical literature that we do not traditionally designate as poetry. He prefers not to name certain parts of the bible as poetry and other parts as prose, but rather to view Hebrew literature as parts of a continuum in which certain common elements are found in varying degrees. See Kugel, *Idea of Biblical Poetry*, 59-95, esp. pp. 68-70, 85, 87, 94. For a different perspective see A. Berlin, *The Dynamics of Biblical Parallelism* (Bloomington, IN: Indiana University Press, 1985) 12-16.

[7] Kugel looks at parallelism in biblical poetry as being synthetic, rather than synonymous or antithetical. Kugel, *Idea of Biblical Poetry*, 57.

[8] Ibid., 51, 52, 55-57.

Adele Berlin also sees a "what's moreness" often in biblical poetry, although she considers Kugel's nomenclature too vague. She prefers to speak of "disambiguation" and "ambiguity," or of sameness and difference. Both are present in the parallelisms of biblical poetry.[9]

While both Kugel and Berlin see a "what's moreness" to much of biblical poetry, Kugel focuses on the two halves of the line as the locus of this "what's moreness," whereas Berlin thinks it can be present throughout the poem.

Robert Alter also sees a "forward movement" in much of Hebrew poetry.[10] Like Berlin, he sees this as occurring not only intralinearly but also interlinearly and in the larger structure of the whole poem.[11] Alter finds that in much of biblical poetry there is a movement of "consequentiality" or "intensification." By "consequentiality" Alter means that there is a temporal progression in the events written about (e.g., I ran to the well, and then I drew water). By "intensification" he means the amplification of an idea or an image to greater and greater degrees.[12] Two of Alter's examples of intensification are Num 24:4 and Job 30:10. Num 24:4 reads "who beholds visions from the Almighty,/ falls down with eyes unveiled." The vision of the first clause becomes an "ecstatic seizure" in the second clause. Job 30:10 reads "They despised me, drew away from me,/ and from my face they did not hold back their spittle." The second clause describes a "more extreme" action than does the first clause. Alter notes, however, that many psalms exhibit intricate patterns that function in other ways than to intensify or to specify the message.[13]

[9] A. Berlin, *Dynamics of Biblical Parallelism*, 2, 98, 99, 130, 135, 136, 138-140. Interestingly, Kugel and Berlin have very similar views on the "what's moreness" of Isa 1:3, although Berlin does go beyond Kugel at certain points. See Berlin, *Dynamics of Biblical Parallelism*, 97, 98.

[10] R. Alter, *The Art of Biblical Poetry* (New York: Basic Books, 1985) 9-15.

[11] Ibid., 14-26 (for interlinear developments), and 27-61 (for developments within the larger poem).

[12] Ibid., 29, 43-46, 63-65.

[13] Ibid., 84. For some other studies of biblical poetry see e.g., S. Geller, *Parallelism in Early Biblical Poetry* (Decatur, IL: Scholars, 1979); Idem, "Theory and

Thus, all three of these authors agree that biblical poetry is often characterized by a dynamic movement rather than by a static parallelism.[14] Kugel's open-ended characterization of this movement as a "what's moreness" seems preferable for my purposes than any kind of specification of the types of movement because of the great diversity of types of progression found in the Psalms: a diversity that, Alter notes, defies a simple categorization. While Kugel focuses on the clauses in the line as the locus of movement, Berlin and Alter argue that it may also occur over larger areas of the poem. My own readings of the Psalms make me appreciate the "what's moreness" as occurring intralinearly, interlinearly and throughout the poem.[15]

At this point the question which should be asked is whether or not the presence of parallel pairs in biblical poetry weakens the "what's more" hypothesis. Parallel pairs are words which are usually found together (e.g., day/night, black/white). Mitchell Dahood has claimed that there are 1,019 parallel pairs that are common to

Method in the Study of Biblical Poetry," *JQR* 73 ('82) 65-77; T. Collins, *Line Forms in Hebrew Poetry* (Rome: Pontifical Biblical Institute, 1978); D. Grossberg, *Centripetal and Centrifugal Structures in Biblical Poetry* (Atlanta: Scholars Press, 1989); M. O'Connor, *Hebrew Verse Structure* (Winona Lake, IN.: Eisenbrauns, 1980).

[14] So too P. Landy, "Poetics and Parallelism: Some Comments on James Kugel's *The Idea of Biblical Poetry*," *JSOT* 28 (1984) 61-87, pp. 64, 65. This seems to me a better approach to biblical poetry than the attempts to look for meter in these poems. The vowels and stress marks in the Massoretic Text were placed there "well over a millennium after the composition of these poems and centuries after Hebrew had ceased to be the vernacular." (R. Alter, *Art of Biblical Poetry*, 4.)

The recognition of the inadequacy of Lowth's categories was implicitly witnessed to by the proliferation of the types of parallelism which were proposed. Moves toward an explicit critique of characterizing biblical poetry in terms of the *parallelismus membrorum* came from those who noted both the freedom of the biblical poets in this regard and the numerous instances in which the rule seemed to be broken. See, e.g., N.H. Ridderbos, *Die Psalmen: Stilistische Verfahren und Aufbau mit besonderer Berücksichtigung von Ps 1-41* (BZAW, 117; Berlin/New York: De Gruyter, 1972) 11, 13. Thus, we are dealing with a historical wave which crested with the proposal of a new organizing principle for biblical poetry.

[15] See also P. Landy, "Poetics and Parallelism," 72-75. Landy argues against Kugel's view of there being a relative disjunction between the second clause of the line and the rest of the poem in the Psalms and Song of Songs.

Ugaritic and Hebrew.[16] Although the number of Hebrew parallel pairs is debatable, the problem remains: How can there be a "what's moreness" to biblical poetry if a word in the second clause simply forms the other half of a parallel pair with a word found in the first clause? Would this not indicate that the poet had no choice of words in the second clause but was governed by the convention of the parallel pair? If this is so, then is it not the case that the second term adds no new dimension to the poem but is simply a cultural given?

Of course, there is the problem of what a word pair is. How many times do two words have to appear together before they are considered to be a stock pair: once, twice, five times? Does the occurrence of two words in association with each other in both Ugaritic and Hebrew constitute such a parallel pair, as many assume? I am not arguing against the existence of this literary convention. Clearly it exists in biblical poetry. One should not assume, however, that any pair of words that appears in conjunction with each other a couple of times is a parallel pair. A certain degree of frequency is needed before this can be inferred.

What about legitimate parallel pairs? Do they argue against the "what's more" dimension of Hebrew poetry? By no means. Alter has noted that at times the normal sequence of parallel pairs is changed in biblical poetry or a new term is substituted in "ostensibly formulaic pairings."[17] These break the stereotypical aspect of the pair and can be used to convey an added dimension as the poem progresses. Kugel has argued that the parallel pairs often highlight by their fixity other elements in the line: elements which carry the meaning of the poem forward.[18] Further, it may be argued that even parallel pairs may be used in poems to move the meaning forward by means of the semantic and thematic connections which are made between them and other elements of the

[16] See M. Dahood, "Ugaritic-Hebrew Parallel Pairs," *Ras Shamra Parallels*, ed. L. Fisher (vols. 1, 2, 3; Rome: Pontifical Biblical Institute, 1972, 1975, 1979).
[17] Alter, *Art of Biblical Poetry*, 13.
[18] Kugel, *Idea of Biblical Poetry*, 29, 30, 39.

poem.[19] For example, Kugel notes that "ox" and "ass" are a parallel pair which meant "beasts of burden."[20] Yet, we saw how, when used in Isa 1:3 in the context of the ox knowing its owner and the ass its master's trough, the terms "ox" and "ass" no longer designated beasts of burden generically; certain differences between these animals were highlighted by the poet.

This is not to claim that all parallel pairs function to move the meaning along, but simply that their presence does not necessarily detract from a progression of meaning in biblical poetry.

The question which presents itself is how is this "what's moreness" achieved? It is a theoretical question which has immense practical implications because the answers to it may enable us to be more sensitive in our interpretations of biblical poetry. My purpose is not to deal with types of progression in biblical poetry, as did Alter, but rather to treat the means by which the "what's more" dimension of biblical poetry is achieved. Before looking at this literary critical approach, however, let us look at why historical criticism is of limited value in our interpretation of the psalms.

Psalms: Accepting Their Mysterious Past

Were the psalms originally independent, private songs, or were they composed for the cult, or were some from the first category and some from the second category? It is difficult to determine the actual situation in which the psalms were composed because the psalms mention very few historical events besides those in the people's distant past (e.g., the time of the patriarchs, of Egypt and the Exodus). As a result, it is almost impossible to use the history of the period to interpret the psalms.

[19] Perhaps Alter, *Art of Biblical Poetry*, 13, was thinking along similar lines when he wrote the following:

> What is constantly exploited in literary expression is not merely the definable referendum of the word but also the frame of reference to which the word attaches...the related semantic fields toward which it points, the level of diction that it invokes, the specialized uses to which it may be put.

[20] See Kugel, *Idea of Biblical Poetry*, 33.

So too, we have very little information on how the psalms were used in the cult, or for that matter of temple worship in general at the time of the psalmists. The psalms themselves are our major source of information on worship in ancient Israel.[21] Thus, one must beware of circular arguments in explaining a psalm on the basis of the Israelite cult.

This difficulty in historical reconstruction is reflected in the differences in the identifications of royal psalms, the theories of an annual enthronement of Yahweh, and in the speculations regarding both cult prophets and the *Sitz im Leben* of the individual laments.

A royal psalm is a psalm which deals with the Davidic dynasty. There is no agreement as to which, and how many psalms are royal psalms.[22] Similar disagreements occur as to what constitutes a royal psalm: What are the characteristics that must be found in order to call a psalm a royal psalm? In conjunction with this, the question of what is metaphor and what refers to the king is not an easy one to answer; many scholars note that a number of psalms seem to have undergone a "democratization" process whereby what originally referred to the king was later applied to the community. Thus, it must be asked if a certain image was always a metaphor, or if it refers to the king, or if it once referred to the king and in a later redaction was used metaphorically to refer to the people.

An enthronement psalm is one which presumably is about the ritual enthronement of Yahweh at the autumnal Feast of Booths. Sigmund Mowinckel proposed such a festival which would be similar to the *akitu* rites in Mesopotamia in which Marduk's original battle and victory over the forces of chaos was ritually reenacted.[23] Our understanding of this ritual has been

[21] S. Mowinckel, *The Psalms in Israel's Worship* (Oxford: Basil Blackwell, 1962) vol. 1, 35, 36.

[22] See, e.g., the differences in the following scholars. J. H. Eaton, *Kingship and the Psalms* (SBT, 32; Naperville: A. Allenson, 1976) 27-84; A. Johnson, *Sacral Kingship in Ancient Israel* (Cardiff: University of Wales, 1967); S. J. Croft, *The Identity of the Individual in the Psalms* (JSOTS, 44; Sheffield: JSOT, 1987).

[23] See J. D. Pritchard, *Ancient Near Eastern Texts Relating to the Old Testament* (Princeton, NJ: Princeton University Press, 1969) 331-334; S. Mowinckel, *The Psalms in Israel's Worship* (vol. 2; Nashville, TN: Abingdon, 1962).

refined,[24] however, and there is no consensus that such an annual reenthronement occurred in Israel, nor is there agreement by those who hold to such a thesis on precisely what happened in this ritual and which psalms witness to it.

A number of scholars think that this ritual occurred at the autumnal Feast of the Booths during the time of the Davidic dynasty. Mowinckel proposed that at this time Yahweh was enthroned as King, that is, Yahweh's power over chaos at creation and in the realm of history was made present for the people. Mowinckel noted that, in Zechariah 14:16-17, one finds the ideas of Yahweh's kingship, his dominion over the waters and the autumnal festival attached to each other. Of course, this is a post-exilic text, one which is later than the time of the Davidic dynasty. It has also been pointed out that Psalms 29, 68, 84, 93 link up Yahweh's kingship in Jerusalem with Yahweh's control of the rain. Mowinckel also thought that it was probable that the king's enthronement was recelebrated at this time; he did not see any evidence, however, for a ritual humiliation of the king during this ceremony.[25] Aubrey Johnson, John Eaton and Helmer Ringgren wrote that during this festival the Davidic king was ritually humiliated and then reenthroned.[26] Johnson's reconstruction is based on psalms (e.g., Pss 89, 18, 118) that are not considered by Mowinckel to be enthronement psalms.[27] Steven Croft has also criticized the theory of the ritual humiliation of the king and proposed a different view of the king's role in the autumn festival.[28]

A similar difficulty in historical reconstruction is witnessed to by the theory of the cult prophet. Aubrey Johnson argued for the existence of cult prophets during the monarchy. He was preceded in

[24] See, e.g., J. Castelot & A. Cody, O.S.B., "Religious Institutions of Israel," *The New Jerome Biblical Commentary*, eds. R. Brown, SS., J. Fitzmyer, S.J., R. Murphy, O. Carm. (Englewood Cliffs, NJ: Prentice Hall, 1990) 1253-1283, p. 1281.
[25] S. Mowinckel, *Psalmenstudien II* (Kristiana: J. Dybwad, 1921); Idem, *The Psalms in Israel's Worship* (vol.1; Nashville, TN: Abingdon, 1962) 60-66.
[26] A. Johnson, *Sacral Kingship in Ancient Israel*, 112, 113, 118, 120, 121, 126, 134, 135; J. H. Eaton, *Kingship and the Psalms*, 131-135, 199; H. Ringgren, *King and Messiah* (Oxford: Oxford University Press, 1955).
[27] S. Mowinckel, *The Psalms in Israel's Worship*, 253-255.
[28] Croft, *Identity of the Individual.*

this view by Mowinckel. According to Johnson, the job of the cult prophet was to be a spokesman both for Yahweh and for the people. "He was not only a giver of oracles; he was also expert in the technique of addressing Yahweh, i.e., in the offering of prayer."[29] This has been used to explain the prophetic elements in the Psalms and the cultic material found in the prophets. On the other hand, W. Bellinger's study of the "prophetic elements in psalms of lamentation" led him to question whether we can speak of cult prophets. According to Bellinger, the divine response to a lament could have been given by a priest. Further, Bellinger notes that the presence of oracular forms in the Psalter and cultic forms in the prophetic corpus does not argue necessarily for a cultic prophet.[30]

Finally, it should be noted that some scholars have postulated that the official cult was not the setting of a whole category of psalms: the individual laments. Erhard Gerstenberger, Klaus Seybold and others have proposed that the setting for the individual laments was the individual's home to which a ritual specialist came.[31] If they are correct, then we need to look at a different type of cultic activity as the setting for a number of psalms.

Thus, a brief survey of some views on the questions of royal psalms, an enthronement festival, the cult prophet and the *Sitz im Leben* of the individual laments shows how difficult it is to reconstruct the situations behind the psalms. The argument is not that an attempt to determine a psalm's *Sitz im Leben* is unimportant or hopeless. One must be cautious, however, about using a hypothetical social context as the basis for interpreting a psalm.[32]

[29] A. Johnson, *The Cult Prophet in Ancient Israel* (Cardiff: U. of Wales, 1962) 75.

[30] W. Bellinger, *Psalmody and Prophecy* (JSOTSS, 27; Sheffield: JSOT, 1984) 91-94.

[31] E. Gerstenberger, *Der bittende Mensch: Bittritual und Klagelied des Einzelnen im Alten Testament* (WMANT, 51; Neukirchen-Vluyn: Neukirchener, 1980) 134-160; K. Seybold, *Das Gebet des Kranken im Alten Testament* (BWANT, 99; Stuttgart: Kohlhammer, 1973) 171-175; R. Albertz, *Weltschöpfung und Menschenschöpfung* (Stuttgart: Calwer, 1974); Idem, *Personliche Frömigkeit und offizielle Religion* (Stuttgart: Calwer, 1978).

[32] In this context it should be noted that R. Knierim, "Old Testament Form Criticism Reconsidered," *Int* 27 (1973) 448-450, has cautioned us that a form (genre) need not have a particular *Sitz im Leben*.

Psalms: Experiencing the Presence of Mystery

A literary critical approach to the Psalms as poetry can help us refrain from imposing upon them an interpretation based upon a questionable *Sitz im Leben*.[33] Thus, my attention will now be turned to how meaning accrues in psalmic poetry: how the "what's moreness" is achieved in the poetry of the Psalter.[34]

Generally, it can be said that a piece of literature conveys not only ideas but also feelings. These feelings are integrally related to the meaning of a text. Therefore, we have to be sensitive both to the ideas and to the feelings in a text. A text's feelings are conveyed in precisely the same manner as are the text's ideas: through the selection and arrangement of terms, sentences, images, and events.

I propose five specific guidelines for the interpretation of the poetry of the psalms: guidelines which will help us be sensitive to the "what's moreness" of psalmic poetry.

First, the use of different words and images add to the meaning of a text. Even apparent synonyms add different connotative dimensions to the poem. New images and new words awaken new

E. Davis, "Exploding the Limits: Form and Function of Psalm 22," *JSOT* 53 (1992) 93-105, noted that in representing reality the poet achieves a meaning which is often prior to and anticipates cultural conceptions and social constructions. She concluded that the full range of the meaning of a poem can only be found within the poem itself, and not in historical facts or social uses "behind the text."

[33] According to Westermann, the psalms originated not so much in the cult as in the more generic situation of "speaking to God as plea and as praise" which occurs in the cult and elsewhere. See C. Westermann, *The Praise of God in the Psalms* (Richmond, VA: John Knox, 1961) 154, 155; Idem, *The Psalms: Structure, Context and Message* (Minneapolis, MN: Augsburg, 1980) 14-16.

[34] No claim is being made that literary critical methods, in contrast to historical critical ones, can offer us anything like the certainty achieved by Lewis Carroll's famous egg: "I can explain all the poems that ever were invented – and a good many that haven't been invented just yet." L. Carroll, "Humpty Dumpty," *The Annotated Alice: Alice's Adventures in Wonderland and Through the Looking Glass*; ed. M. Gardner (New York: Bramhall House, 1960) 270. What is being asserted is that literary criticisms, such as poetic criticism, can ground us in, and open us to, dimensions of the text.

feelings because different words have different "evocative values." Thus, Alter wrote:

> Six inches and half a foot may be the exact quantitative equivalents, but they are not true synonyms, as the eighteenth century novelist Tobias Smollet was perfectly aware when in *Peregrine Pickle* he described a character with a grotesque face overshadowed by a nose half a foot long – which for the affective reader is a good sight longer than six inches.[35]

Similarly, Berlin makes the following point about Isa 1:3b ("Israel does not know;/ My people does not understand"). The choice of "my people" as a parallel term for "Israel" instead of other possible terms such as "Ephraim" or "House of Jacob, "adds an emotional tone, a closeness to God, and the irony that God's people does not realize that it is God's people."[36] Thus, we have to be aware that different words evoke differing types and ranges of responses in the reader. These evocations may come both through the words' etymological associations and through the use of the words. In regard to the second means it should be noted that words have histories; they develop stories through their use and they may carry one or more of these word-tales over into their successive manifestations in human discourse and literature. In order to tell the etymological associations or word-tales which may be alluded to in a particular usage, one needs to view the word from the following perspective on how meaning develops in the psalter.

Second, not only the selection of terms and images, but also their arrangement play a key role in conveying the meaning of a poem. When a term is placed in a context it is colored by the context and takes on shades of meaning from it. This can be seen in the use of the term "waters" (*mayim*) in Ps 124:3-5 and in Ps 42:1.

> ...Then they would have swallowed us up alive,
> when their anger was kindled against us;
> then the flood would have swept us away,
> the torrent would have gone over us;

[35] Alter, *Art of Biblical Poetry*, 13.
[36] Berlin, *Dynamics of Biblical Parallelism*, 137.

then over us would have gone
  the raging waters (*mayim*). (Ps 124:3-5)

As a deer longs
  for flowing streams (*mayim*),
so longs my soul
  for thee, O God."(Ps 42:1)

Clearly, we have different aspects of "waters" being stressed in the two citations, and it is the context in which "waters" is placed that gives meaning to this term. The context of Ps 124:5 leads us to interpret "waters" in this verse as a force which threatens to overwhelm and destroy us. The image is that of sinking beneath stormy waters. On the other hand, the image of Ps 42:1 is of water as the basic necessity of all of life, and this is conveyed by the context of the hart longing for flowing waters.

Third, an image or phrase is developed through its repetition at various points in the poem. New aspects of meaning are given to it as it is placed in new contexts. Thus, one should not suppose that all uses of an image in the poem mean the same thing. Caution must be used in explaining an image or a phrase on the basis of the use of the same or a similar image or phrase elsewhere in the psalm or in another psalm. Unfortunately, this has been an all too common practice in Psalm criticism. The recasting of the phrase in a different context, the juxtaposing of the phrase with different elements and the repetition of the phrase at a different point in the poem nuance the meaning of the phrase. We need to be sensitive to what Alter has called the "fine recasting of the conventional" through which the psalmist has created a new poem.[37]

Fourth, we must see how the different images in a poem relate to each other in order to determine the thrust of the poem. There is an overarching idea(s)-feeling(s) to which the disparate images in a poem contribute: the poem's unity arising from its metaphorical diversity. (A poem's diverse images build to convey an overarching idea and an overarching feeling which are integrally related to

[37] Alter, *Art of Biblical Poetry*, 112, 113.

each other.) The individual images were not intended to be literary worlds unto themselves; to interpret them separately is to miss the fact that they are parts of one poem.[38]

Fifth, in searching for the overarching idea(s)-feeling(s) of the poem there is a real danger that we will confuse the metaphors for the meaning they are intended to express. It is often difficult in the Psalms to distinguish between what is actually happening to the psalmist and what is the psalmist's metaphorical expression. Thus, in the introduction to his treatment of Ps 38, Arnold Anderson injects a helpful word of caution when he writes that "it would be impossible to say whether a particular detail belonged to the conventional word-pictures of trouble, or whether it was an actual description of a particular experience."[39]

The language used to describe situations does betray the psalmist's experience of these situations, be they the psalmist's external or internal experience. Where doubt exists as to whether or not an external experience is being referred to, it seems exegetically safer to look at the way the situation is described to explore what internal experience this description implies. The way in which one speaks or writes about matters betrays the internal attitude which one has to them. Thus, Ps 40:12 expresses the attitude of being overwhelmed.

> For evils have encompassed me
>   without number;
> my iniquities have overtaken me,
>   until I cannot see;
> they are more than the hairs of my head;
>   and my heart fails me.

Ps 46:9 expresses the attitude of the peaceful power of God, regardless of whether or not the psalmist experienced the termination of actual wars.

[38] Similarly, C. Broyles, *Conflict of Faith and Experience*, 28.
[39] A. Anderson, *The Book of Psalms* (NCB; London: Oliphants, 1972) 1.301. A. Weiser, *The Psalms* (OTL; Philadelphia: Westminster, 1962) 227, makes the same type of comment about the imagery in Ps. 23.

He makes wars cease to the end of the earth;
 he breaks the bow, and shatters the spear,
he burns the shield with fire!

One can foresee these types of inner responses being useful to people in numerous situations.

Sensitivity to the manifold connections in a psalm, and to the ways in which these linkages are made, is crucial if one is to be open to the meaning of the psalm. The five guidelines found in this chapter show ways in which the transfer and buildup of meaning between different parts of the poem occurs.

PART II

TRUST, SECURITY AND RELATIONSHIPS

We find delight in the beauty and happiness of children that makes the heart too big for the body.
Ralph Waldo Emerson, "Illusions,"
The Conduct of Life

CHAPTER 3

PSALM 131 AND EMOTIONAL SECURITY

> What the mother sings to the
> cradle, goes all the way
> down to the coffin.
> Henry Ward Beecher,
> *Proverbs from Plymouth Pulpit*

At Our Limits

All children and adults experience fear, fatigue and pain. How we react to these experiences is determined to a large degree by the support or lack of support which we have during these times. A number of psychologists claim that the type of parental care that is given in these situations is important in establishing a person's basic approach to social relationships throughout one's life.

This chapter begins with an exploration of the psychoanalytical interpretive construct labeled attachment theory. The purpose is to present the effects of different types of parental behavior on children who are fearful, in pain or tired. An interpretation of Psalm 131 follows. The chapter concludes with observations on the help that this psalm can provide for adults and for effective parenting when children are anxious, weary or in pain. While attachment theory provides a strong heuristic tool for discerning certain bases of inappropriate relations, the transformative ability of attachment therapy is weak, and it can be greatly strengthened by considerations and practices derived from Psalm 131. This can be of great benefit to all parents.

Different Types of Children: Perspectives from Attachment Theory

Attachment Theory

The founder of attachment theory is John Bowlby.[1] Attachment theory states that every human being needs comfort in times of danger, suffering or fatigue. Succinctly put, one encourages emotional health and socialization by encouraging the autonomy of one's child while being ready to provide a secure base by means of comforting a child who is fearful, in pain or tired.[2] Bowlby called the behavior displayed in times of fear, fatigue or pain "attachment behavior." He did not wish to label this "dependent behavior" because of the "adverse valuation" which the word "dependency" has.[3] "Dependent behavior" has been used to refer to a stage which should be outgrown. According to Bowlby, attachment behavior is natural for one at any stage of life during times of fatigue, fear or pain.[4] The attachment figure is an older, stronger person, although healthy adolescents and adults will also seek attachment to other figures.[5]

Children's Secure or Insecure Attachments to Parents

All individuals seek to feel secure, but the way in which they do this varies from person to person depending on how one's parents have responded to one's needs for security in times when one was

[1] J. Bowlby, *Attachment and Loss*, vol. 1: *Attachment* (New York: Basic, 1969); vol. 2: *Separation* (New York: Basic, 1973); vol. 3: *Loss, Sadness and Depression* (New York: Basic, 1980).
[2] J. Bowlby, *A Secure Base* (New York: Basic, 1988) 12.
[3] In this light, Bowlby also said that the labels "childish" and "regressive" do not fit this type of behavior and that they are the products of inaccurate theories. See *A Secure Base*, 82.
[4] Ibid., 12, 27, 62. According to Bowlby, such behavior may also occur when the "caregiver" is, or appears to be, inaccessible. See *A Secure Base*, 82.
[5] Ibid., 3, 27, 46, 120, 121. In the novel *The Touchstone* (repr.; New York: Harper, 1991) 53, 56, Edith Wharton describes a young man just out of college who curries the favor of an older author who can "carry him lightly and easily over what is often a period of insecurity and discouragement."

fearful, tired or in pain. If the parent was "available and responsive to the child's distress signals," the child learns to actively seek comfort from the parent during such times. Some parents, however, reject the child's requests for comfort or are not consistently available to comfort the child. This leads to the child's having a lack of confidence that he or she will receive comfort in these situations and consequently to alternative and unhealthy ways of seeking to relieve distress. Let us now look more closely both at the different forms of parenting in these situations, and at the different types of attachment behavior that they engender.

Mary Ainsworth and her colleagues studied twenty-three infants throughout their first year of life. These infants were from white, middle-class families in Baltimore. The researchers studied them in their homes for three hours every three weeks throughout the first year of life in order to see how their mothers acted towards them. Ainsworth and colleagues also placed these infants in the Strange Situation.[6]

The Strange Situation is a procedure which is designed to test how secure or insecure infants and young children are in their attachment to their mothers.[7] The procedure is as follows. The child is introduced to a new room, to toys and to a stranger. First, one observes how a child reacts while in the presence of his or her mother in this strange situation. The mother leaves the room twice and returns twice. The way that the child reacts when the mother is present, when the mother is away and as soon as the mother returns shows what type of attachment it has to its mother, be it a secure type or an insecure type of attachment.

Ainsworth and her colleagues found three distinct types of behavior exhibited by the one year olds in the Strange Situation. These were labeled as (1) secure attachment, (2) insecure-

[6] M. Ainsworth, "Social Development in the First Year of Life: Maternal Influences on Infant-Mother Attachment," J. Tanner, ed., *Developments in Psychiatric Research* (London: Tavistock, 1977) 1-20.

[7] As Bowlby, *A Secure Base*, 9-11, notes, "in most, perhaps all" cultures, mothers tend to be the attachment figure for children.

ambivalent attachment and (3) insecure-avoidant attachment. Those children who had a secure attachment relation to their mothers were more explorative when their mothers were present in the Strange Situation, and they came back to their mothers or exchanged glances with their mothers in the course of their explorations; their mothers were used as a secure base from which to make sorties into the world. As noted, the mothers were taken away from their children. Those children who, on the basis of the evaluation of the relationship between child and mother in the home, seemed to have a secure attachment to their mothers joyfully greeted their mothers upon their return.

In the Strange Situation those children who, on the basis of observation in the home, were judged not to have a secure attachment to their mothers acted differently from the secure group. Some, both in their mother's presence and apart from it, were passive and did not explore much. Others alternated between seeming independence and ignoring their mother on the one hand, and anxious attempts to find her on the other; they did not, however, seem happy when they found her "and often they struggled to get away again."[8]

The Determinative Parental Characteristics

Ainsworth and her colleagues found a correlation between the types of mothering which the child received at home and how the child acted in the Strange Situation; they found that different types of mothering led to either a secure attachment or to one of the two different types of insecure attachment.

The characteristics of mothers of children with secure attachment relations are as follows. Such mothers tend to be constantly "tuned-in" to their children's needs and natural rhythms; they tend to pay attention to details of their children's behavior. The other mothers tend to ignore the children or to be unaware of them

[8] M. Ainsworth, "Social Development in the First Year of Life," 1-20.

for a time. This lack of attention often causes the mothers to respond inappropriately to the infant's needs when they become aware of these needs. On the other hand, the "tuned-in" mothers frequently check the signals which their children are giving.[9] The children of mothers who show this kind of sensitivity display a secure attachment to their mothers, while those whose mothers are not sensitive lack such a secure attachment as evidenced by their behavior in the Strange Situation.[10]

A second characteristic of mothers who are secure attachment figures is that many hold their infants lovingly for long periods of

[9] The following poem may be very helpful as an aid to attending more to the child's needs and interests. It may sensitize us to the child's perspective, the tragedy of not responding to it sufficiently, and to the limited time in which to respond to it. As such, it can help us to make children's needs and interests a higher priority in our lives. Although I have looked through the standard library sources, I have been unable to identify either the author of this poem or where it was published.

My Son Grows Up

My hands were busy through the day.
I didn't have much time to play
The little games you asked me to.
But when you'd bring your teddy bear
And ask me please to share your fun,
I'd say: "A little later, son."
I'd tuck you in all safe at night
And hear your prayers, turn out the light.
Then tiptoe softly to the door...
I wish I'd stayed a minute more.
For life is short, the years rush past
A little boy grows up so fast.
No longer is he at your side,
His precious secrets to confide.
The teddy bears are put away,
There are no longer games to play,
No good-night kiss, no prayers to hear
That all belongs to yesteryear.
My hands, once busy
Now are still.
The days are long and hard to fill.
I wish I could go back and do
The little things you asked me to.

[10] M. Ainsworth et. al., *Patterns of Attachment* (Hillsdale, NJ: L. Erlbaum, 1978) 139, 142-143; Bowlby, *A Secure Base*, 131.

time. The children of those who did so in Ainsworth's study tended to develop secure attachment relations to their mothers.[11] This shows the importance of touch for the infant in the development of secure attachment relations.

A third characteristic of secure attachment figures is that they engage in more direct communication with their children by means of "eye contact, facial expression, vocalization and showing or giving toys." The result is that these children themselves engage in direct communication with their mothers both when they are content and when they are distressed, whereas children with insecure attachment relations only engage in direct communication with their mothers when they are content.[12] Thus, children with insecure, attachment relations are cut off from direct relations with an attachment figure precisely when they need it most: when they are distressed.

Fourth, Bowlby noted the importance of emotional communications for the establishment of secure, attachment relations. The initial bond between mother and infant is formed by means of "emotional expressions." "Although supplemented later by speech, emotionally mediated communication nonetheless persists as a principal feature of intimate relationships throughout life."[13]

The second, third and fourth characteristics of secure attachment figures are their entering into tactile, direct and emotional communication with their children. One may surmise that tactile and emotional communication strengthen the sense of security which the child feels. Direct communication may provide confidence in the child that the way to secure attachment relations is open when needed.

[11] M. Ainsworth, et al., *Patterns of Attachment*, 139.

[12] Bowlby, *A Secure Base*, 131,132.

[13] Ibid., 121. Bowlby notes that throughout one's life the most important communications are expressed emotionally, and that there is "no information more vital for constructing and reconstructing working models of the self and the other than information about how each feels about the other." See *A Secure Base*, 156,157.

The Benefits of Strong Bonding

On the basis of their study of attachment relations in young children, Mary Main and Donna Weston have argued that children who have a secure relation to both parents are the most confident and competent children. They will explore boldly. Those with a secure relationship with only one parent do not exhibit these qualities to the same degree, and those without a secure relation to either parent are the least confident and competent.[14] This shows the importance not only of the mother in the development of secure attachment relations, but also of the father.

Studies of children from infancy through five years of age have corroborated the findings of Ainsworth and her colleagues.[15] These studies have shown that a child who experiences secure attachment relations tends to comfort others when they are in distress. Securely attached children also develop a sense of inner confidence: they are more self-reliant. They have a capacity to give and to receive care from others, and they display more ego-resiliency, which is "the capacity to flexibly engage the environment to maintain organized behavior in the face of high arousal, and to recoup following stress."[16]

[14] M. Main & D. Weston, "Quality of Attachment to Mother and to Father Related to Conflict Behavior and the Readiness for Establishing New Relationships," *Child Development* 52 (1981) 932-940.

[15] M. Main & J. Stadtman, "Infant Response to Rejection of Physical Contact by Mother: Aggression, Avoidance and Conflict," *Journal of the American Academy of Child Psychiatry* 20 (1981) 292-307; M. Main & D. Weston, "Quality of Attachment to Mother and to Father," 932-940; K. E. Grossmann, K. Grossmann & A. Schwunn, "Capturing the Wider View of Attachment: A Reanalysis of Ainsworth's Strange Situation," C. Izard & P. Read, ed., *Measuring Emotions in Infants and Children*, (New York: Cambridge University Press, 1986); L. Stroufe, "Attachment-Classification from the Perspective of Infant-Caregiver Relationships and Infant Temperament," *Child Development* 56 (1985) 1-14. R. Arend, F. Gove & L. Stroufe, "Continuity of Individual Adaptations from Infancy to Kindergarten: A Predictive Study of Ego-resiliency and Curiosity in Preschoolers," *Child Development* 50 (1979) 950-959.

[16] L. Stroufe, "The Role of Infant-Caregiver Attachment in Development," in *Clinical Implications of Attachment*, eds. J. Belsky & T. Nezworski, (CP; Hillsdale, NJ: L. Erlbaum, 1988) 26, 27, 29, 34; C. Zahn-Waxler, M. Radke-Yarrow & R. King, "Childrearing and Children's Prosocial Initiations Toward Victims of Distress," *Child Development* 50 (1979) 319-330.

Children, like adults, have different temperaments. Thus, one child may be more prone to distress than is another child. The first type of child may require more to create the sense of "felt security" which is generated by attachment relations.[17] Research has shown, however, that children with all types of temperaments may develop secure attachment relations if the care giver is sensitive to their individual needs.[18]

May Main, Nancy Kaplan and Jude Cassidy studied the verbal responses of parents and their six year olds who had been tested in the Strange Situation five years earlier. The results tended to be the same: those children classified in one category at one year old tended to be classified in the same category at six years of age.[19] The degree of the persistence of attachment behavior has not been studied beyond the sixth year of a child's life; a study by R. Rogers Kobak and Amy Sceery has shown, nonetheless, the same type of correlation between the type of care an attachment figure provides and the type of behavior found in young adults.[20]

Kobak and Sceery studied fifty-three first year college students during the course of their academic year. They found that those students who exhibited a secure attachment looked for support from others when they were distressed, and that they displayed greater ego-resiliency.

[17] J. Belsky & T. Nezworski, "Clinical Implications of Attachment," J. Belsky & T. Nezworski, *Clinical Implications of Attachment* (CP; Hillsdale, NJ: L. Erlbaum, 1988) 10.

[18] L. Stroufe, "The Role of Infant-Caregiver Attachment in Development," 23; K. Rubin & S. Lollis, "Origins and Consequences of Social Withdrawal," J. Belsky & T. Nezworski, eds., *Clinical Implications of Attachment* (CP; Hillsdale, N.J.: L. Erlbaum, 1988) 219-252.

[19] M. Main, N. Kaplan & J. Cassidy, "Security in Infancy, Childhood and Adulthood: A Move to the Level of Representation, " I. Bretherton & E. Waters, eds., *Growing Points in Attachment: Theory and Research* (Chicago: University of Chicago, 1985) 66-104.

[20] R. Kobak & A. Sceery, "Attachment in Late Adolescence," *Child Development* 59 (1988) 135-146.

The Emotional and Social Scars From Insecure Ties

In their study, Ainsworth and her colleagues found that mothers of children with insecure-ambivalent relations do not function consistently as attachment figures when the child needs such a figure. In its most extreme forms this lack of consistency is accompanied by prolonged separations from the child and by parental threats to abandon the child. Insecure-ambivalent children are uncertain if the care giver will be there when he or she needs the care giver. As a result, they tend "to be prone to separation anxiety," to be clinging and afraid to explore.

The third type of attachment behavior is insecure-avoidant attachment. The parents of the child who manifests this type of behavior have repeatedly rebuffed the child's attempts to seek comfort and protection. The child who has experienced such behavior from his or her attachment figure tends to alternate between avoiding others and bullying others.[21]

Those first year college students studied by Kobak and Sceery who had an insecure-ambivalent attachment, caused by the attachment figure's failure to provide consistent care when the child needed it, focused their attention on the distress and on the attachment figures. This focus inhibited "the development of autonomy and self-confidence." The students who had insecure-avoidant attachment relations, caused by the attachment figure's rebuffing the child's requests for comfort during times of fear, fatigue or pain, did not acknowledge distress

[21] M. Ainsworth, S. Bell, & D. Stayton, "Individual Differences in Strange Situation Behavior of One-Year-Olds," H. R. Schaffer, ed., *The Origins of Human Social Relations* (London: Academic, 1971) 17-58.

The behavior of all of the one-year-olds whom Ainsworth and her colleagues studied corresponded closely to one of these three types of attachment relations. P. Crittendon, "Relationships at Risk," J. Belsky & T. Nezworski, ed., *Clinical Implications of Attachment* (CP; Hillsdale, NJ: L. Erlbaum, 1988) 136-174, has argued that there are "sub-groups" of infants who don't fall into these categories, and so who can incorrectly be classified as secure. While more precision in our categories of attachment behavior is certainly possible and desirable, we will see that a number of studies have shown the usefulness of these three categories.

and did not seek support. They tended to be more hostile toward others.[22]

Thus, a number of age groups have been studied by means of a number of different methods. Kobak and Sceery, for example, used the adult attachment interview developed by George, Main and Kaplan to study the first year college students.[23]

The following two areas would be interesting to explore. First, Bowlby noted that a fear of opening up to attachment relations in the future is characteristic of those who have not had secure, attachment relations. There is another consequence which can be postulated. One might expect that the effects of rejections from those whom one seeks to develop an attachment to in adolescence or in the adult years would be exacerbated in those who have not experienced secure, attachment relations in the past. These people have no secure base to which they can fall back and no means to seek comfort from others in such a situation. Further studies may establish the above proposal as a corollary of attachment theory.

Another fruitful avenue of research would be the study of whether or not certain cultural conceptions make it more difficult for some groups to enter into secure attachment relations. For example, boys in our culture have been taught not to express their fatigue ("tough it out"), pain ("boys don't cry") or fear ("don't be a sissy"). One can infer that such attitudes would make it harder for boys to engage in secure attachment relations.[24]

[22] R. Kobak & A. Sceery, "Attachment in Late Adolescence," 136, 142, 144. Sceery (p. 143) postulated that the hostility shown by the insecure-avoidant group is hostility toward the parent for rejecting attachment; this hostility is displaced so as not to endanger the situation with the parent. This is intriguing, but it may need to be nuanced. In the situation where one parent has fled there would be no need to fear endangering the relation with that parent; hostility toward that parent could still be the underlying reason, however, for the hostility which the child shows.
[23] C. George, N. Kaplan & M. Main, "The Attachment Interview for Adults," Unpublished manuscript, University of California, Berkeley.
[24] This would especially be the case when the boy's parents have subscribed to these cultural attitudes; even when the parents have not accepted these attitudes, however, their presence in the larger culture would influence boys to a certain degree.

Why the Different Types of Parenting?

"A mother's feeling and behavior" towards her child is influenced by the type of mothering that she experienced from her own mother. By means of the Adult Attachment Interview, Main and Goldwyn studied parents whose children had been assessed six years ago in the Strange Situation. They found that seventy-three percent of the parents had experienced the same type of attachment relationship to their own parents that their children had shown towards them six years ago. This indicates that parents tend to pass on to their children the type of attachment relations which they themselves experienced.[25]

Some parents had to care for their parents when they were young. Their parents had inverted the parent-child relationship by expecting to be cared for by their children. This makes the child the attachment figure. When such children became parents they often inverted the parent-child relationship in a similar way.[26] Further, mothers who in one way or another experienced a disturbed childhood interacted less with their infants. This is a time in the baby's life when almost all of its interaction is with its mother![27]

How Long and How Far-Reaching the Consequences?

Attachment relations produce internal working models of attachment. These are mental representations of the self in relation to attachment. They tell one what kind of responses to expect in times of fear, pain or tiredness. These responses are the result of the type of attachment which one has had with an attachment figure: internal working models evolve from a child's experience

[25] Bowlby, *A Secure Base*, 15, 126; M. Main & R. Goldwyn, "Adult Attachment Classification System," Unpublished Manuscript, University of California, Berkeley; D. Morris, "Attachment and Intimacy," G. Stricker & M. Fischer, ed., *Intimacy* (New York: Plenum, 1983) 305-323.

[26] P. J. Delozier, "Attachment Theory and Child Abuse," *The Place of Attachment in Human Behavior*, C. M. Parkes & J. Stevenson-Hinde, ed. (New York: Basic, 1982) 95-117.

[27] J. Bowlby, *A Secure Base*, 16.

with his or her parents. The three different types of attachment behavior reflect three different types of expectations (internal working models) caused by three different types of experiences of one's parents in situations of fear, fatigue and pain. Internal working models provide rules both for how one responds to "emotionally distressing or challenging situations," and for how one feels in times of distress. In other words, a working model tells a person how to handle distress and how to feel about it.[28]

Thus, we saw how the secure first year college students in Kobak and Sceery's study looked for support from others in stressful situations, and how they exhibited greater ego-resiliency. Their internal working model was of an expectation of support in difficult situations. This enabled them to seek such support and not to be overcome by the difficult situation. On the other hand, the students who were classified as insecure-ambivalent focused on their distress in such a way as to hinder their self-autonomy and responsibility. The insecure-avoidant group refused to acknowledge the distress, and did not seek support. The internal working models of these two insecure groups did not allow them to act and feel in such a way as to provide relief for the distress.

Once established, internal working models tend to be unconscious. Thus, it is possible, but difficult, to change them. If the attachment figure changes the way he or she relates to one then one's attachment behavior may change. Patterns of attachment tend to perpetuate themselves, however, because insecure attachment relations cause a child to act in ways that evoke unfavorable responses from the parent. On the other hand, "a secure child is a happier and more rewarding child to care for, and also is less demanding than an anxious one." A pattern of attachment behavior is harder to change the longer it persists. One expects in present and future relationships the kind of attachment responses which one has already experienced. As a result, those who have not experienced secure attachment relations tend to fear opening

[28] M. Main, N. Kaplan & J. Cassidy, "Security in Infancy, Childhood, and Adulthood," 67.

themselves to such relations in the future. Change may occur as a result of new experiences with one's attachment figure. This is the starting point for attachment therapy.[29]

Realistic Possibilities for Change? Attachment Therapy and a New Parent Figure

Bowlby writes about the role of the therapist who applies attachment theory. He says that the therapist must provide a secure base for the patient; the therapist becomes an attachment figure and this gives the patient the security from which to explore key events in his or her life. The therapist should encourage the patient to explore both these past attachment relationships, as well as the patient's current expectations for intimate relationships, and how the latter may have been influenced by the former. In other words, the therapist should help the patient discover for him or herself the events which have led one to be angry, anxious or aggressive in certain situations. Then the therapist should guide the patient to consider how these events have continued to influence one. This clarifies the basis for the person's current responses. The therapist also attempts to help the patient see how past responses of attachment figures may not have been justified in order that the patient may "feel free to imagine alternatives better fitted to his current life" and to alter his or her responses.[30]

There is a transference relationship that goes on in psychoanalysis. From the perspective of attachment theory, the therapist

[29] Bowlby, *A Secure Base*, 55, 65, 86, 136, 170; J. Belsky & T. Nezworski, "Clinical Implications of Attachment," 5, 6; M. Greenberg & M. Speltz, "Attachment and the Ontogeny of Conduct Problems," J. Belsky & T. Nezworski, ed., *Clinical Implications of Attachment*, 177-209.

[30] Bowlby, *A Secure Base*, 117, 118, 138-143. The therapist also encourages the patient to talk about the type of relationship that exists between patient and therapist. On pp. 144-146 Bowlby treats different attitudes which the patient can have to a therapist who applies attachment theory, and on pp. 147-151 Bowlby catalogues a number of pathogenic situations in childhood that can cause insecure attachments. These pages are well worth reading to help one become aware of the variety of events that can lead to insecure attachments and to consequent problems.

becomes a mother figure who provides a secure base from which the patient can explore past relationships. This enables the patient to see the reasons for the attachment relations which he or she exhibits so as to modify these relations in the present and in the future.[31]

The needs of people who have not had a secure relationship with an attachment figure are great, and so the psychoanalyst, in becoming an attachment figure, must be cautious not to promise more than he or she can give. It is difficult to give one who has not experienced secure, attachment relations the amount of care that he or she needs. Bowlby notes several examples of those who did not have secure, attachment relations as children and who made "rewarding progress" during therapy. He notes, however, that they remained "more sensitive than others to personal misfortune."[32]

A therapy based on attachment theory is a stronger heuristic tool than it is a transformative agent. Its heuristic power derives from the secure base provided by the therapist who becomes a mother-figure for the patient. This security allows the patient to explore in an honest way insecure relations which he or she had with the attachment figure. The transformative weakness of the approach stems from the fact that the therapist as a mother-figure cannot give the patient all the care for which the patient has been longing.[33]

Burch and Hunter are correct when they say that pastoral theologians must critique the philosophical presuppositions of various psychological theories.[34] The attachment theory strand of the psychoanalytical tradition is based on the empirical evidence of studies on children and young adults. A principal tenet of this theory is that:

[31] Ibid., 137.
[32] Ibid., 57, 114.
[33] Ibid., 140, 141.
[34] J. R. Burch & R. J. Hunter, "Pastoral Theology, Protestant," *Dictionary of Pastoral Care and Counseling*, ed. R. J. Hunter (Nashville, TN: Abingdon, 1989) 872.

> The capacity to make emotional bonds with other individuals, sometimes in the careseeking role and sometimes in the caregiving one, is a principal feature of effective personality functioning and mental health.[35]

This concept is congruent with the concern for caring relationships which is found in the biblical traditions.

Psalm 131: The Divine Mother

The Widening Path: An Overview of This Section

Psalm 131 deals with the perspective we should have in relation to events that are either too difficult for us to handle or too difficult for us to understand. These are what cause fear, fatigue or pain. In this section of the chapter a translation of Psalm 131 will be followed first by critical notes and next by an exegesis of this psalm. The chapter concludes with a correlation of my understanding of Psalm 131 with attachment theory, and with the type of psychoanalytic therapy which stems from it.

The New Revised Standard Version Translation of Psalm 131

A Song of Ascents. Of David.
1 O Lord, my heart is not lifted up,
my eyes are not raised too high;
I do not occupy myself with things
too great and too marvelous for me.
2 But I have calmed and quieted my soul,
like a weaned child with its mother;
my soul is like the weaned child that is with
me.
3 O Israel, hope in the Lord
from this time forth and forevermore.

[35] Bowlby, *A Secure Base*, 121.

A New Translation of Psalm 131

My own translation of Psalm 131 is not meant to be a smooth one. It is meant to preserve the different dimensions of meaning of the verbs in the poem as well as to preserve the exact imagery.

A Song of Ascents. Of David.[36]
1 Lord, my heart is not lifted up/haughty,
  and my eyes are not raised/exalted.
I do not walk in paths of great things
  nor in paths which are too surpassing/difficult
    for me.
2 Rather, I have leveled/placed and quieted my soul
  like a weaned child upon its mother,
  like a weaned child upon me [is] my soul.
3 Israel, hope in the Lord both now and forever.

What Richard Hays has said in reference to the interpretation of Paul applies here as well.

> The texts and symbols which grasp and move us most profoundly are almost always polyvalent... Accuracy in interpretation consists not in eliminating all possible ambiguities in the meaning of Paul's language but in tracing attentively its various overtones and ranges of implication.[37]

Hayes is not interested in abandoning the search for the correct interpretation of Paul's writings, but rather in being aware of the full range of implications of various words in order to discover which one or ones are present in the text.

Paul Raabe has dealt with instances of deliberate ambiguity in the Psalter, classifying them as examples of lexical, phonetic or grammatical ambiguity.[38] He notes James Barr's caution against assuming that the full range of meanings of terms must be found

[36] The psalm title could refer to a psalm by David, a psalm about David or a psalm for David, i.e., on behalf of David. The *lĕ* prefix admits all of these interpretations.
For a discussion on *maʿălôṯ*, here translated as "ascents," and views on how Pss 120-134 received this designation, see A. Anderson, *The Book of Psalms*, 2:847.

[37] R. Hays, *The Faith of Jesus Christ* (SBLDS, 56; Atlanta: Scholars Press, 1983) 266.

[38] P. Raabe, "Deliberate Ambiguity in the Psalter," *JBL* 110 (1991) 213-227.

in each use of these terms;[39] Raabe adds, however, that the determination of whether or not the context supports such ambiguity serves as both a control against such an error and as evidence that there is *deliberate* ambiguity in the text. The following translation reflects my interpretation of several instances of deliberate lexical ambiguity in Psalm 131. The following remarks show how the context supports this interpretation.

The Subtleties of the Hebrew Text[40]

Verse 1a – Lord, my heart is not lifted up/haughty
and my eyes are not raised/exalted.

The verb translated "lifted up[41]/haughty" is *gāḇah*. It is used with the word "heart" (*lēḇ*) in the opening line of the psalm. When it is used in such a way it means either to encourage or to be haughty. Here it means to be haughty, as is the case when it is used with heart (*lēḇ*) in Prov 18:12; 2 Chrn 26:16; 32:25; Ezek 28:2, 5, 17. That it has such a meaning in v.1 is shown by the corresponding image in the following colon.

The verb in the clause "my eyes are not raised/exalted" *(rāmû)* means to be high, to be exalted. It is used with "eyes" (*'ênayim*) to refer to pride in Pss 18:27; 101:15; Prov 6:17; 30:13. Thus, this is probably the meaning here as well.

Verse 1b – I do not walk in paths of great things
nor in paths too surpassing/difficult for me.

From the NRSV translation ("I do not occupy myself with things/ too great and too marvelous for me") one might get the impression that a verb of thinking is used. This is not the case; a normal verb for thinking such as *ḥāšaḇ* ("to think") or *dāraš* ("to seek")[42] is not used. The verb *hālak* is used; *hālak* frequently

[39] J. Barr, *The Semantics of Biblical Language* (Oxford: Oxford University Press, 1961). Barr calls this "illegitimate totality transfer."

[40] This is also called the Massoretic Text (MT).

[41] Why the meaning "lifted up" is preserved in my translation will become clear in the next section of this chapter.

[42] From which we get "midrash" which is "a study," but which later comes to be used specifically for an exposition of Scripture.

means "to walk or to go."[43] The first part of v.1b literally reads "I do not walk in paths of great things" because after the verb *hālak* comes the word *bigḏōlôṯ*. The second part of this word means "great things." The initial "*b*" is a prefix and when it is found after the verb *hālak* it often means "in paths of."[44] Thus, the image is of walking in paths of great things.

The second part of v.1b is translated as "too marvelous for me" in the NRSV. The word used here is *pālā'*, which does mean to be surpassing or extraordinary; it also expresses, however, the idea of difficulty.[45] Verse 1b is translated as "I do not walk in paths of great things nor in paths which are too surpassing/difficult for me" because the initial lines of this psalm highlight the difficulty of a certain course of action. Sustaining arguments are found in the following section of this chapter.

Verse 2a- Rather, I have leveled/placed and quieted my soul.

The words translated "rather" are *'im-lō'*, which literally read "if not." These words are hard to translate. Some scholars interpret them as an asseveration.[46] What we can be sure of is that the beginning of verse 2, *'im-lō'*("rather"), links verse 2 to verse 1 whose second through fourth clauses begin with the word *lō'* ("not").

> Lord, my heart is not (*lō'*) lifted up/haughty
> and my eyes are not (*lō'*) raised/exalted.
> I do not (*lō'*) walk in paths of great things
> nor in paths too surpassing/difficult for me.
> Rather (*'im-lō'*), I have leveled/placed and quieted
> my soul...[47]

[43] The *piel* form of *hālak* is used. C. & E. Briggs, *The Book of Psalms* (ICC; New York: Charles Scribner's Sons, 1907) 2:467 propose that this gives emphasis to the verb *hālak*. So too L. Sabourin, *Le livre des Psaumes* (RNS, 18; Montreal: Bellarmin, 1988) 554 who translates it as "pursue." M. Dahood, *Psalms 101-150* (AB; Garden City, New York: Doubleday, 1970) 3:238 says that the *piel* form of *hālak* means "to go to and fro."

[44] BDB, 235.

[45] See e.g., Prov 30:18; 2 Sam 13:2; Deut 17:8; 30:11.

[46] E.g., J. Alexander, *The Psalms* (Edinburgh: 1873; repr.; Grand Rapids: Baker, 1975) 522; L. Allen, *Psalms 101-150* (Waco, TX: Word, 1983) 197.

[47] In the Hebrew text all of these clauses have the word *lō'* as the first or the second word in the clause.

This linkage shows us that verse 2 is to be interpreted in connection with verse 1. We will look at the precise connections between these verses later.

The verb which in the NRSV is translated as "calmed" in the clause "I have calmed and quieted my soul" is *šiwîṯî*, which is the piel form of the verb *šāwāh*. In the *piel* this verb means "to level, to smooth," or "to set, to place."[48] The psalmist is referring to both meanings of this word in Ps 131:2. The arguments appear in the next section of this chapter; at this point the range of meanings which the terms can have is set forth.

The last part of verse 2 reads "like a weaned child upon me [is] my soul." This clause has given both translators and interpreters problems. The difficulty consists in determining how the words "like a weaned child upon me [is] my soul" relate to the words which precede it: "like a weaned child upon its mother." Why is there a shift from the image of the soul being as a child on its mother to that of the soul being as a child upon the psalmist is the question.

It has been suggested that the phrase "like a child upon me [is] my soul" is a scribal insertion.[49] Others delete the Hebrew word translated "upon me" (*ʿālay*) so that both clauses refer to the soul being like a child on its mother.[50]

> like a weaned child upon its mother
> like a weaned child [is] my soul.

Leopold Sabourin also proposed that both phrases present the image of the child being upon its mother. He suggests that there was a textual corruption whereby the reference to the child being upon its mother, *ʿāley*, became *ʿālay* ("upon me"). Such a corruption would be produced by no more than the mistranslation of one vowel.[51] This textual emendation does not have support in the manuscript tradition.

[48] BDB, 1000,1001.
[49] E.g., by the editors of the BHK^3.
[50] E.g., P. Skehan, *Studies in Israelite Poetry* (Washington, DC: CBA, 1971) 61.
[51] L. Sabourin, *Le livre des Psaumes*, 554.

Finally, some suggest that the original reading of the second phrase was not "like a weaned child" (*kaggāmul*), but rather "is weaned" (*tiggāmēl*).[52] This would form the sentence "my soul is weaned" so that the two phrases would read as follows:

> like a weaned child upon its mother,
> my soul is weaned.

In support of this emendation one could note that a verb is found at this point in some Septuagintal manuscripts. Leslie Allen has argued convincingly, however, that this was a corruption of the original Septuagintal reading.[53]

The preceding attempts to explain the phrase "like a weaned child upon me [is] my soul" rely in one way or another on textual emendations. In the absence of strong manuscript support for these emendations, however, it is wiser to interpret the Hebrew text as we have it.

This phrase has both an aesthetic and a suasive function. The repetition in verse 2b creates a parallelism between the threefold response of the psalmist (v. 2) and the threefold description of courses the psalmist does not take when faced with surpassing difficulties (v. 1). The psalmist's attempt to link these two sections by means of the *lō' – 'im-lō'* ("not" – "Rather") connection has already been noted.[54] The linkage also occurs through the similarity of form between the two sections. In verse 1a we have two succinct half-lines with the same syntactic pattern: "Lord, my heart is not lifted up, my eyes are not raised too high" (*YHWH lō' gāḇah libbî wĕlō' rāmû 'ênay*). Besides the initial address to *YHWH* at the beginning of the verse and the connecting word at the beginning of the second half-line ("and-" *wĕ*) the pattern is identical: "not" (*lō'*) followed by a third person, plural, perfect Qal verb which is in turn succeeded by a substantive with the first person singular pronominal suffix which serves as the subject.

[52] E.g., S. Mowinckel, *Psalmenstudien I.* (Kristiana: J. Dybwad, 1921) 132.
[53] L. Allen, *Psalms 101-150*, 197.
[54] See supra, pp. 50-51.

Such a syntactic parallelism is found neither in the half-lines in verse 1b ("I do not walk in paths of great things nor in paths too surpassing/difficult for me") nor in the first line of verse 2 ("Rather, I have leveled/placed and quieted my soul like a weaned child upon its mother"). The words "not" (*lō'*) and "I walk" (*hillaktî*) in the first colon in verse 1b have no counterparts in the second colon in verse 1b, and the same is true of the word translated "for me" (*mimmennî*) in the second colon. The words *'im-lō'* ("but") in the first half-line of verse 2 are not paralleled in the second half-line of this verse, and "my soul" (*napšî*) in the second half-line is not mirrored in the first.

Like verse 1a, the words "like a weaned child upon its mother, like a weaned child upon me, my soul" exhibits a short, three word parallelism. In each half-line there is a *kě* ("like") inseparable preposition attached to the word signifying "weaned child" (*gāmul*). These are followed first by "upon" (*'al*) words and then by objects of this preposition: "its mother" (*'imô*) and "my soul" (*napšî*).

Thus, verse 2b ("like a weaned child upon me, my soul") creates a parallelism between verse 1 and verse 2. Verse 1a ("Lord, my heart is not lifted up, my eyes are not raised too high") is balanced by the second line in verse 2 ("like a weaned child upon its mother, like a weaned child upon me, my soul"). They bracket verse 1b and the first line in verse 2. The words "like a weaned child upon me, my soul" in verse 2b have an aesthetic function; they establish a parallelism which contrasts two sets of responses.[55] This is not the only function of verse 2b. In the next section of this chapter, it will be pointed out that verse 2 encourages a certain type of faith response on the part of the reader.

[55] E. Greenstein, "How Does Parallelism Mean?" in S. Geller, E. Greenstein & A. Berlin, *A Sense of Text: The Art of Language in the Study of Biblical Literature* (Winona Lake, IN.: Eisenbrauns, 1983) 69-70 notes a number of examples where parallelism highlights "thematic oppositions." This is especially prevalent in the Wisdom Literature. Greenstein does not mention Ps.131:2b, but his work is not meant to be a catalogue of the appearance of this feature in the Hebrew Bible.

Ps 131:3 – O Israel, hope in the Lord, both now and forever.

This verse may be an appendix added to the psalm. The words "O Israel, hope in the Lord" are found in Ps 131:3 and in Ps 130:7a. These words are not found in the Septuagintal version of 130:7a. Claus Westermann thinks that these words were added to both psalms because both were originally psalms of the individual used later as communal psalms during the pilgrimages.[56]

On the other hand, some consider 130:7a and 131:3 as being part of the original psalm which presented the individual as an example to the entire community.[57]

When Life Is Too Difficult: The Interpretation of Psalm 131

As we have seen in the prior section, verse 1a ("Lord, my heart is not lifted up, and my eyes are not raised too high") is the psalmist's assertion that he is not proud. The problem in verse 1 is in determining what verse 1b ("I do not walk in paths of great things, nor in paths too surpassing/difficult for me") means. Some scholars interpret this line as saying that the psalmist has abandoned his ambitions, or his impossible ambitions.[58] One may wonder why the psalmist would advocate this check on human aspirations. Anderson suggests that possibly the ambitions were unjust, whereas Weiser proposes that the dreams are not abandoned; rather, the psalmist now has "the balance of mind that enables him to be satisfied with what is given to him."[59]

[56] C. Westermann, *The Living Psalms* (Grand Rapids: Eerdmans, 1989) 120, 121.
[57] See e.g., A. Anderson, *The Book of Psalms* (NCB; London: Oliphants, 1972) 2.878.
[58] C. & E. Briggs, *The Book of Psalms*, 2.466; A. Anderson, *The Book of Psalms*, 2.878. The note in the NAB says that the psalmist is free from worldly ambition. So too H. Kraus, *Psalmen* (BKAT; Neukirchen-Vluyn: Neukirchener, 1978) 1:1053 interprets v. 1c as a claim that the psalmist does not strive for riches, power or for the overcoming of opposition.
[59] A. Anderson, *The Book of Psalms*, 2.878; A. Weiser, *The Psalms* (OTL; Philadelphia: Westminster, 1962) 777.

What these interpretations do not treat is the fact that the psalmist is writing about matters which are "too difficult" (*niplā'ôṯ mimmennî*). As has been noted, the word *niplā'ôṯ*, coming from *pālā'*, has the meaning of "to be difficult" or "to be surpassing or extraordinary."[60] When it is used with the preposition *min* it means to be "too difficult" (Gen 18:14) or "too extraordinary" (Prov 30:18) for one,[61] and this is the way it is used in this verse in Ps 131. Thus, the psalmist has not abandoned his ambitions, but rather he has handed over the excess, what is too difficult for him, to God. What the psalmist has abandoned is the attempt to do or to understand what is beyond him ("too surpassing/difficult"); he is no longer banging his head against the wall. He interprets such activity as a sign of pride and asserts that he is not acting in this way which manifests pride ("Lord, my heart is not lifted up/haughty, and my eyes are not raised/exalted"- Ps 131:1a).

In verse 1 the psalmist asserts that being concerned with things beyond one's power is a strain. The psalmist uses a variety of spatial images to convey this point. To concern one's self with things too difficult to understand is like one's heart and eyes being lifted up. It is like thinking envisaged as walking through paths of great things and through paths too surpassing/difficult. It is a strain.

The psalmist claims that a better response to matters that are beyond one's power is to hand over the excess to God. This is expressed by imagery which is both in contrast to, and in response to, the straining imagery found in verse 1. Thus, the psalmist asserts that he has leveled/placed (*šāwāh*) and quieted his soul. Recall that the verb *šāwāh* can mean "to level" or "to place."[62] The leveling aspect of *šāwāh* is in contrast to the lifting up (*gāḇah*) of the heart and the raising up (*rāmû*) of the eyes written about in verse 1.[63] The placing aspect of *šāwāh* is in con-

[60] See supra, p. 50.
[61] *KB*, 3.876.
[62] See supra, p. 51.
[63] M. Dahood, *Psalms 101-150* (AB; Garden City, New York: Doubleday, 1970) 239 suggests that translating the *šāwāh* verb in this verse as "I have kept level" brings out the contrast with thoughts too lofty for the psalmist. Thus, Dahood sug-

trast to the image of "walking (*hillaktî*) in great things" found in verse 1.[64]

The phrase "like a weaned child upon his mother" refers both to how the psalmist has quieted (*dāmam*) and to how he has leveled/placed (*šāwāh*) his soul (v. 2).[65] The image of a weaned child upon his mother is an image of a quieted child; it is also, however, a fixed and leveled image. The child is set upon its mother. There is no "walking in paths of great things," no straining over great matters for the young child; the world is mediated through mother. In other words, instead of straining over matters too difficult for him (v. 1) he has placed his soul like a child placed on its mother.[66] This is not a retreat from the difficulties of life; it is a taking comfort in the divine mother when the situation becomes too great and difficult for one.

gests that the word *gĕḏōlôṯ* in the clause "I do not occupy myself with things too great (*gĕḏōlôṯ*) and too marvelous for me" (NRSV translation) should be translated as "lofty matters" rather than as "great (matters)." This is moot. While the *šāwāh* verb is to be viewed against the backdrop of "elevated" terminology in this psalm, the loci of this terminology appears to be the words "to be lifted up," "to be raised too high," and "too surpassing/difficult" in v. 1.

[64] A. Weiser, *The Psalms*, 777 thinks that behind the words "I have calmed and quieted my soul" lie many struggles against ambitions and arrogance. Similarly, D. Grossberg, *Centripetal and Centrifugal Structures in Biblical Poetry* (SBLMS, 39; Atlanta: Scholars Press, 1989) 46. This is speculative. V. 2a tells only about the posture which the psalmist advocates in the face of difficulties too great for him, and not about his history which eventuated in the proposal of this type of stance.

[65] The word used for child (*gāmul*) refers to a weaned child. Thus, the image is not of a child who is quieted because it is nursing, as is the impression given by translations which place the child at the mother's breast. See, e.g., the RSV translation.
2 Macc 7:27 indicates that children were weaned around age three.

[66] A. Weiser, *The Psalms*, 777 writes that v. 2 expresses the idea that the psalmist now desires God for God's own sake and not as a means to satisfy the needs of the psalmist. This view neglects the fact that the mother imagery in the psalm is found as a response to things that are too difficult for the psalmist. The psalmist does portray God as an answer to needs, but the needs are emotional ones and not physical ones. The child is a weaned child, and so the needs are not physical ones. The psalmist is experiencing matters too great and too difficult to handle and so he returns to the divine mother; it is the emotional needs of the psalmist which find attention in this psalm. Emotional needs are never outgrown; they recur at different times throughout our lives.

Following the phrase "like a weaned child upon its mother," the psalmist wrote "like a weaned child upon me [is] my soul." These words relate the experience of the weaned child upon its mother to the state of the psalmist's soul. The repetition of the image of the weaned child also produces a calming effect to show the calm experience of the psalmist.

Finally, in verse 3 ("Israel, hope in the Lord, both now and forever") the psalmist encourages Israel to adopt towards God the posture of a weaned child upon its mother's lap. This verse presents hope as rest in the Lord in the face of situations too difficult to handle (vv. 1, 2). Thus, Psalm 131 is not expressive of a *c'est la guerre* attitude. God will act and Israel is to adopt a restful posture that manifests a confident expectancy of salvation.

The Divine Mother and Attachment Theory

Psalm 131 advocates a type of relationship to God that is similar to the type which attachment theory says is necessary in situations which are too difficult for us. The perspective found in Psalm 131 can help those who have not experienced secure attachment relations and can help all parents to be secure attachment figures for their children.

The two respects in which attachment theory and Psalm 131 are similar are that each treat reactions to situations which are too difficult for us, and each stresses the value of a certain type of trust in these situations. To begin the process of correlating attachment theory and Psalm 131 each of these points will be treated in the context of a short review of the salient features of attachment theory and therapy.

Psalm 131 treats what is too difficult for us; attachment theory is concerned with behavior when one is fearful, tired or in pain. What causes fear, fatigue or pain are matters which are too difficult for us. We saw that attachment theorists say that when one is fearful, in pain or tired one needs an attachment figure: someone to provide comfort and a secure base during these times. If these needs are consistently met during such times, the child becomes confident, self-reliant and shows a good degree of ego-resiliency. In addition, such children tend to comfort others who are in distress, and they are able to request and to receive care from others when they themselves are in distress.

Mothers who provide secure attachment relations to their children display the following characteristics: (1) they are "tuned-in" to their children's needs; (2) they hold their infants for long periods of time; (3) they engage in more direct communication with their children than do other parents; (4) they engage in emotional communication with their children. The capacity of the mother to provide secure attachment relations to her children depends upon the type of attachment relations which she herself experienced as a child. In such a way a type of attachment relation tends to perpetuate itself.

Attachment relations produce internal working models which tell us what to expect from others when one is tired, fearful or in pain. The longer a certain type of attachment exists, be it an insecure one or a secure one, the harder it is to change. Change is possible, however. As an aid to such change, the therapist becomes an attachment figure, offering a secure base from which to explore past events in one's life. The goals are (1) to see how past attachment relations continue to be influential, (2) to see how past attachment responses by one's parents may not have been justified, and (3) to imagine both new, alternative attachment responses by attachment figures and alternative responses to fear, fatigue or pain by the patient. The problem is that the needs of one who has not experienced secure attachment relations are so great that it is difficult for the therapist to give the amount of care that such a person needs.

This leads us to the second point at which attachment theory and Psalm 131 intersect, namely, the value of trust in difficult situations which cause fear, fatigue or pain. According to Teresa Nezworski and her colleagues the basic issue in attachment relations is trust.[67] If there is trust that one will be comforted when

[67] T. Nezworski, W. Tolan, J. Belsky, "Intervention in Insecure Infant Attachment," in J. Belsky & T. Nezworski, eds., *Clinical Implications of Attachment*, 379.

fearful, tired or in pain, then one will develop a secure attachment, the healthy life style that comes from such relations, and the ability to provide children with secure, attachment relations. Psalm 131 deals with the basis for trust in such situations. A person can trust because God is present as the divine mother to provide comfort in situations which are too difficult.

Let us now look at how the perspective of Psalm 131 can help both those parents who did not experience secure attachment relations as a child, and those who did experience such relations, so that all parents may provide a secure base for their children.

Aid for Parents Who Have Not Experienced Secure Attachment Relations

There are two ways in which Psalm 131 can help parents who have not experienced secure attachment relations. First, as we have seen the psychotherapist becomes a new attachment figure for such a person; the therapist's presence as an attachment figure, however, is often not enough for this person's great needs. [68] It is difficult to reverse the effects of years of neglect. The needs of some mock the gear[69] of the psychotherapist.

Psalm 131 presents one whose presence is great enough for such needs; Psalm 131 presents the image of God, the divine mother, who is always present when life is too difficult, when we need an attachment figure. The caring attachment figure of God as the divine mother ("like a weaned child upon his mother") is present to us as our souls are present to us ("like a weaned child upon me, my soul"); indeed, we are called upon to adopt this posture toward God ("Israel, hope in the Lord both now and forever"). Thus, one can rely on the divine mother whenever one feels overwhelmed or tired or in danger. The

[68] See supra, pp. 45-46.

[69] To use one of Adrienne Rich's images. See lines 42-45 of her poem "Double Monologue" in A. Eastman, ed., *The Norton Anthology of Poetry* (New York: Norton, 1970) 1177-1178.

psychoanalyst may not have the time to be present, but the divine mother does.[70]

The second way in which the perspective of Psalm 131 can help parents who have not had secure attachments is by helping them to reclaim a past filled with secure attachments as a basis for present maturation and care for children. Recall that the psychotherapist who engages in Bowlby's type of attachment therapy attempts to help the patient explore past attachment relations. The goal is to show the patient how past responses of attachment figures may not have been justified in order that the patient may "feel free to imagine alternatives better fitted to his current life" and to alter his or her behavior.[71]

The perspective of Psalm 131 shows why it is legitimate to imagine alternative responses to one's need for secure attachment during times of pain, fatigue or fear. It is because the divine mother was always there during these times in one's past ("Israel, hope in the Lord both now and forever" – 131:3) providing a secure base of emotional support and care. For this reason those who have not experienced secure attachments can review their past from the perspective of the secure attachment with the divine mother which they had in the past, but did not recognize. To look at their past from this perspective enables people to reframe their past in order to reclaim significant aspects of it which have gone unnoticed.

The Brief Therapy Center of the Mental Research Institute in Palo Alto, California calls our attention to reframing. This is the process of changing the frame in which a person perceives events by changing one's view of, or feelings regarding, these events. This can change both the significance which one attaches to these events and the way in which one responds to them. Donald Capps has noted how the parables of Jesus and the Book of Job accom-

[70] In a conversation my colleague, Barbara Turner, noted that the church must model this care because "God's presence is mediated by community. There have to be signs of grace in the community even if the community will not be fully adequate."

[71] Bowlby, *A Secure Base*, 117, 118, 138-143.

plish such a reframing and he has shown how these reframings can guide us in many types of pastoral care.[72]

As one remembers incidents in the past when an attachment figure was needed and either was not present or did not provide the care needed, one can look at the divine mother's response to such situations; the divine mother was always there to provide care in times which were too difficult (Psalm 131). In such a way these voids in a person's life can be seen to have been moments when there was care and support which came from the divine mother. One's history, the personal story from which one lives, can be reframed when looked upon from a different perspective, and this reframing of the past can bring one emotionally and socially into a different present and into a different future.[73]

The degree to which the patterns of behavior developed in childhood can be changed is a disputed point among psychologists. Although it may at first seem to be at an angle to my own view, the view of Leslie Stroufe appears to be realistic.

> Development... is not a blackboard to be erased and written upon again. Even when children change rather markedly, the shadows of the earlier adaptation remain and, in times of stress, the prototype itself may be clear.[74]

[72] P. Watzlawick, J. Weakland & R. Fisch, *Change: Principles of Problem Formation and Problem Resolution* (New York: W. Norton, 1974); D. Capps, *Reframing: A New Method in Pastoral Care* (Philadelphia: Fortress, 1990).

[73] What we need is input from Jewish and Christian psychotherapists who utilize attachment theory in their therapies; we need studies that carefully document the effects of the use of reframing one's past from the perspective of the divine mother as presented in Psalm 131. The progress which this group makes in their capacity to undertake exploration and to enter into caring, compassionate relations with others must be measured against a group which has not attempted to reframe its histories from the perspective of Psalm 131.

[74] L. Stroufe, "Patterns of Individual Adaptation from Infancy to Preschool: The Roots of Maladaptation and Competence," in M. Perlmutter, ed., *Minnesota Symposia on Child Psychology* (Hillsdale, New Jersey: L. Erlbaum, 1983) 16:73, 74. See also L. Stroufe, "The Role of Infant-Caregiver Attachment in Development," in J. Belsky & T. Nezworski, *Clinical Implications of Attachment*, 24. This dovetails with Bowlby's experience of a couple of patients who made rewarding progress in therapy, but who remained susceptible in stressful situations. *A Secure Base*, 57, 114.

Stroufe is correct in stressing the difficulty of a change in behavior pattern, especially in times of stress; it can be argued, however, that the past may be reclaimed as a basis for a healthy present and future, although such a reclamation is a time-consuming process. Through frequent reflections on the past and present from the perspective of Psalm 131 one can create a new "prototype," to use Stroufe's terminology, upon which one's life may be based. Patience and persistence in viewing life through the perspective of Psalm 131 will be required because of the accumulated weight of the many years in which some have lived from an insecure "prototype;" change is possible, however.

Attachment theory deals with the secure attachment relations which are necessary in order to be a care giver. This is congruent with the witness of the scriptures that it is God's love for us that is to draw out a similar response in us.[75] From a biblical perspective, one should not minimize either God's will to heal, or the transformative power of the Word of God to bring us into touch with this healing. Psalm 131 puts us in touch with God as our secure base which enables us to become secure bases for children. The power of a therapy which reclaims one's history from the perspective of Psalm 131 is rooted in the powerful, transformative love of God.

Richard McCormick used Philip Rieff's metaphor of "climates" as public assumptions which have sunk into the unconscious of a society and which are more influential about where a society is going than are a society's laws. According to McCormick, "climates of addictiveness" lead to a "silent slavery." Our tradition attempts to establish "climates of grace" so that we may not be enslaved by "climates of addictiveness." "Climates of grace" are transformative. "Good climates support good people. It is no accident that children of good, loving people are often comfortable with themselves."[76] There is a transformative power in the "climates of grace" found in our tradition.

[75] See, e.g., 1 John 4:7-19, especially v. 19 ("We love, because he first loved us.").
[76] R. McCormick, "Discernment in Ethics: What Does It Mean?" Paper Presented at Marquette University, Milwaukee, Wisconsin, 27 November 1990; P. Rieff, *The Triumph of the Therapeutic* (Chicago: University of Chicago, 1987).

God is the primary attachment figure. In this light, it is interesting that Dahood noted that Ps 27:10 expresses a sentiment similar to the one found in Ps 131:2.[77] Ps 27:10 reads as follows. "Though my father and my mother abandon me,/ yet Yahweh will receive me." Reframe the primary attachment relationship which the parent experienced as a child and you create a new pattern of attachment relations between this parent and his or her own child. The literary dynamics of Psalm 131 – when received in faith and appropriated for past or present situations which may overwhelm one by causing fear, fatigue or pain – puts the parent in the presence of the love that is not mocked by his or her needs.

By providing such a resource from our tradition we should not think that we are truncating the biblical passage and making it merely a servant to psychotherapy. Christianity should be integrally involved in whatever promotes human health. Further, no harm is done to Psalm 131 because this psalm is about comfort and rest in God, the Divine Mother, in situations that are too difficult. What attachment theory does is to allow us to see a little more clearly the situations to which Psalm 131 can respond. The therapeutic present in Psalm 131 can contribute greatly to providing secure attachment relations.[78]

One may suggest that not only societies have climates, but so do the groups which make up societies, including families. The "climates" of the larger, inclusive group and that of the smaller groups need not be identical to each other, although they mutually influence each other. "Climates of grace" may transform families which have earlier been characterized by unhealthy climates.

[77] M. Dahood, *Psalms 101-150*, 239.

[78] D. Capps, "Bible: Pastoral Use and Interpretation of," in *Dictionary of Pastoral Care and Counseling*, ed., R. J. Hunter (Nashville, TN: Abingdon, 1989) 84; Idem, *Biblical Approaches to Pastoral Counseling* (Philadelphia: Westminster, 1981) 45 has also argued that the bible may inform and modify the therapeutic practices derived from psychotherapeutic theories and methods which are used in pastoral care. He suggests that in time these theories and methods may be judged by theologians on the basis of how well they conform to the "world disclosive" biblical texts. Cf. R. Lambourne, *Community, Church and Healing* (London: Darton, Longman & Todd, 1963).

I am grateful to my teacher, Bernard Tyrell, who recognized the therapeutic implicit in our religious heritage. See B. Tyrell, *Christotherapy* (New York: Seabury, 1975); Idem, *Christotherapy II: The Fasting and Feasting Heart* (New York: Paulist, 1982).

Aid for Parents Who Have Experienced Secure Attachment Relations

It seems natural that parents comfort their child when the child is fearful, tired or in pain; it often happens in these situations, however, that the parents do not give enough comfort. There are at least two reasons why this is the case. First, in these situations the child requires not just the normal amount of attention and sensitivity, but rather a great amount of these qualities. These are extranormal situations which require much out of a parent. This leads to the second reason why it is often the case that not enough comfort is given when a child is fearful, tired or in pain: the parent cannot always muster the extra energy that is necessary in these situations. The parent is often overburdened with other concerns and with other tasks. As Bowlby noted, preoccupation with other things or being worried about other things may contribute to parental insensitivity.[79]

The person is only able to function as a care giver for a child's emotional needs to the degree that his or her care is centered on the child and not on him or herself. Jay Belsky and Russell Isabella have noted that if a mother is to promote a secure attachment by being sensitive to the child's needs then "she must be able to decenter from self, appraise the needs of another, and meet those needs in a nonnarcisstic manner. In many cases being psychologically mature means being able to do just such things."[80] This is where the image of one's soul being leveled and placed on God comes in (Ps 131:2). Viewed in relation to the image of putting aside things too difficult (Ps 131:1), verse 2 is an image of trust in the care of the divine mother.[81] The perspec-

[79] Bowlby, *A Secure Base*, 48.
[80] J. Belsky & R. Isabella, "Determinants of Attachment Security," in *Clinical Implications of Attachment*, ed., J. Belsky & T. Nezworski (CP; Hillsdale, New Jersey: L. Erlbaum, 1988) 50, 51.
[81] In his own way Charles Peguy attempted to provide images which would enable one to rest in God in the face of excess difficulties. See C. Peguy, *God Speaks: Religious Poetry* (New York: Pantheon, 1965). See especially his poems "Sleep" (pp. 27-31), "Abandonment" (pp. 32-36) and "Night" (pp. 106-122) in this book.

tive of Psalm 131 leads one to not be overburdened with things too difficult to handle, but rather to hand over the excess to God. This enables the parent to have sufficient emotional resources to provide the degree of comfort necessary when the child is fearful, tired or in pain.

Psalm 131 also helps parents live with and in situations which are too difficult to understand. Being unable to live without all the answers is a sign of mental illness. There are some who are driven so that they are unable to rest. That which is unanswered, which they cannot grasp, drives them to "walk in paths of great things... in paths which are too surpassing/ difficult." Their hearts and eyes are raised too high; their life is a strain. Their souls are not leveled and placed quietly as a weaned child on its mother; they cannot live separated from all the answers and so they do not mature. They cannot wait/ hope (*yaḥēl*) for the Lord (131:3); they must have all of the answers.

The first act of *Faust* opens with the following soliloquy from Dr. Faust.

> I've studied now to my regret,
> Philosophy, Law, and Medicine
> and – what is worst- Theology
> from end to end with diligence.
> Yet here am I a wretched fool
> and still no wiser than before.
> I've become Master, and Doctor as well,
> and for nearly ten years I've led
> my students a merry chase,
> up, down, and every which way -
> and find we can't have certitude.
> That is too much for heart to bear! [82]

Faust finds that he does not have the ability to understand what he wishes to understand.

[82] *Faust*, Pt.1, Sc.1, l.354-365. This translation, as well as the one which follows it, is from S. Atkins, *Johann Wolfgang von Goethe, Faust I and II* (Cambridge: Suhrkomp/ Insel, 1984).

The god that dwells within my breast
can deeply stir my inmost being;
the one that governs all my faculties
cannot realize its purposes.[83]

His anguish causes him to plan to take his life.

There are things which we cannot grasp (the suffering of children etc...).[84] With these matters we can choose one of three options: (1) forsake the God Whose meanings we cannot grasp, (2) manipulate our reasoning to apparently grasp the ungraspable, or (3) allow ourselves to be grasped by God.

To be able to live with uncertainty in certain things while hoping in God is to reach a greater stage of maturity just as a child who is weaned has reached a greater stage of maturity. Of course, the image of weaning is an image of separation on one level, but it is also one of maturation and growth towards the ability to enter into deeper relations.

Psalm 131 presents a way to live maturely without all of the answers. Not having all the answers need not cause anxiety nor inability to let go of the attempt to answer all of the questions. One can let go and live relaxed and trustingly because one is being held by God like a child held by its mother; but the child is weaned. The message of Psalm 131 is that when one cannot grasp, let go and be grasped by God.

Psalm 131 can also help parents who have had secure attachment relations to reclaim parts of their past in which their attachments could have been more secure. There are times in which all of us wish that we had had more comfort, care and sympathy.

[83] Ibid., Pt.1, Sc.3, l.566-569.

[84] In this light one must question if the media bring people more than they can handle. One is almost bombarded with news about every societal and environmental distress at all hours of the day and night through radio, T.V. and newspapers. While people must keep abreast of the world's news in order to act responsibly and sensitively to human pain, there is such a thing as there being too much for one individual to reasonably and responsibly handle. One may often question if the choice of items which are deemed newsworthy is the result of a concern for human pain and suffering or the result of the attempt to market the news through the sensationalism that sells.

Psalm 131 calls our attention to the fact that the divine mother was always there during these times, and by so doing it clarifies the richness of the care which is our heritage.

In this light it should be noted that in his last essay in *A Secure Base* Bowlby wrote about how important events in the first three years of life are difficult to reclaim. It may be suggested that what we cannot reclaim by memory we appropriate through our imagination. One can imagine how God, the divine mother, responded to the emotional needs which one experienced in the first three years of life. For those who had a secure attachment figure this can be a way of reappropriating the richness of the emotional care that was present from one's origins.[85] For those who have not had a secure attachment figure this can be a way of reframing their lives from the outset. The lives of this latter group have been marked by an emotional void which is best filled with this type of meditation. In imagining God in this way both groups are only reclaiming the care that God has shown to people during these years.[86]

In conclusion, Psalm 131 presents us with the image of the divine mother who is present to comfort us when life is too difficult. The image is of a direct and tactile relation to God during these times: we are as children upon the lap of the divine mother (v. 2). The image is one of having our emotional needs attended to: the child is comforted not because it is nursing – the child is weaned (*gāmul*) – but rather because it is being cared for in the midst of things which are too difficult for it (v. 1). The image is of the divine mother always being tuned in to our needs because we

[85] One may note the transformative effect of such a reclaiming of the first year of one's life on the character Barabbas, in Par Lagerkvist's *Barabbas* (New York: Random, 1989).

[86] Perhaps we need to appropriate our vast and rich heritage of paintings on the Madonna and child for this type of exercise. These paintings could aid us in imaginatively claiming God's care for us from birth. In *Mary: The Feminine Face of the Church* (Philadelphia: Westminster, 1977) 78, Rosemary Radford Ruether wrote that we need to image God as nurturer: as the "ground of being and its continual power for aspiration to new being." Psalm 131 provides us with such an image and perhaps our heritage of Madonna and child paintings could also provide us with helpful images of God as nurturer.

are encouraged to hope in God both now and forever (v. 3). As we have seen, being tuned in to the child's needs and engaging in direct, emotional and tactile relations are characteristics of secure attachment figures.[87] Psalm 131 presents us with the image of the divine mother who can provide the secure attachment relations which all need as a basis for providing such relations to their children.[88]

[87] See supra, pp. 36-38.
[88] See the appendix for a literary elucidation of the need for secure attachment relations throughout life, and the difficulties in providing such relations when there are family divisions.

CHAPTER 4

PSALM 23 AND THE CHILD'S CONFIDENCE IN RELATIONSHIPS

Therefore, I summon age
to grant youth's heritage.
R. Browning, "Rabbi Ben Ezra"

If it is true that a secure base needs to be maintained for the healthy growth of the child, it is equally true that this base must be a loving and a relaxed one. The daily environment of the home and the emotional and social development of the child are inextricably intertwined. Psalm 23 is a great resource for providing parents with the basis for maintaining a loving and relaxed atmosphere in the home.

The program for this chapter is to first explore psychological and literary perspectives on the effects of stress on the family, next to interpret Psalm 23, and finally to show how this psalm can aid parents in their attempts at creating a nurturing family life.

Space To Be a Child: Psychological and Literary Perspectives

There have been numerous psychological studies on the detrimental effects of stress on the family. The following sampling will illustrate my point.

Financial difficulties often cause stress. In a study of twenty divorced fathers and twenty-five divorced mothers, Clarke-Stewart and Bailey have determined that there is a correlation between the degree of psychological stress which these parents experienced and the ability to provide for one's self without financial support from the spouse. The men were found to be generally better off financially, to have more stable jobs, less stress and more "psychological satisfaction."[1]

Stress caused by financial problems often filters down to the children, as was shown by a study of one hundred and five sixth, seventh and eighth graders. Some came from farm families and some did not. It was found that parents of children from farm families reported more financial stress and depression. Their children, in turn, displayed significantly more depressive symptoms. The researchers discovered a connection between family financial stress and the children's reports of depressive symptoms.[2]

Stress manifests itself in the family not only in depression but sometimes also in child abuse. Lawson and Hays studied twenty-three abusive couples and twenty-three non-abusive ones. The groups were matched in age, education, income and occupation. They found that there was no significant difference in abuse among those who had a high self-esteem and those who had a low self-esteem. However, using "The Recent Life Changes Questionnaire" to measure stress, they discovered significantly higher mean stress scores in abusive couples.[3]

The more stresses that a child is exposed to the harder it is for a child to adjust to different situations and groups. In a study of fifty-six urban eleven to thirteen year-olds, researchers found a correlation between the number of stressful circumstances the child experienced and his or her difficulty in adjustment as determined by parents, teachers and the children themselves.[4]

This brief selection of studies highlights some of the difficulties experienced by children in stressful situations. From these one

[1] "Adjusting to Divorce. Why Do Men Have It Easier?," *Journal of Divorce* 13 (1989) 75-94.

[2] D. Clark-Lempers, J. Lempers & A. Netusil, "Family Financial Stress, Parental Support and Young Adolescents' Academic Achievement and Depressive Symptoms," *Journal of Early Adolescence* 10 (1990) 21-36.

[3] K. Lawson & R. Hays,"Self-Esteem and Stress as Factors in Abuse of Children," *Psychological Reports* 65 (3, 1989) 1259-65.

[4] W. Work, G. Parker, E. Cowen, "The Impact of Stressors on Childhood Adjustment: Multiple Perspectives," *Journal of Community Psychology* 18 (1990) 73-78.

may surmise that the children of families under stress may have a difficult time socializing with their peers. This, in fact, was one of the results of a massive study of school children in Minnesota and Texas.

Roff, Sells and Golden have conducted a study on the social adjustment of children.[5] It was a five year project in which about forty thousand third through sixth graders were tested, five thousand of which were studied in the second through the fifth years as follow-up samples.

Their study showed that there is a correlation between a family's financial situation, stress, parental child-rearing habits and children's socialization. Peer acceptance is associated with the family background of the child and with the parents' child-raising attitudes and practices. These promote certain types of characteristics in children: characteristics which either attract or repel others. Among other things (e.g., health, athletic ability, appearance), peers respond to one's intelligence, ego development and personality traits. These attributes are promoted by certain parental qualities: a loving, rather than a rejecting response to the child, casual "rather than punishing or demanding mothers' attitudes," and "agreement between parents in expressed child-rearing attitudes."

These parental habits are present in families in the higher socio-economic levels to a significantly greater degree than they are in families in the lower levels. The former group of families experience less stress than the latter group. Family harmony and cohesiveness are conducive to developing socially appealing characteristics in children and instability, tension and unhappiness in families hinder the growth of the desired traits. Families in higher socio-economic strata live in more comfortable settings and expe-

[5] M. Roff, S. Sells & M. Golden, *Social Adjustment and Personality Development in Children* (Minneapolis: University of Minnesota, 1972) 146, 147, 179. Cattell's Teacher Ratings and Bower's Class Play procedure were among the instruments used for the test. Interestingly, it was found that there was no correlation between the peer status of the child doing the rating and the child who was being rated. In addition, the researchers discovered that children had a good idea of their degree of acceptance or rejection by peers.

rience less deprivation. As a result they are less prone to tension and stress than are families in lower socio-economic strata who experience more "stressful and tension-producing family situations." More stress increases the chances of family instability, tension and unhappiness. Often, this leads to rejecting-demanding parental attitudes and practices and to disagreement on child raising. The result is that the children in these families develop characteristics – such as low self-esteem, poor intelligence and an attitude of hostility towards others – which are not desirable to their peers.

Less tension enhances the possibilities for family cohesiveness and harmony. Often, this leads to loving and casual parental attitudes and practices as well as to expressed agreement on child raising practices. This, in turn, leads to socially appealing characteristics in their children: characteristics such as intelligence, high self-esteem and the acceptance of others. Children with these traits have an easier time with transitions in life.[6]

Thus, this study by Roff, Sells and Golden has shown how a child's social adjustment is influenced greatly by types of parental attitudes and behavior, and how these attitudes and behavior in turn are influenced by the degree of stress in the family. Once again we see how stress adversely touches children.[7]

[6] Roff, Sells and Golden have a few caveats. First, while intelligence was found to be stimulating and appreciated by peers in the high or middle socio-economic levels, it was not found to influence acceptance by peers in the low socio-economic levels. Second, it is possible to have some characteristics associated with low peer acceptance and to still be highly accepted by one's peers if the child has "enough positive attributes to overcome the effect of such liabilities."

[7] Not surprisingly even attachment relations, described in the previous chapter, are adversely affected by stress and again there may be a correlation with different socio-economic groups. Thus, T. Nezworski, W. Tolan and J. Belsky, "Intervention in Insecure Infant Attachment," 378-82, found a correlation between insecure attachment and "families under stress."

J. Belsky and R. Isabella, "Maternal, Infant, and Social-Contextual Determinants of Attachment Security," 45, 80, note the effect of economic and social factors on secure attachments. In most children from the middle-class who have been studied in terms of attachment behavior the rate of attachment is between 65-70%; in children from the lower economic class, however, some researchers report lower rates (i.e., 55%). So, too, parents of securely attached children tended to

A novel by Frederick Buechner also helps sensitize us to how stress affects parenting and to the havoc it plays on children's emotional and social lives. In *A Wizard's Tide*[8] Buechner writes about a year (1936) in the life of the Schroeder family. It is the time of the Great Depression and the story is told from the perspective of Teddy Schroeder. The story is about certain events that occur in the Schroeder family during the end of Teddy's tenth and the beginning of his eleventh year. The emotional climate is very unstable in Teddy's home. Teddy's father was fired a few weeks before the story begins, and he "sometimes talked about how depressed he felt." This loss of his job has contributed to his depression. The situation caused Teddy's mother to be angry, and "she sometimes said such terrible things that she felt sorry about them afterward."[9]

Reading is one of Teddy's favorite pastimes and one of the reasons for this is that books provide a stable world: "a book didn't make you laugh one time you read it and scare you out of your wits the next."[10] It is the fighting between his parents that scares Teddy. He reads the books in the Oz series. In one of the books there is a magic word that would "transform anything into anything else if only you knew how to pronounce it." Teddy practices pronouncing it in different ways with the hope that he will come upon the correct pronunciation and use it to change the situation which made his father depressed and his mother angry. He would give his father money and his mother dresses and change the cocktails his father drank so that his father's face would no longer "feel clammy and cold when he came to kiss him and Bean good night."[11]

think, to a significantly greater degree than did the parents of insecurely attached children, that their neighbors were helpful and/or friendly. Belsky and Isabella note that the risk of insecure attachments is greater as the amount of stresses which the family experiences increases (pp. 86, 87).

[8] Frederick Buechner, *A Wizard's Tide*, San Francisco: Harper & Row, 1990.

[9] Ibid., 2-4.

[10] Ibid., 4.

[11] Ibid., 4, 5, 10. See W. Saroyan's short story, "The Oranges,"in W. Saroyan, ed., *The Saroyan Special* (New York: Harcourt, Brace & Co., 1948) 42-45 for a poignant tale of how economic difficulties play themselves out in a child's emotional life.

Teddy is insecure because of the fighting in the house. When Teddy's parents fought, "it made him afraid that the very ground they were standing on would split apart like an earthquake and they would be swallowed up into it." At his party on his eleventh birthday, what brings him the most joy is not the presents, games or cake, but the fact that all are on their best behavior and so no one would start fighting. Just sensing that his parents were going to have a fight made his stomach turn and "the top of his head go cold as ice."[12]

This is a story of a child who is suffering because of the lack of a strong bond between his parents. His security is in the bond that created him.

> He thought to himself that the loveliest and nicest thing he could remember for a long time had already happened. It had happened downstairs when his father's suntanned forehead and his mother's golden hair had touched just for a moment. For as long as that moment lasted he believed that there was no sad or scary thing in all the world that could ever touch any of them.

Unfortunately such moments were rare, and Teddy is anxious and careful how he acts so as not to get his parents upset; otherwise the fighting might begin again.[13]

Teddy is a child whose whole life revolves around his parents' relationship to each other precisely because this relationship is so insecure. We read that he wakes up one beautiful morning but what makes it beautiful to him was that everyone in the house was "feeling happy." All the sounds that morning are nice because "at least for the time being everybody was in the right place doing the right thing and it gave him a very good feeling." There is no room to be a child because the parental relationship is in frequent need of repair. The carefree days of childhood are replaced by attempts to tend to the relationship of parent to parent.

In a poignant passage we read about all the reasons why Teddy liked rainy days. The enumeration begins with all of the wonderful sounds, sights and smells of a rainy day; it ends with the claim

[12] Ibid., 14, 21, 22.
[13] Ibid., 14, 37.

that what he liked most about rainy days "was that it not only gave you a good excuse for staying inside at home all day if you felt like it but that it made home seem homier and cozier that it did any other time." Again, the focus is on the unstable home and the yearning for a comfortable, secure home.[14]

The home, and the relationship between his parents which is the basis of the home, must be attended to because it is so unstable. So Teddy listened carefully to what went on around the house.

> "It was as if he felt he had to keep track of everything that was going on in the house pretty much all the time so in case anything went wrong he would be prepared for it even if there was nothing he could do about it."[15]

There are some things for which Teddy can not prepare. Once, Teddy was caught in the middle of a fight which his parents were having. His mother gave him the car keys and told him not to give them to his father because his father was in no shape to drive. The scene takes place in his parents' bedroom, and Teddy is acutely aware that he is where he does not belong.

His father discovers that Teddy has the keys, and he pleads with Teddy over and over again to relinquish the keys. Teddy is torn by mother's instructions and father's pleading, and he pulls the cover on his father's bed up over him. He tries, but no magic word will put everyone back in their own beds where they belong. With his father still pleading and the blankets still over him, he feels "so tired his whole body ached," and, "still holding the car keys tight in his fist," he falls "fast asleep in his father's bed."

One day something happens to Teddy that makes his fears and his insecurities "fade away." It is the coming of his maternal grandmother, "Dan," for a visit. Everyone is nice to each other when Dan is around because Dan is so peaceful and content that it makes others in the family feel that way, and "it's when you're feeling like that, of course, that you're apt to be nicest."[16]

[14] Ibid., 38, 40, 41, 47.
[15] Ibid., 48. *Sturm und Drang* make for good novels but for poor family life.
[16] Ibid., 60.

Thus, with the sensitivity of a litterateur, Buechner describes how stress moves from parents to children with the result that children concentrate too much on the parental relationship. This emotional constriction and unease is relieved by the arrival of a peaceful, contented person who makes others feel as she does.

From the preceding psychological studies and literary portrait, we have seen that stress often causes unease in both parents and children and that a peaceful familial environment is important for the social adjustment of a child. Children need emotional space: a freedom from nagging and from tension. They need an internal space that is unencumbered by stress and the effects of stress in order to go out comfortably and confidently into the world. Thus, it is important that parents be given resources for handling potentially stressful situations in order that they might maintain the comfortable environment in the home as much as possible.

Psalm 23 and Liberated Space

Psalm 23 presents the peace which can exist at all times because of God's attention to our needs. It expresses the confidence that God will provide for our physical and emotional needs and will protect us in times of danger. This counters the tensions and stresses of life, and encourages the parental attitudes which promote emotional space and healthy social characteristics in children.

The Reading

Psalm 23

A Psalm of David

1 The Lord is my shepherd, I shall not want.
2 He makes me lie down in green pastures.
He leads me beside still waters;
3 he restores my soul.
He leads me in right paths
for His name's sake.

4 Even though I walk through the valley of the
shadow of death, I fear no evil
for you are with me, your rod and your staff
they comfort me.

5 You prepare a table before me
in the presence of my enemies;
you anoint my head with oil,
my cup overflows.
6 Surely goodness and mercy shall follow me
all the days of my life;
and I shall dwell in the house of the Lord
for length of days.[17]

Refreshment for the Whole Person: The Interpretation of Ps 23:1-3a

This psalm presents the psalmist through the use of two distinct images: that of a sheep (vv. 1-4) and that of a man (vv. 5, 6). Corresponding to these images are the images of God as a shepherd (vv. 1-4) and as a host at a party (vv. 5, 6).[18] In verses 1-3a the

[17] This translation is from the NRSV with the exception of the phrase "the valley of the shadow of death" in verse 4 and the last half line of the psalm. The NRSV translates these respectively as "the darkest valley" and "my whole life long." In both cases I have opted for a literal translation. The reasons for these choices will become clear later in this chapter.

[18] Most exegetes would argue that God and the psalmist are presented first respectively as shepherd and sheep and then as host and guest. See C. O'Connor, "The Structure of Psalm 23," *LS* 10 (1985) 207, 208, nn. 7, 8 for a listing of scholars who hold this view. C. & E. Briggs, *The Book of Psalms* (ICC; New York: Charles Scribners' Sons, 1906) 1:207 proposed that God is only presented as shepherd in this psalm. E. Power, "The Shepherd's Two Rods in Modern Palestine and in Some Passages of the Old Testament," *Bib* 9 (1928), 434-442, proposed that *šulḥān* ("table") in v. 5a is the result of dittography because the next word begins with the letter *nûn*. He said that the word in v. 5a was *šelaḥ*, which means "spear." In such a way he proposed that the shepherd imagery is carried through the first part of v. 5.

J. Morgenstern, "Psalm 23," *JBL* 65 (1946), 17, 18, and L. Kohler, "Psalm 23," *ZAW* 68 (1956) 227-34, proposed that the shepherd image extends even to the last two hemistiches of v. 5. They argue that the oil refers to the oil used to heal a cut on a sheep, and they adduce Ezek 34:16 and Isa 40:11; oil is not used in this way in these two passages. Morgenstern proposed that the cup referred to in Ps 23:5 refers to the trench which the shepherd digs to water the sheep; he could find, however, no such use of *kôs*.

shepherd-sheep imagery is used to show the complete well-being which is God's gift. The following considerations support this thesis.

In verse 1 the psalmist writes that because the Lord is David's shepherd, David will not want.[19] The verb "to want" in English can mean either to lack or to desire something. For this reason the NRSV translation "I shall not want" is ambiguous. The verb in verse 1 is *ḥāsēr*. It means "to lack, to need, to decrease, to take away."[20] The result of the Lord being David's shepherd is that God will always provide for David's needs.

Verses 2, 3a ("He makes me lie down in green pastures./ He leads me beside still waters;/ he restores my soul") make it clear that what the Lord provides is shalom: well-being.[21] Some commentators have interpreted the images in verse 2 as referring to food and drink, others to rest for the person, and still others to "contentment for both body and mind."[22] This last interpretation appears to be correct for the following reasons.

[19] The name "David" is used because of the superscription which relates this psalm to David. The use is simply one of convenience; it does not indicate that I think this psalm was written by, about or for David.

Some have proposed that the shepherd imagery alludes to the Exodus. The only passage which is adduced is Isa 63:11-14, and this passage shares none of the specifics of the shepherd imagery which are found in Ps 23. E. Beaucamp, "Vers les pâturages de Yahweh," *BVC* 32 (1960) 47-57, proposed that the shepherd imagery in Ps 23 refers to the hope of a return from the exile. Although we have the shepherd-sheep imagery used of God and the people in Ezek 34, Jer 23:1-8, 31:9-14, Isa 40:11, 49:9, it is only in Ezek 34 that this image used in a way similar to its use in Ps 23; there is, however, no shift from shepherd-sheep imagery to host-guest imagery in Ezek 34 as we find in Ps 23.

[20] BDB, 341; KB, 2.325.

[21] M. Dahood, *Psalms 1-50* (AB 16; Garden City, NY: Doubleday, 1966) 145, 146, 148, 149 proposed that verses 2, 3, 6b refer to the afterlife whereas verses 4-6a refer to this life; the only argument that he gives to support this view is that "water forms an essential element in the description of the Elysian Fields." This is hardly sufficient proof for his interpretation of the "still waters" of verse 2 as a reference to the afterlife. A. Anderson, *The Book of Psalms*, 1:197, also thinks that Dahood's view is unlikely.

[22] For food and drink, see, e.g., C. & E. Briggs, *The Book of Psalms*, 1:209. For those who see these images as referring to rest, see, e.g., S. Mittmann, "Aufbau und Einheit des Danklieds Psalm 23," *ZTK* 77 (1980) 4,16; J. Alexander, *The Psalms*, 108. Cf. R. Tomback, "Psalm 23:2 Reconsidered," *JNSL* 10 (1982)

Verse 1 is the thematic statement of the psalm: because the Lord is David's shepherd, David will not want. This is dealt with in the following verses. The words "I shall not want" do not specify what David will not lack. This openness leads to an inclusive interpretation of verse 1, and this is the first argument for interpreting verse 2 as referring to sustenance for the whole person.

A second argument comes from the choice of images used in verses 2, 3a. If the psalmist had only wished to stress the rest that the Lord provides, other images besides the natural food and drink of sheep (i.e., grass and water) could have been used. Conversely, if the psalmist had only wished to stress the provision of food and drink, it is puzzling why certain terms appear in verses 2, 3a. In verse 2a "He makes me lie down" (*yarbîṣēnî*) is used instead of an "eating" verb such as *rā'āh*, which is used of sheep in Ezek 34:3, 18.

Ps 23:2b also takes up the idea of rest and refreshment found in 23:2a. Although the NRSV translates verse 2b as "He leads (*nāhal*) me beside still waters," the editors note that in Hebrew it is "beside waters of restfulness." The Hebrew term *mĕnûḥôṯ* comes from the verb *nûaḥ* which means "to rest, to settle down, to be quiet or to make quiet."[23]

Ps 23:3a ("he restores my soul") also treats the rest which God gives. The verb "restores" (*šûḇ*) and the form in which it is found in this verse[24] means "to bring back." Thus, it is often translated figuratively in verse 3a along the lines of "he refreshes my soul." Such a translation is warranted given the imagery of rest and refreshment found in verse 2; however, the original meaning of *šûḇ* as "to bring back" should not be forgotten. Ps 23:3a is expressing the idea that God brings one's soul back to rest and to refreshment.[25] Thus, the choice of images and terms in verses 2,

93-96. For those who see it as referring both to food and drink on the one hand and to rest on the other, see e.g., W. Oesterley, *The Psalms* (London: SPCK, 1959) 183.

[23] BDB, 628.

[24] I.e., the *polel*.

[25] Cf. the uses of *nepeš* ("soul") and *šûḇ* ("to bring back") in Ps 19:8; Prov 25:13; Ruth 4:15.

3a supports the interpretation of verse 2 as referring to God's provision of both physical and emotional sustenance.[26]

The final argument for this interpretation of verse 2 comes from the fifth verse. In verse 5 we find linked together imagery referring both to physical and emotional well-being. Verse 5 reads: "You prepare a table before me in the presence of my enemies;/ you anoint my head with oil, my cup overflows." The first clause speaks of physical sustenance. The overflowing cup in the final clause is clearly a symbol of joy.[27] The interconnection of images of physical and emotional well-being in verse 5 argues that this is the type of idea being expressed in verse 2 as well.

The Lord treats the psalmist as a shepherd who leads his sheep to green pastures, to waters of restfulness. Resting in verdant pastures and being led beside waters of restfulness are images that evoke the fullness of nature, the restorer of peace, and therefore the psalmist follows verse 2 by stating the effect of this relationship with God: "he brings back (*šûḇ*) my soul."

We have in verse 2 the imagery of nature, the great expander of a person's spirit. The human spirit is continually being constricted by the pressures of life. The images of lying down both in green pastures and beside waters of restfulness express the idea of nature, the great enlarger of the spirit, as showing who God is to us.

We have seen that the images in verses 2, 3a are those of being in touch with nature at its root, with nature the great spirit-expander and with nature as sustainer. The images in these verses also convey the idea of safety: the sheep may "lie down" and be

[26] The possibility exists that *yarbîṣēnî* ("he makes me lie down") in v. 2 also signifies the safety that the psalmist experiences in God's presence. The sheep may lie down and be at rest because the shepherd is watching over them (v. 2). This would adumbrate the idea of security in God which is more fully expressed in vv. 3, 4.

[27] For the interpretation of the cup as signifying sustenance but with an "additional suggestion of exhilaration" see, e.g., J. Alexander, *The Psalms*, 109; A. Weiser, *The Psalms*, 231. A. Anderson, *The Book of Psalms*, 1:198,199, points to five passages in which oil is a symbol of joy: Pss 45:7; 92:10; 133:2; Eccl 9:8; Amos 6:6.

at ease because the shepherd is there. Through these multidimensional images, the psalmist conveys the experience of God's shalom: God's peaceful well-being.

The Shalom Which Dissipates Stress

Stress can be caused by difficulties, by the anticipation of difficulties and by the inordinate pursuit of refreshment. The first two ways are obvious; the third, perhaps, needs some clarification. We often go to excess in seeking to relax and by so doing we bring more stress upon ourselves. The problems which societies experience with alcohol, drugs and/or weight control are examples of this tendency. There is a basic need which these binges do not satisfy and, if unchecked, they can add stress to the family and turn us away from our children. Psalm 23 leads us to the experience of God's peace as the answer to our heart's desire; it also dissipates stress and moderates us in our entertainments. First, we look at how Psalm 23 can do this and next at the experience itself to which it leads.

The concept of "defamiliarization," elucidated first by some English Romantic poets and later by the Russian Formalists, is helpful in clarifying the way that poetry can lead to new types of experiences.[28] Poetry is a "defamiliarizing language ... which restores to awareness what otherwise goes unnoticed."[29] It does so by the use of similes, metaphors and images which present the familiar in an unfamiliar way. This process "short-circuits" the ordinary way in which we view things and enables us to perceive

[28] This concept in the English Romantic poets is found, for example, in the following works. Samuel T. Coleridge, *Biographia Literaria*, ed., J. Shawcross (Oxford: Oxford University Press, 1954); Percy Bysshe Shelley, "The Defence of Poetry," in *Shelley's Literary and Philosophical Criticism*, ed., J. Shawcross (London: Humphrey Milford, 1932) 120-159.

[29] J. Custer, "The Poetics of Complaint at the Limits of Theology," (S.T.D. diss., Pontificia Universitas Gregoriana, 1987) 13, 17-18, 20. Cf. P. Ricoeur who wrote about the "poetic function" as the attempt to redescribe reality so as to show what goes unnoticed. P. Ricoeur, "Biblical Hermeneutics," *Semeia* 4 (1975) 75-88, p. 88; Idem, "Philosophy and Religious Language," *JR* 54 (1974) 71-85, pp. 79-80.

and experience something in new ways. Thus, the psalms can mediate to the reader experiences which are radically different from ordinary experiences and perceptions.[30]

Psalm 23 mediates the experience of the peaceful abiding in God which is the deep longing within the human heart. This is done especially through the images found in verses 1-3a. We have already looked at the meaning of these images in the preceding section. As a point of entry for appreciating their significance, let us look at how the image of lying down outdoors is used in some twentieth century American literature. This may help remove "the film of familiarity,"[31] caused by the frequent repetition in private and liturgical prayer, from the initial verses of Psalm 23.[32]

A number of writers have expressed the idea of deep peace by means of the imagery of lying down outdoors. There is something about this image which is expressive of humanity's deepest longings. In *The Professor's House*, Willa Cather writes about two of her characters lying separately and at different times on a rock looking up at a mesa and on a sandy beach. They come into contact with "Desire under all desires, Truth under all truths;" they feel a total presence, a participation in the whole rather than in the parts.[33]

In her chef d'oeuvre *My Antonia*, Cather describes how the nine-year-old Jim Burton, soon after his arrival on the Nebraska prairie, went to his grandmother's garden. It was a good distance from the farm house and surrounded by tall, red, prairie grass.

[30] Percy Bysshe Shelley, "The Defence of Poetry," 156, said that poetry "creates anew the universe, after it has been annihilated in our minds by the recurrence of impressions blunted by reiteration."
[31] Ibid., 156.
[32] Similarly, in his poem "Whitmonday," L. MacNeice cited parts of Ps 23:1-2 and called them "familiar words of myth," yet he wondered if "perhaps there is something in them" and then radically reinterpreted them. See E.R. Dodds, ed., *The Colected Poems of Louis MacNeice* (2nd rev. ed.; London: Faber & Faber, 1979).

See W. Holladay, *The Psalms through Three Thousand Years*, 359-69, for a study of how Psalm 23 has become "an American Secular Icon."
[33] W. Cather, *The Professor's House* (New York: Random House, 1973) 250-53, 263-67.

> I sat down in the middle of the garden ... and leaned my back against a warm yellow pumpkin ... The earth was warm under me, and warm as I crumbled it through my fingers... I kept as still as I could. Nothing happened. I did not expect anything to happen. I was something that lay under the sun and felt it, like the pumpkins, and I did not want to be anything more. I was entirely happy. Perhaps we feel like that when we die and become a part of something entire, whether it is sun and air, or goodness and knowledge. At any rate, that is happiness; to be dissolved into something complete and great. When it comes to one, it comes as naturally as sleep.[34]

Here too Cather uses an image of resting outdoors as expressive of a peace which is described as a participation into the whole.

Thus, the image of lying down outdoors has been used to express an abiding in the whole which is the deepest longing of humanity:[35] "Desire under all desires, Truth under all truths." Perhaps these twentieth-century examples can help us reclaim the beauty and the profundity of Ps 23:2, 3a: "He makes me lie down in green pastures/ besides waters of restfulness He leads me and gives me rest./ He brings back my soul."[36] We may now have an easier time seeing how such an experience would "bring back" (*šûḇ*) one's soul (v. 3a). These are the effects of God as shepherd so that we will not lack or suffer a decrease in what we really need (v. 1). Difficulties, anticipated problems and the pursuit of refreshment need not cause excess stress if we abide trustingly in the God Who leads us to the deep peace which we desire (v. 2), the recreation from which there is no diminution (v. 1), the shalom which brings back our souls (v. 3a).

Symbolic worlds not only help us to interpret our experiences, but they make the experiences themselves possible.

[34] W. Cather, *My Antonia* (Boston: Houghton Mifflin, 1977) 17, 18.

[35] See also J. Agee's short story "Knoxville: Summer 1915" in W. Huck and W. Shanahan, *The Modern Short Story* (New York: Van Nostrand Reinhold, 1968) 360-63, E. Wharton's *Summer* (New York: Macmillian, 1981) 13, 35-36 and R.P. Warren's "Star-Fall," *Now and Then: Poems 1976-1978* New York: Random, 1978) 23-24 for the use of imagery of lying outdoors to express a deep peace.

[36] This is my translation based on my exegetical observations found on p. 79.

> Symbols shape my experience. I perceive the rotation of the earth on its axis in relation to the sun as the sun rising, because of my symbolic world. I do not perceive the same phenomenon as god rising from the death of night, though someone in another symbolic world might well perceive it that way.[37]

Psalm 23 evinces a symbolic world which creates a certain type of experience for those who make it their own. Psalm 23 reflects, reflects on, and leads us into peace, which is the result of a certain type of openness to God's presence. Reflecting on these words, while taking time to allow God to give us rest, relieves stress and enables us to provide a loving and a relaxed home; this, as we have seen, is the type of milieu conducive to the social adjustment and the social development of children.

Different cultures reinforce different values. A Bishop of the Marquesas Islands once noted the importance for the Marquesans of being a peaceful person.

> A "man of peace" is the highest form of praise. A Frenchman asks, "Is he intelligent?" An American asks, "How much money does he have?" An Englishman asks, "Is he a gentleman?" The Marquesan asks, "Is he a man of peace?"[38]

Perhaps, in the light of the discoveries of the effects of peace on the social development and adjustment of our children, we may be encouraged to concentrate more on being people of peace and on Psalm 23 as a means to it.

Encompassed by Goodness and Love: The Interpretation of Ps 23:3b-6

In verses 3b, 4 we read that God as shepherd leads the psalmist in right paths and protects the psalmist even if the psalmist walks through "the valley of the shadow of death" (*bĕgê' ṣalmāweṯ*). The phrase refers most likely to the dark valleys through which the

[37] L. Johnson, *The Writings of the New Testament: An Interpretation* (Philadelphia: Fortress, 1988) 16.

[38] D. Grieve, producer, J. Heminway, writer, *In Search of Paradise* (New York: Granada Television International, 1991).

sheep are led.[39] These had many caves which sheltered wild beasts and robbers. Even there the psalmist will not fear because God's presence with rod and staff brings comfort (v. 4).[40]

There is a word play which causes the reader to link up God's providing rest and refreshment (*nāhal* used with the image of "waters of restfulness" – v. 2) with God's showing us what to do ("He leads me [*nāḥāh*] on right paths for his name's sake" – v. 3) with God's comforting us in difficult times ("Even if I walk in the valley of the shadow of death I will fear no evil for you are with me. Your rod and staff they comfort [*niḥam*] me" – v. 4). The deep peace that God gives us (*nāhal* and the "waters of restfulness" – v. 2) is the reality both in which God will lead us to do what is right (*nāḥāh* – v. 3) and in which God will comfort us in times of difficulty (*niḥam* – v. 4). The waters of restfulness are a spring underlying all paths which we take in our life.[41]

In verse 5 the image changes. The psalmist is now presented as a person whom God has invited to a feast. Verse 5 reads as follows.

> You spread a table before me
> in the presence of my enemies;
> You anoint my head with oil,
> my cup overflows.

How is verse 5 to be interpreted? There have been two major proposals put forth. Some claim that verses 5, 6 refer to the conclu-

[39] C. & E. Briggs, *The Book of Psalms*, 1:209. E. Leslie, *The Psalms* (Nashville, TN: Abingdon, 1949) 283, 284, also notes that these gorges are the primary referent of this phrase. He also thinks that it is likely that this phrase figuratively alludes to "the psalmist's dangerous illness." This may be too specific.

[40] The term *yĕnaḥămunî* in v. 4b may mean "they comfort me" or "they console me." J. Morgenstern, "Psalm 23," 17, proposed the reading "they reassure me." M. Dahood, "Stichometry and Destiny in Ps. 23,4," *Bib* 60 (1979), 418, has proposed the reading *yanḥûmĕnî*, "they guide my destiny." In all of these readings we get the idea of security in the presence of enemies.

S. Mittmann, "Aufbau und Einheit," 11, thinks that v. 4b is a later addition. Even if this is the case the idea of the security given by God is expressed in v. 4a (*lō'-'îrā' rā'*).

[41] The words of Percy Bysshe Shelley, "A Defence of Poetry," 126, are apt. Poetry has a "harmonious recurrence of sound which is scarcely less indispensable to the communication of its influence than the words themselves."

sion of the thanksgiving sacrifice in the temple,[42] while others claim that verse 5 expresses the psalmist's vindication in the presence of his enemies.[43]

In support of the former thesis, the following passages have been adduced: 1 Sam 1:3, 9; Pss 22:25-31; 63:4; 116:12-19. This last citation may be the clearest allusion to a thanksgiving sacrifice. Kraus noted that in this last passage there is a reference to the worshiper who takes the "cup of salvation" (Ps 116:13 – *kôs yěšû'ôṯ*).[44] Beyerlin proposed that verse 5 refers to a sacrificial meal; he did not specify it as a thanksgiving meal.[45] The reference to the enemies in verse 5 has not been explained by proponents of the sacrificial meal thesis; none of the passages which they cite can explain the enemies. A tithe, freewill, votive or thanksgiving offering was to be eaten in the presence of one's family, servants and a Levite (Deut 12:17-18), not in the presence of one's enemies.

As noted, others interpret the reference to the enemies as a sign of the vindication of the psalmist; his enemies must watch as

[42] A. Weiser, *The Psalms*, 230; S. Mittmann, "Aufbau und Einheit, 18; M. Mannati, *Les Psaumes* (Paris: Desclée De Brouwer: 1966) 1:239; C. Stuhlmueller, *Psalms I*, 152, 153. A. Anderson, *The Book of Psalms*, 1:195, 196, also sees this as "a reasonable working hypothesis." Cf. H. J. Kraus, *Psalmen* (BKAT; Neukirchen-Vluyn: Neukirchener, 1978) 1:337, 339-341. E. Vogt, "The 'Place in Life' of Ps.23," *Bib* 34 (1953), 194-211, is even more specific in his interpretation; he proposed that this psalm belonged to the setting of a banquet that was held after a sacrificial offering.

[43] E.g., L. Jacquet, *Les Psaumes et le coeur de l'homme* (Gembloux: Duculot, 1975) 1.561; J. Morgenstern, "Psalm 23," 15. In this light see El Amarna, 100, 33-35 where we read of the following report to Pharaoh: "may he give gifts to his servants while our enemies look on."

[44] Kraus, *Psalmen* 1.339. Kraus also noted that a possible connection between Ps 23:5 and the thanksgiving meal comes from the phrase "You prepare a table (*taʿrōk...šulḥān*) found in this verse. *ʿrk šulḥān* is also used in Ps.78:19; Prov. 9:2; Is.21:5. I note, however, that in none of these three passages is it used in the context of the cult.

[45] W. Beyerlin, *Die Rettung der Bedrängten in den Feindpsalmen der Einzelnen auf institutionelle Zussamenhänge untersucht* , (FRLANT 99; Göttingen: Vandenhoeck & Ruprecht, 1970) 111, 113, 115. Beyerlin provides no arguments for his view; rather, he says that the fact that v. 5 refers to a sacrificial meal is *ganz ohne Frage*.

God prepares a feast for the psalmist. In this regard, it has been argued that the oil (*šemen*) in verse 5 is a sign of honor.[46] Jacquet cited the following passages in which *šemen* is used to support the thesis that in Ps 23:5b it is a sign of respect: Pss 45:8; 92:11; 104:15; 133:2; Amos 6:6; Eccl 9:8; 2 Sam 12:20. In addition, he noted the use of *muron* (a Greek word for oil) in Wis 2:7; Matt 26:7; Luke 7:36-50.[47] In Ps 104:15; Amos 6:6; Eccl 9:7-9 *šemen* (oil) and *yayin* (wine) appear together. In 2 Sam 12:20; Pss 45:8; 92:11; 133:2 *šemen* is mentioned without any reference to wine, as is the case with *muron* in Matt 26:7; Luke 7:36-50.

Interestingly, among the passages which Jacquet adduces to show that oil alone can signify honor, only in Ps 45:8 does *šemen* have this connotation and here it is also a sign of joy because it is the "oil of gladness" of which this verse speaks. The *šemen* in Ps 133:2 and in 2 Sam 12:20, and the *muron* in Matt 26:7 and in Luke 7:36-50, are not signs of respect. In Ps 92:11 the anointing of the psalmist's head with oil is placed in the context of the treatment of the psalmist's enemies; the oil is not, however, a sign of honor which vindicates the psalmist in the presence of his enemies. It is the psalmist who sees the downfall of his enemies (Ps 92:10,12), and not the enemies who see the psalmist's anointing (Ps 92:11).

More important are the passages in which anointing one's head with oil (*šemen*) is written about in conjunction with wine (*yayin*) because this is the type of combination found in Ps 23:5: the clause "my cup overflows" refers to a cup of wine. There are three other passages of this type: Ps 104:15; Amos 6:6; Eccl 9:7, 8.[48] In each of them *šemen* and *yayin* are signs of joy. In Ps 104:15 this is shown by the words that are used with *šemen* and *yayin*: "and wine to gladden the heart of man, oil to make his face shine, and bread to strengthen man's heart." *Šemen* and *yayin* are

[46] L. Jacquet, *Les Psaumes*, 1.561; S. Mittmann, "Aufbau und Einheit," 12.
[47] L. Jacquet, *Les Psaumes*, 1.561.
[48] Wis 2:7, a passage cited by Jacquet in this regard, does not explicitly treat an anointing with oil.

also signs of joy in Amos 6:6. This verse is part of the judgment oracle found in Amos 6:4-7. Those "who drink wine in bowls and anoint themselves with the finest oils" (6:6) are those who are enjoying a party (6:4, 5). In describing the judgment upon them, Amos 6:7 explains the meaning of the images found in Amos 6:4-6 by saying "and the revelry of those who stretch themselves shall pass away."

In Eccl 9:7, 8 *šemen* and *yayin* are also signs of joy. Eccl. 9:7 shows that the *yayin* is a sign of joy: "Go, eat your bread with enjoyment, and drink your wine with a merry heart; for God has already approved what you do." (Eccl 9:7). Eccl 9:9 reads "Enjoy life with the wife whom you love." In this context the reference to anointing one's head with *šemen* (Eccl 9:8) clearly is meant to be a sign of joy; "Let your garments be always white; let not oil be lacking on your head" (9:8).

If we wish to understand the reference to enemies in Ps 23:5, we must interpret it in terms of the context in which the psalmist has placed it. The psalmist writes that the enemies are present when the Lord as host prepares a table (*šulḥān*) for the psalmist. Thus, it is in the context of the prepared table that one must interpret the mention of the enemies. Verse 5b shows us that the table is to be interpreted in the context of a celebration because when anointing the head with *šemen* is mentioned in conjunction with *yayin* both are signs of joy. Thus, the enemies must be interpreted in terms of the psalmist's participation in the *merriment* of the feast and not in terms of the psalmist's exaltation over, nor vindication of the psalmist before, his enemies.[49]

[49] Kings, priests, and apparently some prophets were anointed with oil. See, e.g., 1 Sam 10:1; 16:1,13; Ps 45:8; 1 Kgs 1:39; 2 Kgs 9:1,3,6; Ps 89:20; Exod 28:41; 29:7. Some argue that the individual written about in Psalm 23 is David, and that Psalm 23 refers both to David's flight from Jerusalem when Absalom revolted and to the events that occurred after this insurrection (2 Sam 15-19). See e.g., J. Lundbom, "Psalm 23: Song of Passage," *Int* 40 (1986), 5-18, pp. 12-14; J. Perowne, *The Book of Psalms* 4th ed. (Grand Rapids: Zondervan, 1966) 249. It is difficult to pin down the basic images in Psalm 23 to these specific events. Moreover, because *šemen* is used in conjunction with the overflowing cup in Ps 23:5 it does not seem that it refers to the anointing of David.

As we have seen, verse 4 shows that in difficult times the psalmist does not fear because God is with him and comforts him. Verse 5 goes on to say that not only does the Lord comfort the psalmist in difficult times so that the psalmist does not fear (v. 4), but also that God's presence is so profound that God gives the psalmist reason to even rejoice in these times! As we have seen, the words "you anoint my head with oil,/ my cup overflows" (v. 5b) refer to the participation in the merriment of a feast. To be able to put aside one's cares and enjoy one's self when enemies are present shows the great confidence, peace and joy which God has given the psalmist.

This is the reason that the image shifts from sheep-shepherd (vv. 1-4) to guest-host (v. 5): the sheep imagery was not capable of sustaining the "what's more" dimension the psalmist wished to express in verse 5. To move from comfort in times of danger (v. 4) to the actual letting down of one's guard and rejoicing in times of danger (v. 5) requires the move to human imagery.[50]

There are two other ways in which the psalmist expresses how great is the shalom which God gives in difficult times. First, the NRSV has translated the first part of Ps 23:5b as "you anoint my head with oil." The verb *māšaḥ* ("to anoint") is not used here; rather the *piel* form of the verb *dāšēn* is used. *Dāšēn* means "to be fat, to grow fat or to make fat."[51] Koehler-Baumgartner suggest translating the *piel* of this verb as "to refresh, reanimate, reinvigorate, strengthen."[52] That this is a good way to translate *dāšēn* in Ps 23:5b is shown by an analysis of the use of *dāšēn* and its noun form *dešen* in the Hebrew Scriptures. *Dešen* means "fatness" or

[50] See D. Sylva, "The Changing of Images in Ps 23,5.6," *ZAW* 102 (1990) 111-116, pp. 111-114.

Interestingly, the shift of images from God's taking care of cattle by providing them water and grass to the image of wine and oil for the joy of people is found in Ps 104:10-15. The starting point for the shift is not, however, the image of protection of animals in times of danger. Rather, Ps 104:10-15 is about the water which God provides for every creature: the water which enables the growth of the bread, oil and wine.

[51] *BDB*, 206.

[52] *KB*, 1.224. They give the word "*erquicken*" as the meaning of the *piel* of *dāšēn*.

"the ashes of victims mixed with fat." When it means "fatness," it conveys the idea of abundance and luxuriance.[53]

Dāšēn and *dešen* are used in three interrelated ways: (1) to express the idea of the riches of the harvest,[54] (2) to designate the gift of the abundance of nature to people,[55] and (3) to describe the beneficial effects of God's blessings on people.[56] These blessings, expressed in terms of fatness, bring joy to people.

> The light of the eyes rejoices the heart,
> and good news makes the bones fat (Prv 15:30).
>
> Then shall the young women rejoice in the dance,
> and the young men and the old shall be merry.
> I will turn their mourning into joy.
> I will comfort them and give them gladness for sorrow.
> I will give the priests their fill of fatness (*dāšen*)
> and all my people shall be satisfied with my bounty,
> says the Lord (Jer 31:13,14).
>
> You crown the year with your bounty;
> your wagon tracks overflow with richness (*dāšen*).
> The pastures of the wilderness overflow;
> the hills gird themselves with joy,
> the meadows clothe themselves with flocks,
> the valleys deck themselves with grain,
> they shout and sing together for joy (Ps 65:11-13).

Thus, "to be made fat" (*dāšēn*) is to experience the delights and the bounty of nature and so to be joyous and reinvigorated.

The words "you anoint (*dišantā* – "make fat") my head with oil" in Ps 23:5b lead one to think both about the oil of joy that is put on a guest's head at a party, because of the words "my head with oil," and about the delight in the bounty of nature, because of the use of the verb *dāšēn* ("to make fat/ to reinvigorate"). This richly variegated joy imagery envelops the reader in the experience of God's shalom. Not only is there no need to fear in the

[53] *BDB*, 206.
[54] Is 30:23; Pss 65:11;92:15; Jud 9:9.
[55] Dt 31:20; Job 36:16; Ps 36:8; Is 55:2.
[56] Prov 15:30;28:25;11:25;13:4.

presence of enemies, but one can also let down one's guard and enjoy one's self in the presence of enemies by being reinvigorated (*dāšēn*) by the bounties of nature which God provides.

Another way in which the psalmist expresses the great shalom which God gives is found in the words which the NRSV translates as "my cup overflows." These words are literally "my cup saturation." *Rěwāyāh* means "saturation" and its verbal form, *rāwāh*, means "to saturate, to drench, to drink one's fill."[57] Thus, this image, like the preceding one about the oil, is not only an image of joy but also one of full participation in the bounty of the harvest.

It is not only the meaning of *rěwāyāh* that emphasizes the idea of the psalmist's participation in nature's bounty, but also the type of construction found in the second colon ("my cup saturation") in verse 5. "My cup saturation" is a verbless noun clause and *rěwāyāh* ("saturation") is a noun used as the predicate of this clause. A substantive is used predicatively in such a clause when no adjectival form of the word exists or when the attribute is emphasized. This latter case appears to be the reason for the use of *rěwāyāh* in Ps 23:5.[58] There is a corresponding adjective (*rāweh*) that could have been used. Thus, the use of the substantive *rěwāyāh* as the predicate in a verbless noun clause also highlights the degree of participation in the fruits of the harvest. In such ways the psalmist expresses the extraordinary experience of God's shalom.

Verse 6 reads "Surely goodness and mercy shall follow me/ all the days of my life;/ and I will dwell in the house of the Lord for length of days."[59] This verse summarizes the significance of the images found in verses 1-5. Verse 6a ("Surely goodness and mercy will follow me/ all the days of my life") summarizes the psalmist's experiences as expressed in verses 1-4. The verb *rāḏap̱*

[57] *BDB*, 924

[58] *GKC*, 452.

[59] The Hebrew form which the RSV editors translated as "dwell" is *šḇt*. The Masoretes gave it the vocalization *šaḇtî* ("I will return"); the NRSV editors chose the vocalization *šiḇtî* ("I will dwell"), however, and this reading is supported by the LXX and by Symmachus' version.

("to follow") in verse 6a is telling. It can mean to pursue "especially with a hostile purpose," to chase or to persecute.[60] As such it alludes to the sheep image in verses 1-4. The sheep are in danger of being attacked when they are in the open (vv.1-3) and particularly when they are in dark valleys (v. 4). *Rāḏap̱* alludes to this because *rāḏap̱* can have the meaning of pursuing for hostile reasons. In spite of the possible danger from lurking enemies, the sheep have experienced security and care from the shepherd (vv.1-4). The psalmist abstracts from this experience and writes "Surely goodness and mercy will follow me/ all the days of my life" (v. 6a), not evil from lurking enemies.[61]

Some say that verse 6b ("and I will dwell in the house of the Lord/ for length of days") refers to the temple.[62] It appears that verse 6b refers to the Lord's house that is implied in verse 5. The psalmist changes the images in verse 5 from that of the sheep and the shepherd (vv. 1-4) to that of the guest and the host. What is implied in this shift of images is a shift of location from the open fields to the house of the Lord as host.

I propose that the following factors, viewed in conjunction with each other, argue that verse 6b refers to verse 5. First, verse 6a refers to the psalmist's experience in verses 1-4 by means of the word "follow" (*rāḏap̱*). Secondly, "house of the Lord" in verse 6b correlates with the image found in verse 5. Thirdly, both verse 6a and verse 6b specifically deal with the course of the psalmist's life (v. 6a – "all the days of my life" [*kol yĕmê ḥayyāy*]; v. 6b – "for length of days" [*lĕ'ōrek yāmîm*]). What emerges from this complex of facts is that verse 6 is a summary verse: verse 6a summarizes the significance for the psalmist's whole life of the images found in verses 1-4, and verse 6b does the same to verse 5. The images in the two lines in verse 6 mirror the images in verses 1-4, 5.

[60] *BDB*, 922, 923.
[61] So too S. Mittmann, "Aufbau und Einheit," 16, 17.
[62] L. Jacquet, *Les Psaumes*, 1:562; J. Pederson, *Israel, Its Life and Culture* (London: Oxford University Press, 1940) 188, 451.

What this relation of verse 6 to the preceding verses shows is that "the house of the Lord" in verse 6b must be interpreted in the context of the implied house of verse 5. Verse 5 does not refer to the temple, but rather to a certain type of experience which God provides for the psalmist.[63] Thus, "the house of the Lord" in verse 6b does not refer primarily to the temple in order to express (1) the wish to dwell forever in the temple or (2) the desire to join the priestly ranks, or (3) simply the experience of God's security throughout the psalmist's life;[64] rather, "I will dwell in the house of the Lord/ for length of days" (v. 6b) alludes to the profound peace and joy which God gives the psalmist in difficult times (v. 5).[65] The phrase "house of the Lord" in verse 6b may be a double entendre; it refers primarily to the experience referred to in verse 5, but it may also secondarily allude to the temple as sanctuary to reinforce the ideas of peace and joy.

[63] C. & E. Briggs, *The Book of Psalms*, 1.211 wrote that "the conception that Yahweh is the host to those partaking in sacrificial meals in His temple is not uncommon." They adduce Pss 5:5; 15:1; 27:4; 61:5; 84:5. While these passages treat of God's tent or house, however, they do not portray God as a host as is the case in Ps 23.

[64] S. Mittmann, *Aufbau und Einheit*, 13-15, 20) and J. Alexander, *The Psalms*, 108, wrote that Ps 23:6b conveyed this idea while H. Kraus, *Theology of the Psalms* (Minneapolis: Augsburg, 1986) 159, 160, wrote that v. 6b referred to the temple as a symbol of this idea.

[65] See D. Sylva, "The Changing of Images in Ps 23,5, 6," 114-116.

One wonders if the psalmist of Ps 100 was influenced by an understanding of "house of the Lord" in Ps 23:6c as referring to the temple because in Ps 100:3,4 the image of God as the shepherd and the people as the sheep is followed by an exclamation to "enter his gates with thanksgiving and his courts with praise." The words "house of the Lord" in Ps 23:6b refer, however, primarily to the house of the Lord that is implied in verse 5, and we have seen that the imagery in verse 5 refers not to the temple but rather to a certain type of experience of the security of God.

The remarks of S. Croft, *Individual in the Psalms*, 48, are pertinent.

> The meaning of a given term cannot be satisfactorily derived from its parallels in Hebrew poetry ... If a word means one thing in one psalm it does not necessarily have exactly the same meaning in all the others. Comparison of the meanings of the words ... in different psalms has been helpful in the analysis, but the immediate context in which the word stands must also play a major role in the discovery of its meaning. Allowance must be made both for the tradition and for individual usage within that tradition.

The Effects of Fear and the Theotherapy of Psalm 23:3b-6

Norman Cousins has noted that strong emotional disturbances weaken one's health.

> Depression follows panic just as surely as a hangover follows excessive drinking. When the human body suffers profound endocrinal disruptions as a result of pervasive, crushing fear or other profound emotional disturbances, depression is an almost automatic aftermath and depression is an intensifying cause of illness. The mood of the patient, therefore, is hardly of less concern than the disease he is called upon to treat.[66]

In short, great emotional distress produces a spiraling, downward cycle that affects the person's health adversely. On the other hand, peace and joy enable people to function well.[67] There are times when we can feel overwhelmed by real or perceived adversaries or adversities: when we don't feel that we can let go and enjoy ourselves and experience the healing properties of relaxation, enjoyment and laughter. In such circumstances Psalm 23 can be a powerful aid to releasing these very qualities of life.

The adversaries are first mentioned in verse 4 of Psalm 23, along with the possibility of their engendering fear. The psalmist need not fear because of God's powerful presence ("your rod and your staff, they comfort me."). In fact, God's shalom is so great that the psalmist can even relax, and thoroughly enjoy the bounties of the harvest at a festive gathering at which the enemies are present (v. 5). Verse 6 tells us that the future is secure: one will be pursued by goodness and steadfast love rather than by enemies (v. 6a), and one can expect the great shalom in the face of adversity whenever one needs it (v. 6b). This verse quells anxieties and fears of future adversities.

Thus, Psalm 23 can be a tremendous help to parents as an emotional safety-net. No matter what the adversity, Psalm 23 assures us

[66] N. Cousins, *The Healing Heart*, 204, 205.

[67] A similar insight is expressed in the maxim, "A tranquil mind gives life to the flesh, but passion makes the bones rot" (Prov 14:30).

that we need not fall into the depths of fear because of God's continual protection and profound shalom. As such a safety-net, Psalm 23 prevents both the depression that follows great emotional disturbances, and the consequent inability to care for children well.

PART III

THE BASIS OF TRUST

PSALMS OF GOD'S STEADFAST LOVE (*ḤESEḎ*) AND FAITHFULNESS (*'ĔMEṮ*)

The previous section treated the importance of trust for the emotional and social development of children. In order to provide children with this bedrock of confidence, parents themselves need to feel secure. If they are weighed down with worries they do not have the requisite psychic energy, and they cannot create the comfortable and relaxed environment which fosters the psychosocial growth of youth. We saw how Psalms 131 and 23 provide a theocentric foundation for parental trust.

The purpose of this part of the book is to explore three psalms (Psalms 117, 107, 92) which can strengthen this confidence by their treatment of God's steadfast love and faithfulness which undergird it.[1]

[1] See K. Doob Sakenfeld, *The Meaning of Hesed in the Hebrew Bible* (HSM,17; Missoula, MT: Scholars Press 1978), 2-15, for examples of ways in which *ḥeseḏ* has been translated. Doob Sakenfeld's preferred translation is "loyalty" in the sense of "faithfulness in action." K. Doob Sakenfeld, *Faithfulness in Action: Loyalty in Biblical Perspective* (OBT; Philadelphia:Fortress, 1986) 2-3.

CHAPTER 5

PSALM 117: WHAT WE MEAN BY GOD'S STEADFAST LOVE AND FAITHFULNESS

Why do we call all our generous ideas illusions, and the mean ones truths?
Edith Wharton, *The House of Mirth*

Multum in Parvo

A major factor which discourages all types of trust is human inconstancy. Our experiences of human weakness and fickleness mar our assurances that we can expect steadfast and helpful responses to our needs. This chapter will begin with a brief presentation of a parable and a poem which highlight reasons for the lack of staunchness in responding to others' needs. There follows an interpretation of Psalm 117 which focuses on God's steadfast love and faithfulness. It is suggested that this psalm can strengthen our trust in God.

The Problem with Trust: Human Inconstancy

The Parable of the Importunate Friend:Luke 11: 5-8

How long will someone be there when we need this person? We have all had the experience of asking too much of someone. We know what it's like to find out that a person who has helped us before is unable or unwilling to help us again. We recall the pain of dashed expectations, of having relied on a person and feeling hurt when he or she was not there for us. The Lukan parable of the man who goes to his friend at midnight – while primarily concerned with the need for a shameless persistence (*anaideian*) in prayer – presents such a rejection poignantly.

> And he said to them, "Which of you who has a friend will go to him at midnight and say to him, 'Friend, lend me three loaves; for a friend of mine has arrived on a journey, and I have nothing to set before him'; and he will answer from within, 'Do not bother me; the door is now shut, and my children are with me in bed; I cannot get up and give you anything'? I tell you, though he will not get up and give him anything because he is his friend, yet because of his importunity he will rise and give him whatever he needs. (Luke 11:5-8)

This parable is part of a larger section on prayer found in Luke 11:1-13. Verses 9-13 are sayings which Luke uses to show that if a friend will give you a favorable reply to a difficult request how much more certain it is that the heavenly Father will answer you.

The parable in verses 5-8 stresses the difficulty involved both in making and in answering the request.[1] The friend must struggle to respond to the call for help. Luke notes that it is midnight (v. 5), the door is shut and both the friend and his family are already in bed (v. 7). The use of verbs of "rising" also highlights the arduousness

[1] This is often overlooked in modern studies. See, e.g., H. Conzelmann, *The Theology of St. Luke* (New York: Harper and Row, 1981); F. Craddock, *Luke* (Int; Louisville: John Knox, 1990); G. Caird, *The Gospel of St. Luke* (New York; Seabury, 1963); E. LaVerdiere, *Luke* (NTM, 5; Wilmington: Glazier, 1980); F. Danker, *Luke* (PC; Philadelphia: Fortress, 1987); A.R.C. Leaney, *A Commentary on the Gospel According to St. Luke* (2nd ed.; London: A.& C. Black, 1966); R. Tannehill *The Narrative Unity of Luke- Acts- Volume 1: The Gospel According to Luke* (Philadelphia: Fortress, 1986); J. Creed, *The Gospel According to St. Luke* (New York: St. Martin's, 1969). B. Scott, *Hear Then the Parable* (Minneapolis: Fortress, 1990), 87, 91, minimizes Luke's presentation of how hard it is to meet such a request by such statements as "it is inconceivable that a neighbor would not meet the needs of hospitality," and "refusal is inconceivable."

Others note some of the indicators of the difficulty the friend would have in granting the request, but not those which deal with the trouble involved in making such a request. Thus, E. Ellis, *The Gospel of Luke* (rev.ed.; Greenwood, SC: Attic, 1974) 165, and J. Fitzmyer, *Luke X – XXIV* (AB; Garden City, NY: Doubleday, 1985) 912, say that getting up to give bread would disturb and wake the whole family. A. Plummer, *The Gospel According to Luke* (Edinburgh: T. & T. Clark, 1922) 299, and I.H. Marshall, *The Gospel of Luke* (NIGTC; Grand Rapids: Eerdmans, 1978) 464, note the *kopos* ("trouble") which this request causes for the friend who is in bed.

of getting up at that hour to give bread to a friend. Three times in the course of verses 7-8 such verbs are used. These circumstances show that the requester has brought trouble (*kopos* – v. 7); it has not been easy, however, for the one in need to ask for such a favor.

There are textual signals that the borrower realizes the trouble he is causing. He begins by addressing the man indoors as "friend" (*Phile* – v. 5). This calls to mind their close relation. Further, he says the reason for his asking for bread is because his "friend" (*philos* – v. 6) has come to him on a journey and he has nothing to offer. The word *philos* occurs as the first word of his address and at the beginning of the reason for his request. The use of this term twice in such a short compass has the effect of linking the "friend" who is in bed to the "friend" who is in need of bread. In such a way the one who was sleeping is made to see this awkward request in the light of his own future need. The first *philos* may someday be in the position of the second *philos* and wish hospitality from a friend of a friend.

The one in need also makes a modest request. He does not ask to be given the loaves of bread but rather that his friend "lend" (*chrēson*) him three loaves (v. 5).[2] Elsewhere in verses 5-8, Luke uses verbs of "giving" (*paratithēmi* and *didōmi*) four times; the request is, however, the more modest one of lend, not give.

The borrower has attempted to justify (*philos* – vv. 5-6) and to soften (*chrēson*) his request. After all, he is coming at midnight. Both the knowledge of his imposition and his consequent uncomfortableness are reflected in the way in which he words his address. It has not been easy for borrower or lender.

On the other hand, there is no support for the views of I. H. Marshall, *Gospel of Luke*, 464, 465, that the bolt on the door might be hard to remove or that the door had been "closed 'long ago'." *Ēdē* (v. 7) means "already," not "long ago." Only when used with *pote* does it have the meaning of "at length." See *BAGD*, 344.

There is also no support for the view that the friend and his family would have to rekindle a fire, grind wheat, make it into dough and bake more bread. So J. Grassi, *God Makes Me Laugh* (GNS, 17; Wilmington: Glazier, 1986) 107.

[2] This is the only use of *kichrēmi* in the NT.

The request is not initially granted. It is jarring to read about this denial because we sympathize with the one who is asking for bread. We understand his situation and the way in which he makes his petition. On the other hand, knowing how difficult it is to be awakened in the middle of the night to attend to someone, we sympathize with the man who was asleep.

The parable concludes with the claim that because of his *anaideian* the friend will give as much as is needed.[3] This vignette also paints a realistic picture of the difficulty involved in finding constant support. The one needs bread and the other rest. Initially, need meets need and comes up empty-handed.

As a result of our experiences of the limited capacity that we have for sustained giving,[4] we are inclined to question the temporal limits of the other's supportive presence. We tend to live emotionally with the expectation that at some time in the future constancy will be replaced by inconstancy.

Which Raison d'Être?

Another fact which mars our expectation of support is the fickleness of the human heart. George Herbert wrote about this in his poem "Giddinesse."[5] The choice of a poem by Herbert is appropriate because his poetry is so imbued with the psalms.

> Oh, what a thing is man! how farre from power,
> From settled peace and rest.
> He is som twentie sev'rall men at least
> each sev'rall houre.

[3] Just how *anaideia* is to be translated and whose *anaideia* is being referred to is moot. *Anaideia* is a *hapax legomenon* in the NT. It is usually translated as "importunity," "persistence" or "shameless persistence." Scott, *Hear Then the Parable*, 88-91, writes, however, that in the Greek literature from the classic through the patristic periods the term is used to mean "shamelessness." Along with K. Bailey, *Poet and Peasant* (Grand Rapids: Eerdmans, 1976) 128, Scott claims that the *anaideia* is that of the one who was sleeping.

[4] As B. Pym has eloquently put it, there lurks "in most of us . . . that desire to do good without too much personal inconvenience." *The Sweet Dove Died* (New York: Dalton, 1978) 11.

[5] See, e.g., H. Fisch, *Poetry with a Purpose*, 113, who claimed that perhaps more than any other Western poetry from his time on, Herbert's poetry is influenced by the Psalter.

One while he counts of heav'n, as of his treasure:
But then a thought creeps in,
And calls him coward, who for fear of sinne
will lose a pleasure.

Now he will fight it out, and to the warres;
Now eat his bread in peace,
And snudge in quiet: now he scorns increase;
Now all day spares.

He builds a house, which quickly down must go
as if a whirlwinde blew
and crusht the building: and its partly true,
His minde is so.

O what a sight were Men, if his attires
did alter with his minde;
And like a Dolphines Skinne, his clothes combin'd
with his desires!

Surely if each one saw another's heart,
there would be no commerce,
No sale or bargain passe: all would disperse,
and live apart.

Lord, mend or rather make us: one creation
Will not suffice our twin:
Except thou make us daily, we shall spurn
our own salvation.[6]

Inconstancy in our support for others is not only the result of the limited amount of energy which we have to expend, but also stems from the capriciousness of the human heart.

Epigrammatic Psalm 117: The Foundation of Our Faith

The Reading

1 Praise the Lord, all nations. Extol him, all
peoples[7]

[6] A. Hecht, ed., *The Essential Herbert* (New York: Ecco, 1987) 106, 107.
[7] V. 1b may read "extol him, all people" or "extol him, all gods." The MT's *'ummîm* ("peoples") has a masculine plural ending and elsewhere in the OT

2 because his steadfast love has prevailed over us
and the faithfulness[8] of the lord is forever.
Praise the Lord[9].

Literary Characteristics of the Hebrew Text

Psalm 117 is the shortest psalm in the Psalter. It is a song of praise with this genre's characteristic marks of imperatives in the summons to praise, which both begins and concludes the psalm, and the word *kî* ("because") at the beginning of the reason for extolling God (v. 2). This psalm is structured as an *inclusio* with the injunction to praise the Lord coming as the first and last words.[10]

The psalm progresses in the following manner. In verse 1 all peoples are called to praise Yahweh. The twofold call is mirrored in verse 2 which gives two reasons for the summons: "because his steadfast love has prevailed over us and the faithfulness of the Lord

'ummāh ("people") takes a feminine plural ending. Therefore, M. Dahood, *Psalms III*, 152, has suggested that the word should be repointed so as to read *'ēmîm*, "gods." Others emend the word to *lĕ'ummîm*, "peoples."

[8] A. Weiser, *The Psalms*, 721, and A. Anderson, *The Book of Psalms*, 2:796, translate *'ĕmeṯ* as "truth." This word can mean "firmness, faithfulness or truth" (*BDB*, 54). When applied to God and linked to the word *ḥeseḏ* ("steadfast love"), however, it refers to loyalty ("faithfulness"), the two terms often forming a hendiadys. So N. Glueck, *Hesed in the Bible* (Cincinnati: Hebrew Union, 1967) 6, 14, 73, 102. Similarly K. Doob Sakenfeld, *Hesed in the Hebrew Bible*, 32-34, said that adding the word *'ĕmeṯ* to *ḥeseḏ* gives an emphasis on the certainty of the *ḥeseḏ*: "that which can be relied on or counted upon." Her analysis is based on some passages in which *'ĕmeṯ* is used alone.

[9] The LXX places "Praise the Lord" (*halĕlû-yāh*) in v. 2 at the beginning of Psalm 118. H. Kraus, *Psalms 60-150*, 390, notes, however, that other psalms (i.e., Psalms 104, 105, 106, 113, 115, 116) end this way. Many Hebrew manuscripts place all of Psalm 117 as the conclusion of Psalm 116 or as the beginning of Psalm 118. The original integrity of Psalm 117 is disputed. I will be interpreting Ps 117 in its canonical form of being an independent psalm.

[10] "Praise the Lord" (*Halĕlû et-yhwh*) begins the psalm and "Praise the Lord" (*halĕlû-yāh*) concludes it. M. Dahood, *Psalms III*, 152, has said that the pronominal suffixes referring to Yahweh in words in the second and third cola also contribute to the chiastic structure and L. Allen, *Psalms 101-150*, 117, has said that the double *lāmeḏ*, a letter of the Hebrew alphabet, in the first and the fourth cola does the same. Both proposals seem too fine.

is forever." These reasons lead to several questions, the first having to do with their precise relation to the invocation in verse 1.

Why are the nations called to praise God? Is it on account of the steadfast love and faithfulness which God has shown to Israel, or is verse 2 saying that all of the nations have been the recipient of these qualities of God? Most scholars opt for the former alternative but some opt for the latter or for some combination of the two.[11] There is not enough evidence to come down decisively one way or another on this issue. What is clear is that for the psalmist the way that God has manifested these qualities is reason for universal praise.

The next question is how has God's steadfast love been expressed? It is common to translate the first colon of verse 2 as expressive of the Lord's action toward us; thus, both the RSV and the NRSV read "for great is his steadfast love toward us." The image is one of a love that is not only directed towards, however, but also of one that prevails over. The verb *gāḇar* is used with the preposition "over" (*ʿal*) in the first colon. *Gāḇar* means to be mighty. When used with the preposition *ʿal* ("over") it means to be mighty over, that is, to prevail over[12], as is shown from the use of *gāḇar* with this particle in 2 Sam 11:23; Gen 49:26. *Gāḇar* with *ʿal* may mean to rise over in Gen 7:19.[13] This is a figurative

[11] Thus, J. Eaton, *The Psalms*, 270, L. Jacquet, *Les Psaumes*, 3:297, and H. Kraus, *Psalms 60-150*, 391, wrote that in v. 2 the psalmist is writing about God's steadfast love and faithfulness towards Israel, whereas C. & E. Briggs, *The Book of Psalms*, 2:402, claimed that the verse refers to all people being the object of this divine care. E. Leslie, *The Psalms*, 29, and C. Stuhlmueller, *Psalms II*, 145, think that it is the steadfast love that was expressed towards Israel. Leslie says that in v. 2 the faithfulness is not limited in such a way.

In Rm 15:11 Paul cites Ps 117:1 and interprets it in terms of God's activity in Christ for Israel which leads to the nations glorifying God.

[12] *BDB*, 149. This also appears to be the meaning of *gāḇar min* (*HAL*,54). See 2 Sam 1:23.

[13] This may also be the case in Ps 103:11, however, reading the word *gāḇar* in this verse is moot. Many wish to emend it to *gāḇah* as found in the preceding half-line in this verse. In support of this position it has been noted that the verb *rāḥaq* appears in each half-line in v. 12 and *rāḥam* does the same in each part of v. 13. See L. Allen, *Psalms 101-150*, 17, 116.

extension of the root meaning of *gāḇar* with *ʿal* as to be mighty over, to prevail over. The waters rise, and by so doing prevail, over the land (Gen 7:19).

In Ps 117:2 there is no such figurative extension.[14] The words *kî gāḇar ʿālênû ḥasdô* in verse 2 are best translated "because his steadfast love has prevailed over us."[15] In other words, the image is not only of God's love being directed toward us but also that of its conquering us. The significance of this observation will be treated in the next section of this chapter.[16]

Constant, Conquering Care

As we saw at the beginning of this chapter, both limited amounts of energy and the capriciousness of the human heart encourage the suspicion that inconstancy will prevail over constancy. Parts of our lives are spent attempting to forestall this end by doing things for others which will lead to reciprocal care when we need it. Proceeding from somewhat less than the purest of motives, our insecurity leads us to build alliances very carefully. The payback is a significant part of many people's designs and the *quid pro quo* the way to achieve it. Underlying this end and means is often the threat of a lack of care when we need it. Human inconstancy leads to suspicion and then to potlatching as a means of coercing help.

Psalm 117 provides us with a different set of expectations. The words "his steadfast love (*ḥeseḏ*) has prevailed over us" tell us

[14] On the basis of the use of *gāḇar ʿal* in Gen 7:19 and in Ps 103:11, L. Allen, *Psalms 101-150*, 116, translates Ps 117:2b as "because his loyal love has towered over us." If such a translation is adopted it should be explained in terms of the exercise of a victorious power which is the root meaning of *gāḇar ʿal*.

[15] Translations of this type are given by A. Weiser, *The Psalms*, 721, and A. Anderson, *The Book of Psalms*, 2:196.

[16] L. Allen, *Psalms 101-150*, 116, 118, wrote that Pss 117:2; 103:8 are based on Exod 34:6 which reads in part that God "abounds in steadfast love and faithfulness" (*wĕraḇ-ḥeseḏ wĕʾĕmeṯ*). He has pointed to other similarities between Psalm 103 and Exod 33,34 to buttress his arguments but he has not adduced such evidence for Psalm 117. There does not seem to be enough evidence to make this conclusion about the basis for Ps 117:2.

that God's love has been given to us despite opposition. By saying it has prevailed over us, God's power is linked with God's love for us. With godly power Adonai's steadfast love has been expressed for us and it has triumphed.

This all-powerful love is forever. The next clause in verse 2 reads "and the faithfulness of the Lord is forever." We need not worry that our needs will outlast God's steadfast love because God's faithfulness is eternal. There is no point beyond it to which one may go, no amount of need that can push one from the realm of solicitude to that of unpredictable support. Here need never meets need; here need only and always meets a constant, conquering care.

Instead of having to lobby for support throughout our lives, we can be assured of a care that always prevails over all the demands of our needs. This provides parents with the assurance and emotional stability necessary to attend more fully to the psychological needs of their children.[17]

[17] Similarly, K. Doob Sakenfeld, *Faithfullness in Action*, 149, noted that we need God's loyalty in order to motivate and strengthen our loyalty to others.

CHAPTER 6

PSALM 107
HOW WE PERCEIVE GOD'S STEADFAST LOVE

I think that we may safely trust
a good deal more than we do.
H. D. Thoreau, *Walden*

The Reading

A Song of Ascents

1 O give thanks to the Lord, for he is good;
for his steadfast love endures forever!
2 Let the redeemed of the Lord say so,
those he redeemed from trouble
3 and gathered in from the lands,
from the east and from the west,
from the north and from the south.

4 Some wandered in desert wastes,
finding no way to an inhabited town;
5 hungry and thirsty,
their soul fainted within them.
6 Then they cried to the Lord in their
trouble,
and he delivered them from their
distress;
7 he led them by a straight way,
till they reached an inhabited town.
8 Let them thank the Lord for his steadfast
love,
for his wonderful works to humankind.
9 For he satisfies the thirsty,
and the hungry he fills with good
things.

10 Some sat in darkness and in gloom,
prisoners in misery and in irons,
11 for they had rebelled against the words of God,
and spurned the counsel of the Most High.
12 Their hearts were bowed down with hard labor;
they fell down, with no one to help.
13 Then they cried to the Lord in their trouble,
and he delivered them from their distress;
14 he brought them out of darkness and gloom,
and broke their bonds asunder.
15 Let them thank the Lord for his steadfast love,
for his wonderful works to humankind.
16 For he shatters the doors of bronze,
and cuts in two the bars of iron.

17 Some were sick through their sinful ways,
and because of their iniquities endured affliction;
18 they loathed any kind of food,
and they drew near to the gates of death.
19 Then they cried to the Lord in their trouble,
and he delivered them from their distress;
20 he sent out his word, and healed them,
and delivered them from destruction.
21 Let them thank the Lord for his steadfast love,
for his wonderful works to humankind.
22 And let them offer sacrifices of thanksgiving,
and tell of his deeds in songs of joy!
23 Some went down to the sea in ships,
doing business on the mighty waters;
24 they saw the deeds of the Lord,
his wondrous works in the deep.

25 For he commanded, and raised the stormy
wind,
which lifted up the waves of the sea.
26 They mounted up to heaven, they went down
to the depths;
their courage melted away in their calamity;
27 they reeled and staggered like drunkards,
and were at their wits' end.
28 Then they cried to the Lord in their
trouble,
and he brought them out from their
distress;
29 he made the storm be still,
and the waves of the sea were hushed.
30 Then they were glad because they had
quiet,
and he brought them to their desired
haven.
31 Let them thank the Lord for his steadfast
love,
for his wonderful works to humankind.
32 Let them extol him in the congregation of
the people,
and praise him in the assembly of the
elders.

33 He turns rivers into a desert,
springs of water into thirsty ground,
34 a fruitful land into a salty waste,
because of the wickedness of its
inhabitants.
35 He turns a desert into pools of water,
a parched land into springs of water.
36 And there he lets the hungry live,
and they establish a town to live in;
37 they sow fields, and plant vineyards,
and get a fruitful yield.
38 By his blessing they multiply greatly;
and he does not let their cattle
decrease.

39 When they are diminished and brought low
through oppression, trouble and
sorrow,

40 he pours contempt upon princes
and makes them wander in trackless wastes;
41 but he raises up the needy out of affliction,
and makes their families like flocks.
42 The upright see it and are glad;
and all wickedness stops its mouth.
43 Let those who are wise give heed to these things,
and consider the steadfast love of the Lord.[1]

The leitmotif of Psalm 107 is the continuity of God's steadfast love for people expressed both in the deliverance of them from all types of difficult situations and in the transformation of, and blessing of people in relation to, these problem areas.[2] The examples given in the psalm demonstrate the scope over which divine faithfulness extends. The theopoetic of the psalm involves the stress on God's salvific presence in all of the dimensions of our lives at precisely those points when the situation is most desperate and when we are least capable of responding effectively to it. The psalmist presents reflection on these transperiodic experiences as an aid to living well. As such, the psalm can help foster in parents a confidence and emotional ease in the face of life's problems.

This chapter begins with a discussion of methods of expounding Psalm 107. This will both clarify my means of dealing with this psalm and acquaint the reader with its salient characteristics. The exegesis will proceed expansively in subsequent sections. After focusing on details which affect the sense and translation of the

[1] This is the NRSV version of Psalm 107. This psalm begins the fifth book of the psalter.

[2] J. Eaton, *The Psalms*, 256, noted that God's steadfast love is the theme of the song. The proposal found in this chapter goes on to articulate how the psalm presents God's steadfast love as being demonstrated. E. Blaiklock, *Commentary on the Psalms*, 73, said that the theme of this psalm is gratitude. This is one of the advocated responses to God's *ḥeseḏ*; it is the steadfast love itself, however, which is the psalm's leitmotif. Later, we will look at how the structure of the psalm supports this assertion.

Hebrew text, I will move to an interpretation of the psalm in which the particulars are viewed in the context of the semantic patterns to which they contribute. Finally, I will look at the impact which the psalm can have on effective parenting today.

Interpretative Approaches to Psalm 107

The purpose of this section of the chapter is to determine if there are overarching perspectives which can aid us in our interpretation of Psalm 107. This will entail an analysis of proposals on (1) the source and redaction stratification of the psalm, (2) its genre and (3) allusions in it either to other traditions or to the psalm's *Sitz im Leben*. The following sections of the chapter will include notes on the overtones of the Hebrew text, an interpretation of Psalm 107, and a consideration of its significance as a resource to parents.

The initial question which confronts an expositor of Psalm 107 is which verses to comment on. The issue is one of tradition and redaction and the decision one makes will determine which level of meaning one explores. As will be shortly demonstrated, there are good reasons to view verses 2-3 as a later addition: one which moves the psalm in a different direction from that which it previously took and one which obfuscates much of its theopoetic. These verses, and the stratum of meaning in which they function, will not be treated.

Some have proposed that verses 4-22 or verses 4-32 are the nucleus of the original psalm and that verses 23-32 and/or verses 33-43 were appended to them.[3] Beyerlin has brought forth the following arguments for the secondary nature of verses 23-32. This subsection, which treats the plight and rescue of seafarers in a storm, does not deal with experiences which many in Israel had as do verses 4-22. Further, it has a different meter than the three stro-

[3] See e.g., C. Stuhlmueller, *Psalms II*, 122, who views verses 22-43 as supplemental.

phes in verses 4-22, and it is longer than them. Still further, it has an interest in Adonai as the Lord over nature: an interest not found in verses 4-22. Finally, it does not treat people's sins as do verses 10-22 and implicitly verses 4-9.[4]

These arguments are not suasive to all.[5] My responses are as follows. First, it is true that not many in Israel would have experienced a storm at sea; this fact does not distinguish this strophe, however, from those which came before it. How many were lost in the desert, or prisoners, or sick to the point of death? Second, the metrical question is a difficult and debated one. We know little about the phonology of biblical Hebrew because it was the massoretes of the sixth through the tenth centuries who were responsible for the vocalization of the text. They also provided the accents to the text: marks which are largely cantillation indicators. As a result, the degree of certainty at which we can arrive in our measurement of the meter in biblical poetry is moot. This is so whether we calculate this meter on the basis of accents or whether we count syllables.[6] Finally, we do not know how various sentences would have been intoned at the time in which the biblical poet wrote them: which words in a sentence would have been accented. For all of these reasons, Beyerlin's argument of a dissimilarity in meter is suspect.

In regard to the difference in length between verses 23-32 and the three stanzas in verses 4-22, the following considerations should not be overlooked. Verses 23-32 (ten lines) is longer than the three preceding subsections; verses 10-16 is, however, seven lines long compared to the six-line strophes found in verses 4-9, 17-22. Admittedly, there is a greater difference in length between

[4] W. Beyerlin, *Werden und Wesen des 107 Psalms*, BZAW,153; (Berlin/N.Y.: W. De Gruyter, 1979) 76, 77.

[5] See e.g., L. Allen, *Psalms 101-150*, 62, who is unconvinced.

[6] So too M. O'Connor, *Hebrew Verse Structure* (Winona Lake, IN.: Eisenbrauns, 1980) 138. See O. Loretz, "Kolometrie ugaritischer und hebräischer Poesie: Grundlagen, informationstheoretische und literaturwissenschaftliche Aspekte," *ZAW* 98 [1986] 249-66, for a critique of the numerous Hebrew metric systems which have been proposed.

verses 23-32 and each of the three strophes in verses 4-22 than there is between verses 10-16 and verses 4-9, 17-22; in a certain sense, however, verses 23-32 represent a culmination of the experiences described in the three previous parts. It may be longer, but its extension beyond the length of the previous sections functions in recapitulating them and in taking them one step further. Arguments for this assessment will be given later in this chapter.

There are also reasons to question the disparity in content which Beyerlin sees in these sections. While there are references to sin in verses 10-16 (v. 11) and in verses 17-22 (v. 17), it is difficult to find even an allusion to the people's iniquities in verses 4-9, as Beyerlin contends. Such an attribution can only come about through the proximity of verses 4-9 to verses 10-22; given this consideration, the absence of an unambiguous reference to sinfulness in verses 23-32 is not unusual. It is more likely that in verses 4-9, 23-32 the psalmist does not present sin as the reason for the people's sufferings.

Another substantive difference noted by Beyerlin is that the theme of God's lordship over nature is found in verses 23-32 but not in verses 4-22. Later in this chapter it will be argued that this is part of the psalmist's attempt to demonstrate God's action in every dimension of life. The difference can be understood on the basis of the message of the psalm; there is no need to assign it to another hand in order to explain this feature.[7]

In sum, the reasons adduced for viewing verses 23-32 as a later addition are not compelling. If this unit is secondary, it is certainly well integrated with the stanzas which surround it. The same holds true with verses 33-43. These verses have a very different tone

[7] L. Jacquet, *Les Psaumes*, 3:165, considered vv. 23b-24a, 25b-26a, 27b to be later additions. He viewed the inverted *nun* letters next to these verses in the margins as signs that the massoretes thought that these verses were suspect; this would not explain, however, why this sign is also found before vv. 21, 22. V. 21 is a refrain that occurs also in vv. 8, 15, 31 and so it is hardly suspect. Jacquet, *Les Psaumes* 3:160,166, also deletes verses 29b-30a. His arguments are from the perspective of preserving the amount of accents in a stich found in the preceding pericopes. It has already been noted why counting accents is an unreliable enterprise; in addition, that this was a concern of the psalmist is debatable.

from that of those which precede them, but they too have been coordinated with the bulk of the psalm. Thus, I will interpret the layer(s) of text which is made up of verses 1, 4-43. This is becoming much more common among interpreters of this psalm who see in verses 2-3 an addition which is not incorporated well with the rest of the material. Having clarified which verses will be treated and the reasons for this focus, I will proceed to consider what light can be shed by genre considerations.

The attempt to discern the form of Psalm 107 is both illuminative of the interpretive dilemma which confronts the exegete and instructive as to an approach to this problem. Some scholars focus on the genre of various parts of this psalm and others on the form of the whole. A number of scholars claim that verses 4-32 are a song of thanksgiving,[8] and many note the hymnic and wisdom elements of verses 33-43.[9] Others have stressed the hymnic aspect of the whole psalm. Beyerlin said that although Psalm 107 has components of a song of thanksgiving, these have been subordinated to the hymnic elements in verse 1. He is referring to the imperative "give thanks" (*hōḏû*) and the two "because" (*kî*) words in verse 1. The words "Let them thank the Lord" (*yôdû lyhwh*) of verses 8, 15, 21, 31 correspond to the "give thanks to the Lord" (*hōḏû lyhwh*) of verse 1. The reasons for thanks beginning with the word "because" (*kî*) in verses 9 and 16 relate to the "because" (*kî*) words in v.1. Thus, Beyerlin viewed verses 4-22 as functioning to provide reasons to praise God (v. 1)[10]

Psalm 107 is a mixture of elements proper to different genres: thanksgiving features are found in verses 4-32, hymnic characteristics in verses 1, 33-43 and wisdom traits in verses 33-43. What is instructive is that the thanksgiving (vv. 4-32) is itself an expres-

[8] M. Dahood, *Psalms III*, 80, claimed that it is a national thanksgiving hymn, and A. Weiser, *Psalms*, 470, that it is a communal thanksgiving. See also L. Allen, *Psalms 101-150*, 60 and C. Westermann *Das Loben Gottes in den Psalmen* (Göttingen: Vandenhoeck & Ruprecht, 1963) 76, 80.

[9] M. Lohr, *Psalmenstudien* (BWAT NF3; Berlin: W. Kohlhammer, 1922).

[10] W. Beyerlin, *Werden und Wesen*, 8, 9, 75. Cf. F. Crüsemann, *Studien zur Formgeschichte von Hymnus und Danklied in Israel* (WMANT, 32; Neukirchener: Neukirchener Verlag, 1969) 73.

sion of the praise of God (v. 1), and that this in turn culminates in the sapiential exhortation that the wise person will reflect on these activities of God (v. 43).

Another way of treating Psalm 107 is to interpret it on the basis of the traditions to which it refers or the *Sitz im Leben* for which it was used. A number of scholars have expounded this psalm as expressive of the Exodus[11] or the Exile[12]. Verses 2-3 serve as the basis for such a view. The desert imagery found in verses 4-9, 33-39 can be looked upon as corroborative. The similarities between Psalm 107 and Deutero-Isaiah can also be used to support the thesis.[13] Let us treat individually the foundations for this view.

Verses 2-3 serve as the linchpin for the conception that Psalm 107 refers to the Exile or Exodus, but the linkage is an extremely tenuous one at best. Although a few scholars do not differentiate between the original psalm and later redaction,[14] the bulk of contemporary scholarship views verses 2-3 as an insertion.[15] A convincing argument for this postulate is the artificial connection between verses 2-3 on the one hand and verses 4-32 on the other.

It is clear that whoever was responsible for verses 2-3 attempted to tie these verses to verses 4-32. This is shown by the fact that the latter section consists of four strophes dealing with four sets of problems and verses 2-3 present God as bringing the people back from the four parts of the world. A bond was also created by the

[11] E.g., E. Kissane, *Psalms II*, 174-180; A. Kirkpatrick, *Psalms*, 637, 638; N. H. Snaith, *Five Psalms* (London: Epworth, 1938) 17-21.

[12] E.g., L. Jacquet, *Les Psaumes*, 3:167-173. M. Dahood, *Psalms III*, 81, viewed the psalm's referents as being both the Exodus and the Exile.

[13] Note the following passages in Deutero-Isaiah: Isa 40:3-5; 41:17-20; 42:7; 43:19; 44:3-5; 45:2; 49:9b-10; 50:2; 51:3; 62:12. *Gā'al* ("to redeem") and *gō'ēl* ("redeemer") are found often in reference to Yahweh in Deutero-Isaiah and the people are called the *gĕ'ûlê Yahweh* ("the redeemed of the Lord") in Ps 107:2. Further, the verb *gā'al* ("to redeem") is used with the Lord as the subject in this same verse. In addition, the surprising similarities between Ps 107:3 and Isa 43:5-7 and between Ps 107:16 and Isa 45:2 should be noted.

[14] E.g., M. Dahood, *Psalms III*, 80-90.

[15] E.g., W. Beyerlin, *Werden und Wesen*, 73-74, 78; H. Kraus, *Psalmen*, 909; L. Allen, *Psalms 101-150*, 58.

use of "trouble" (*ṣar*) in verse 2; this term relates verses 2-3 to the *ṣar* mentioned in verses 6, 13, 19, 28.

Just as clear is the fact that the author or editor of verses 2-3 did not effect a coherent unification. While one can see how verses 4-9 could fall under the rubric of being "gathered in from the lands" (*mē'ărāṣôṯ qibbĕṣām* – v. 3a), it does not seem possible to categorize verses 10-32 in this way. There is no movement implied in verses 17-22, and no emigration mentioned in verses 10-16. In verses 23-32 we read of a journey taken in order to do business and not for the sake of repatriation. The connection between verses 2-3 and verses 4-32 is weak. The addition of verses 2-3 may have cast the various parts of the psalm in the light of the Exodus or the Exile, but the images in the rest of Psalm 107 were originally not expressive of these events. To interpret them as such is to miss their meaning to a great degree.

The other argument for the thesis that Psalm 107 refers to the Exile comes from the similarities of parts of it to passages in Deutero-Isaiah.[16] It is difficult to say if there is any direct borrowing between the two, and, if so, who is doing the borrowing. Is this common tradition which a number of authors are using or is Deutero-Isaiah or the psalmist the source of this tradition?

Some scholars have claimed that only parts of the psalm, verses 4-9 or verses 4-22, refer to the Exile.[17] It is possible both that there are such allusions and that some who first heard the psalm would correlate verses 4-9 with the desert experience of the ancestors.[18] There is, however, nothing in these sections which necessitates such an understanding and much in them that indicates that their function is to use the experiences of certain groups to comment on

[16] C. & E. Briggs, *The Book of Psalms*, 2, 358, claimed that the psalmist was dependent on Deutero-Isaiah.

[17] A. Weiser, *The Psalms*; 686; E. Beaucamp, *Le Psautier: Pss. 73-150*, 174, 175; L. Sabourin, *Le livre des Psaumes*, 479. All differ in their assessment of precisely which verses refer to the exile and how these verses function in the context of the psalm. Little evidence is brought forward to buttress this thesis.

[18] C. Stuhlmueller, *Psalms II*, 123, sees the refrain in vv. 8, 15, 21 and 31 as linking God's actions to God's "wonderful works" throughout the long history of Israel.

general types of problems which people encounter. The individual episodes are used as lenses through which to focus on how God acts in various difficulties; they are not the cynosure themselves. That this is the case is indicated by the comprehensive coverage of the full range of human life in the four pericopes in verses 4-32. What is expressed in these verses is an assessment of God's activity in every dimension of our lives.

Finally, there are some who propose that Psalm 107 was used as part of a thanksgiving offering in the temple.[19] In support of this assertion one can note that a variation of Ps 107:1 is found in Jer 33:11 in the context of bringing thanksgiving offerings to the temple. The psalm was undoubtedly used in the temple, but this does not mean that a literary critical interpretation of it is unnecessary or that the knowledge of its *Sitz im Leben* will exhaust its meaning. There was a reciprocity between word and liturgical act in the cult. Each operated in conjunction with the other to interpret the people's experience in the light of their faith and to elucidate faith in the light of experience. A hermeneutic of each is needed. Since it is ambiguous whether the psalm was written for the cult or only used there at a later time, I will focus my exegesis on Psalm 107 rather than on the cultic context in which it was used.[20]

Nuances of the Hebrew Text

The purpose of this section is to point out elements of the Hebrew text that are not apparent in the NRSV translation given at

On the other hand, W. Beyerlin, *Werden und Wesen*, 34, 35, argued that the description in vv. 4-9 does not correspond to the OT descriptions of the Exodus or of the return from the Babylonian Exile.

[19] H. Kraus, *Psalms 60-150*, 327; E. Leslie, *The Psalms*, 301; M. Dahood, *Psalms III*, 80; A. Weiser, *The Psalms*, 685.

[20] The value of such a focus is expressed well by W. Kaiser: "*Dichtung kann und muss zunächst als ein Gebilde betrachtet werden, das völlig selbständig ist, das sich restlos von seinem Schöpfer gelöst hat und autonom ist.*" W. Kaiser, *Das sprachliche Kunstwerk. Eine Einführung in die Literaturwissenschaft* (8th ed.; Berne: Francke, 1962) 289.

the beginning of this chapter. This enterprise will cast light on the shades of meaning of various words and, in the process, clarify aspects of the text which are in need of interpretation in relation to larger segments of the psalm. The meaning of some morphemes, and the connections established by similar phonemes in various terms, will be left for the next section of this chapter. The principle used to determine which to treat in each section was how smoothly the explications of these smaller semantic units fit into a cohesive presentation of the theopoetics of Psalm 107, the subject of the subsection following this one. Three specific elements will be treated in this section: (1) the waves appearing in verses 25b, 29b, (2) the hemistich "their courage melted away in their calamity" (v.26b), and (3) verses 39-40 in terms of their order of appearance in the psalm.

In verses 25b, 29b we read about waves which threaten to swamp the mariners' ships. There are several questions that puzzle interpreters. Does *gallāw* in verse 25b mean "its waves" or "his waves?" If the former then to what precisely does "it" refer? If the latter, it indicates God's waves.[21] Who or what brings these waves? The question has to do with the form of the verb *rûm* ("to raise") used in verse 25b. Finally, are the waves mentioned in verse 29b the waves of the mariners (*gallêhem* – "their waves") or is the Massoretic Text (Hebrew) inaccurate at this point? These problems will be treated in the order in which I have presented them here.

The NRSV translation of verse 25 is as follows. "For he commanded, and raised the stormy wind, which lifted up the waves of the sea." The Massoretic Text reads *wayyō'mer wayya'amēḏ rûaḥ se'ārāh watterômēm gallāw*. The last term can mean either "his waves" or "its waves." A consideration of the antecedents to which this suffix could refer points to *gallāw* as referring to God's waves.

[21] Among others A. Anderson, *The Book of Psalms*, 2:755, and L. Allen, *Psalms 101-150*, 59, opt for *gallāw* as pointing to the sea's waves. According to J. Alexander, *The Psalms*, 447, it points to God's waves.

The difficulty in interpreting *gallāw* in verse 25b as "its waves" is that the nearest antecedent to which it could refer is "waters" (*mayim*) two verses before this (v. 23b). *Gallāw* cannot refer to *meṣôlāh* ("deep") in verse 24b because the latter word is in the feminine gender and *gallāw* has a masculine pronominal suffix. This is also the reason why *gallāw* cannot point back to the feminine *rûaḥ* ("wind – v. 25a) beyond the difficulty of conceptualizing the waves of the wind.[22] Thus, the translation, "its waves," is precluded by grammatical considerations.[23]

An interrelated question is who or what is bringing these waves. The Massoretic Text has *tĕrômēm* ("you raised" or "it raised") as the verb in verse 25b. If this is considered to be a second person singular, masculine *polel* form then verse 25b would be translated as "you raised his waves." Given the context of God's action in verses 24-25, the "you" would have to refer to God and the "his" would be inexplicable. *Tĕrômēm* could also be a third person singular, feminine *polel* form of *rûm* giving us the translation "it (feminine singular apparently referring to the "tempestuous wind") raised his (i.e., God's) waves." It is unusual to read about the wind as the moving force of something which is attributed to God ("his waves"). The context of verses 24-25 argues, moreover, against this reading and for an alternate one.

The best option is that the original reading was "he raised" (*yĕrômēm*); "you raised" or "it raised" (*tĕrômēm*) is easily explained in terms of scribal tendencies. The clause "it raised (*tĕrômēm*) its waves" has the advantage of not making God the source of the problems from which God saves. Thus, it could be considered quite easily as a scribal emendation designed to

[22] The LXX reading (*kai hypsōthē*) would suggest an original *niphal* verb in v. 25b ("its waves were raised"). This runs into the same problem of a logical and proximate antecedent.

[23] A "wave" (*gal*) word is also used in reference to God's waves in Psalm 42:8. M. Dahood, *Psalms II*, 87, argues that just as the abyss of v. 24 is pictured as a mere instrument of Yahweh so "the waves" might appropriately be termed "his". Both he and A. Ehrlich, *Die Psalmen* (Berlin: M. Poppelauer, 1905) 268, take the *b* preposition in *bimṣûlāh* ("in the deep") as instrumental. This interpretation of *bimṣûlāh* may be correct. It harmonizes with other features which I will treat later.

smooth a hemistich that appears to subvert the primary message of the psalm: God's salvation in times of distress.

The context of verses 24-25 supports the "he raised" (*yěrômēm*) reading. The term *yěrômēm* makes God the subject of the action. This is in line with the three clauses in verses 24-25a which treat God as the one who is operative in the sea. It is God whose deeds (*ma'ăśê YHWH*), whose "wondrous works in the deep" (*niplě'ôṯāw bimṣûlāh*) are written about in verse 24.[24] It is God who speaks (*wayyō'mer*) and who brings the tempestuous wind (*wayya'amēḏ rûaḥ se'ārāh* – v. 25a).[25]

Finally, the NRSV of verse 29b is "and the waves of the sea were hushed." The Massoretic Text (Hebrew) reads "their waves (*gallêhem*) were hushed." The NRSV editors and others base their translation on the proposal that "waves of the sea" (*gallê hayyām*) is original and "their waves" (*gallêhem*) is the result of a scribal failure to copy a *yôḏ*.[26] The reading "their waves" in the Massoretic Text (Hebrew) appears correct, however, because it is consistent with a literary feature found in verses 23-32: one which will be delineated in the following section of this chapter.

The next element to be treated in this section of the chapter is Ps 107:26b. The NRSV version of verse 26b reads "their courage melted away in their calamity." The verb which is translated as "melted" is *mûg*. The purpose of the following word study is to clarify the use of *mûg* in Psalm 107:26b. When *mûg* is used metaphorically in the Old Testament, it expresses the fear that either (1) paralyzes or (2) that follows a great catastrophe which

[24] Verse 25 clarifies the works of the Lord which are mentioned twice in verse 24.

[25] The LXX attests to the imperfect *Qal* verb *wayya'amōḏ* which would give us the clause "and the tempestuous wind arose." This is consistent with the LXX rendering of verse 25b as "its waves were raised." The problem with the latter reading is the lack of a logical and proximate antecedent. The difficulty in opting for the former LXX reading (i.e., "and the tempestuous wind arose" – v. 25a) is the context of the three other unambiguous times in vv. 24-25a in which God's action is treated.

[26] The editors of BHS suggest "waves of the sea" (*gallê hayyām*) both for v. 29 and for v. 25b. It is harder to view *gallāw* ("his waves" or "its waves") of v. 25b as a scribal error than it is *gallêhem* ("their waves," v. 29b).

precludes the ability to act or (3) that appears in the context of events that could inspire a crippling fright.

Passages in the first category are Exod 15:15 and Nah 2:7. Exod 15:15 reads as follows:

> Then the chiefs of Edom were dismayed;
> trembling seized the leaders of Moab;
> all the inhabitants of Canaan melted
> away (*nāmōgû*).

Mûg is used in this verse with two other verbs denoting shock and fear. The extent of the dread is shown in the next verse.

> Terror and dread fell upon them;
> because of the the might of your arm, they became
> still as a stone . . . (Ex 15:16a).

Notice that this fear is so great that it results in cataplexy.

In Nah 2:6 one reads that "The river gates are opened, the palace trembles (*mûg*)." This is a reference to the waters of the Tigris inundating Nineveh. It is part of a picture of Nineveh's destruction: a picture which stresses the certainty of its fall by highlighting the efficiency of the invading armies (vv. 4-5), the unpreparedness of the defenders (v. 6) and the unleashing of the mighty Tigris against the city (v. 7). The resultant mind and body-numbing anxiety is described in verse 10.

> Devastation, desolation and destruction!
> Hearts faint and knees tremble,
> all loins quake,
> all faces grow pale!

Twice *mûg* is used of people melting in the context of the upheaval that an earthquake causes. In these cases the people cannot act but must roll with the ground, so to speak. In Ps 75:3 the psalmist has God saying "When the earth totters (*mûg*) with all its inhabitants, it is I who keep its pillars steady."

In 1 Sam 14:6-15 we read of the slaughter of twenty Philistines by Jonathan and his armor-bearer. The result is described in verses 15-16.

> And there was a panic in the camp, in the field, and among all the people; the garrison and even the raiders trembled; the earth quaked; and it became a very great panic. Saul's lookouts in Gibeah of Benjamin were watching as the multitude was surging back and forth.

The first thing to note is that the Massoretic Text (Hebrew) of the second part of verse 16 (i.e., what the NRSV editors translated as "the multitude was surging [*nāmôg*] back and forth") is confusing. Literally, it reads something like "the confusion was melting [*nāmôg*] and going this way." The extent of this confusion, its cause, and the degree to which it precluded all effective action, is shown by the preceding and following verses.

Verse 15 is about a buildup and an expansion of the trembling, convulsion, fear, all of which the term *ḥărāḏāh* ("panic") signifies.[27] This increase and extension reveals the reasons for the benumbed state of the Philistines referred to in verse 16. Verse 15 begins by saying that there was a *ḥarāḏāh* "in the camp, in the field and among all the people." Notice how this convulsive fear is spreading outwards. The next part of this verse reads "the garrison and even (*gam-hēmmāh*) the raiders trembled" (*ḥārḏû*). This is the second use of a *ḥrḏ* term in this verse; this time in its verbal form. The idea appears to be that even the hardened Philistine soldiers, those in the garrison, and their most intrepid raiders are in the grasp of this tremulous terror. The offensive incursions of these stalwart troops are written about in 1 Sam 13:17-18.

The reference to the garrison and the raiders stresses the degree of the "panic" (*ḥărāḏāh*) in the following ways. While the NRSV reads "the garrison and even the raiders trembled," in the Massoretic Text (Hebrew) the clause is "the garrison and the raiders (*hammaṣṣāḇ wĕhammašḥîṯ*), even they trembled;" the words "the garrison and the raiders" are placed as nominative absolutes. This sentence function highlights and focuses on the words placed

[27] See *HAL* 116.

there, giving them a special emphasis in the sentence.[28] This stress on "the garrison and the raiders" also comes through by the choice of the words "even they" *(gam-hēmmāh)* which punch the fact that the "panic" (*ḥărāḏāh*) has affected these warriors.

In the next part of the verse we read that the terror has reached cosmic proportions as even the earth begins to quake. Finally, a *ḥrḏ* word is found for the third time in this verse, the seam that links the diverse elements together in a frightful pattern. What has caused the ecophysiological seizure is "a godly convulsion" (*ḥerdaṯ 'ĕlōhîm* – v. 15).[29] Thus, there is eclampsia within and without; not even the terrestrial base is firm because of the extent of the shakeup.[30] Such a preamble indicates that the melting mentioned in verse 16 refers to an inability to act effectively.[31] This idea is reinforced in verses 20-22 where we read about a panic so great that even though the Israelites are outnumbered and only Saul and Jonathan have swords the Philistines are routed.

Both in Ps 75:4 and 1 Sam 14:16 *mûg* is used to refer to the fear that follows a catastrophe which precludes action. The final group of passages in which *mûg* is used metaphorically to designate fear are in passages of terror that could inspire a paralyzing fright.

In Jos 2:9 Rahab tells the two spies that "the fear of you has fallen upon us, and . . . all the inhabitants of the land melt away before you." The reason for this response is because of the great power of God exercised for Israel and manifested in nature and in

[28] B. Waltke and M. O'Connor, *An Introduction to Biblical Hebrew Syntax* (Winona Lake, IN: Eisenbrauns, 1990) 76.

[29] This is a superlative genitive. According to P. Kyle McCarter, Jr., *1 Samuel* [AB 8; Garden City: Doubleday, 1980] 240) "the shuddering has reached superhuman proportions." Cf. R. Klein (*1 Samuel* [Word 10; Waco: Word, 1983] 132, 137) who interprets these last two words of v. 15 as referring to terror sent by God.

[30] P. Kyle McCarter (*1 Samuel*, 236) notes Stoebe as claiming the v. 15 may be too full. The preceding analysis leads to the conclusion that the fullness of this verse functions to show the extent and cause of the grip of terror.

[31] The Codex Vaticanus manuscript of the LXX interprets this verse as referring to a loss of animation caused by dispiritedness. It does so by concluding v. 15 with the words "and they were not willing to act" (*kai autoi ouk ēthelon poiein*).

decisive military victories. "We have heard how the Lord dried up the water of the Red Sea before you when you came out of Egypt, and what you did to the two kings of the Amorites that were beyond the Jordan, to Sihon and Og whom you utterly destroyed," (2:10). This news of the marshaling of the divine power for Israel has caused a passivity among the inhabitants of the land. "And as soon as we heard it, our hearts melted, and there was no courage left in any of us because of you; for the Lord your God is he who is God in heaven above and on earth beneath" (2:11).

Isa 14:31 is part of an oracle of judgment against Philistia (14:28-31). As with many of the oracles against the nations in Isa 13-23, the judgment redounds to the salvation of Israel.[32] The first part of this verse reads "Wail, O gate; cry, O city; melt in fear, O Philistia, all of you." The reason for this warning is that a great power is coming against them ("For smoke comes out of the north, and there is no straggler in its ranks" – 14:31b). This power is compared to a seraph, a flying serpent. This is shown by the following considerations.

Isa 14:28-32 is arranged according to the centering pattern a b c b' a'. In verse 28 (a) we read of an oracle, and in verse 32 (a') we read about a response to "the messengers of the nation." Both "a" sections deal with a message. Both "b" sections treat a specific report to Philistia, and they do so with great symmetry. In verse 29 (b) the prophet tells "Philistia" not to rejoice "all of you" (*pĕlĕseṯ kullēk* – v. 29a). In verse 31 (b') the prophet adjures them to "Wail, . . . cry . . . melt in fear, O Philistia, all of you (*pĕlĕseṯ kullēk* – v. 31a). Both verse 29b and verse 31b begin with a "for" (*kî*) and a word beginning with a "mss" sound (*miššōreš* ["from the root of" – v. 29] and *miṣṣāpôn* ["from the north" – v. 31]), each having a prefixed *mêm* ("from"). Verses 29b and 31b give the reason for the adjuration in verses 29a and 31a. Philistia

[32] Thus, the account of the destruction of Babylon (13:1-22) is followed by one about Israel's salvation vis-a-vis Babylon (14:1-21). The oracles against Philistia (14:28-31), Moab (15:1-16:4), Damascus (17:1-6) and the oracles in 18:1-6 and 19:1-16 (the latter against the Egyptians) are each followed by oracles of salvation for Israel (14:32;16:5;17:7;18:7;19:16-18, 24-25).

should not rejoice because "from the serpent's root will come forth an adder, and its fruit will be a flying serpent" (v. 29b). Philistia is told to "melt in fear" (V. 31a) because "smoke comes out of the north, and there is no straggler in his ranks" (v. 31b). The "c" element is found in verse 30. It refers to the safety of Israel and to the total destruction of the Philistines. This is reason enough for them to melt in fear but the manner in which their demise is described heightens the fear.

Verses 29b and 31b parallel each other, both treating the means of the Philistine destruction. Verse 29b relates this to the sending of seraphim: flying serpents! It is these seraphim who are the minions of the awesome divine power which Isaiah experiences in his vision (Isa 6); they are the hosts of the "Lord of hosts" who is king (6:1, 3, 5). Thus, the oracle in Isa 14:28-32 provides terrible images both of the slaughter and of the means by which it will be effected. [33]

The uses of *mûg* in other parts of the Old Testament to express fear are in passages which convey, or imply because of the nature of the events described, a paralyzing, or incapacitating fear. This argues for such an interpretation of *mûg* in Ps 107:26.

Some wish to transpose verses 39, 40.[34] The major arguments given for this proposal are as follows. In verse 38 the psalmist writes that God's blessing causes the people to increase greatly. Therefore, it is jarring to read at the beginning of verse 39 that the people are diminished (*wayyim'ăṭû*). On the other hand, if verse 40 ("he pours contempt upon princes and makes them wander in trackless wastes") is placed before verse 39 then the diminishing of this latter verse would refer to the princes and not to God's people. This would reconcile verses 38 and 39. It will be argued in the next section of this chapter, however, that verse 39 ("When they are diminished and brought low through oppression, trouble and sorrow") is viewed best as a restatement of the types of problems

[33] See M. Cahill, "The Oracles Against the Nations: Synthesis and Analysis for Today," *LS* 16 [1991] 121-136, for an informative review of the Oracles against the Nations.

[34] E.g., L. Allen, *Psalms 101-050*, 60; H. Kraus, *Psalms 60-150*, 325.

written about in verses 10-32. If verse 39 is placed after verse 40 then it no longer refers to God's salvation from these types of problems, but rather to God's causing these types of problems for some.

The transposition of verses 39-40 may make an apparently smoother transition between verse 38 and these verses, but it makes for a harsher break between the permuted verses and verse 41a. The words of verse 41a ("he raises [*wayśaggēḇ*] the needy out of affliction [*mē'ônî*]") link up with those being brought low (*wayyāšōḥû*) because of "oppression, trouble and sorrow" (v. 39). If verse 39 is placed after verse 40, then those who are being brought low are the princes (v. 40). This would mean that it is the princes, designated as "the poor" (*'eḇyôn* – v. 41) who are being raised (v. 41). While possible because of their new condition, such a designation is a strange one for those who were just called "princes" (*neḏîḇîm*).

The use of verse 40 ("he pours contempt upon princes and makes them wander in trackless wastes") verbatim in Job 12:21a, 24b also casts suspicion on a transposition which would lead to the interpretation that God is raising the princes, newly named "the poor". Job 12:17-25 treats God's actions against the leaders of the people: counselors, judges, kings, priests, the mighty, the trusted, the elders, princes, the strong, the chiefs of the peoples. All of them are punished, often by being led away (vv. 17, 19, 23, 24), and not one is restored.[35] In fact, after the statement that God

[35] At first glance, it may look like v. 18 ("He loosens the bonds [*mûsār*] of kings, and binds a waistcloth on their loins") is not about the punishment of kings, but this would be a misperception. *Mûsār* can mean "discipline", "chastening" or "correction", and it is often used to refer to the discipline necessary for the acquisition of wisdom. See *BDB*, 416. In Job 12:18a *mûsār* is used in this way to refer to the removal from kings of the quality necessary for them to rule wisely. This is shown by the fact that the same type of action is going on in v. 17, where judges are made fools, v. 20, where speech is taken away from those who are trusted and discernment from the elders, and in v. 24, where understanding is withdrawn from the chiefs of the people.

This similarity explains v. 18b ("and binds a waistcloth on their loins"). This is a chastisement of the kings as is shown from the abb'a' parallelism of vv. 17, 18. In v. 17b and in v. 18a (the "b" elements) we read about God's making leaders

makes leaders wander in a trackless waste (Job 12:24b) – the same words found in the same order in Ps 107:40b – we find the words "They grope in the dark without light; and he makes them stagger like a drunkard" (Job 12:25). There is no subsequent salvation of this group. These considerations lend credence to the Massoretic Text (Hebrew) order of verses 39-40.

The present order of verses 39-40 does not create any discordance. The verb *mā'aṭ* ("to be or become small or diminished")[36] is the final word of verse 38 and the first word of verse 39. The psalmist has operated previously in a similar way; the final word in verse 13b is *yôšî'ēm* ("he saved") and the first word in verse 14a is the similar sounding *yôṣî'ēm* ("he delivered"). Admittedly these are not two uses of the same word as in the case of verses 38 and 39, but they do demonstrate the psalmist's use of similar sounds at the end of one and at the beginning of another line.

More importantly, verse 38, with its claim that God's blessing causes the people to multiply, is a reference to God's actions in relation to the specific problems of finding a fertile place to dwell and of sustenance, treated in verses 33-38. God makes the people fruitful in these areas (vv. 37-38). Verse 39 presents other problems which people encounter ("oppression, trouble and sorrow") and the diminishment which they can cause. The increase of the people in these situations is written about in verse 41 ("he raises the needy out of affliction [*mē'ônî*], and makes their families like flocks"). The "affliction" (*mē'ônî*) of verse 41 links up to the "oppression, trouble and sorrow" (*mē'ōṣer rā'āh wĕyāgôn*) of verse 39b. Accordingly, verses 39-40 will be interpreted in the order found in the Massoretic Text (Hebrew).

unfit for their positions ("and judges he makes fools. He loosens the bonds of kings."). In vv. 17a, 18b (the "a" elements) we read about their lack of, or scanty, clothing ("He leads counselors away stripped, ... and binds a waistcloth on their loins."). This shows that v. 18 is a castigation of kings, a fact emphasized by the repetition in v. 19a of leaders being stripped (v. 19) immediately after the saying about the waistcloth on kings' loins.

[36] *BDB*, 589-590.

Ḥeseḏ-Dimensions of Human Life: The Interpretation of Psalm 107

The psalm is concerned with God's "steadfast love" (*ḥeseḏ*); this is plain from the inclusion which frames it. In verse 1 the psalmist writes "give thanks to the Lord for he is good; for his steadfast love *(ḥeseḏ)* endures forever." The psalmist concludes the psalm with the encouragement to "consider the steadfast love of the Lord" (v. 43b). Thus, the psalm begins and ends with the steadfast love of God. This theme also permeates the whole psalm, *ḥeseḏ* being mentioned in a refrain in each of the four pericopes in verses 4-32 (vv. 8, 15, 21, 31).

The main part of the psalm (vv. 4-42) serves to elucidate how and where God's *ḥeseḏ* is manifested. Verses 4-32 are divided into four subsections, each of which treats a distinct trouble from which God has rescued people. Thus, verses 4-9 are concerned with God's actions for those who were lost in the desert, and verses 10-16 with the deliverance of prisoners. Verses 17-22 deal with God's actions for a group who were on their deathbeds and verses 23-32 reflect on the Lord's rescue of some mariners from a perilous storm. These episodes collectively treat the different types of problems which people encounter: trouble finding sustenance and shelter (vv. 4-9), societal difficulties (vv. 10-16), sickness (vv. 17-22), occupational dangers and the ravages of nature (vv. 23-32).[37] They are narrated in such a way as to inspire confident prayer, based on God's *ḥeseḏ*, in the face of such difficulties. The second part of the body of the psalm, verses 33-42, is an abstraction from and an expansion of the specific experiences related in verses 4-32.

[37] J. Eaton, *The Psalms*, 256, noted that the descriptions in vv. 4-32 need not refer to actual groups, but may be descriptive of God's deliverance from extreme danger. It may also be noted that they treat danger in the different areas in which it is possible to experience it.

Verses 4-32

These verses delineate manifestations of God's goodness and reasons to be thankful for God's steadfast love (v. 1). There are four distinct strophes (vv. 4-9, 10-16, 17-22, 23-32) bound together by a common pattern. The basic structure of the schema has been treated by many. There is a description of a group and a difficulty it has encountered (vv. 4-5, 10-12, 17-18, 23-27), followed by the statement "Then they cried to the Lord in their trouble and he delivered them from their distress" (vv. 6, 13, 19, 28). Next there is an account of God's deliverance of them (vv. 7, 14, 20, 29-30) and the exhortation "Let them thank the Lord for his steadfast love (*ḥesed̠*), for his wonderful works to humankind." (vv. 8, 15, 21, 31). Each strophe concludes with either a restatement of the reason for such thanks (vv. 9, 16) or an exhortation to "go public" with this thanksgiving (vv. 22, 32).

There are important nuances of this pattern which have not yet been noted. The description of the distress in each strophe begins by stating the problem in desperate terms. This is followed by an elucidation of the incapacitation which the difficulty causes. The people cannot save themselves; rather, they have been so weakened by the distress, their life-force so depleted, that they are on the brink of death.[38] The cry to God for help comes at the nadir of each of the four sections, following the depiction both of the serious problem and of the enervation of the group which makes them unable to deal with the difficulty. As we move through these four strophes, the movement is continually down towards the underworld. This, together with the positioning of the cry to God for help, highlights God's salvific power as we move through verses 4-32. I turn to how the preceding structure is fleshed out in these verses.

[38] Beyerlin, *Wesen und Werden*, 32-58, viewed these verses as dealing with God's salvation from the threat of death; he did not, however, cover the other nuances which are noted in this paragraph and which are developed in succeeding ones.

Verses 4-9

Verses 4-9 are about some who are lost in a desert. The desperateness of their situation is highlighted at the outset by writing that "They wandered in a desert (*ḇammiḏbār*), in a wilderness (*bîšîmôn*)." *Miḏbār* ("desert") and *yĕšîmôn* ("wilderness") are also used together in Pss 78:40a; 106:14a. In these verses they are used in different half-lines; they form part of the symmetrical background against which the asymmetrical elements are placed in order to convey the "what's moreness" of these verses. In Ps 107:4a they are placed next to each other and both have the inseparable preposition *b* ("in") attached to them. The effect is to stress the inhospitality of the region in which the travelers find themselves. The inability of the land to provide for their nourishment is stressed by the proximate use of these two nouns denoting barren places. The second half-line in verse 4 ("finding no way to a city to dwell in") shows that the concern is also with finding a habitable place.[39]

The depiction of the wanderers' difficulties continues in verse 5 with an account of their diminishing personal resources. In the desert they are fainting from hunger and thirst. Not only have they not found a way to a habitable city (v. 4b), but they apparently lack the energy to even continue the attempt (v. 5). Death is not far away from those who faint in the desert.[40]

The cry to God for help (v. 6) comes next at the point where it seems that there is no hope for the people. Immediately after the

[39] An alternate reading of v. 4 comes from viewing *drk* as an infinitive absolute. So M. Dahood, *Psalms III*, 81, and M. O'Connor, *Hebrew Verse Structure* (Winona Lake, IN.; Eisenbrauns, 1980). In this case v. 4 would have three clauses referring to (1) a wandering in the desert, (2) a walking in the wilderness and (3) an inability to find a habitable city. This reading, following the MT positioning of the *'aṯnaḥ* under *drk*, also emphasizes the predicament in which the group finds themselves.

[40] M. Dahood, *Psalms III*, 82, translated *napšām bāhem tiṯ'aṭṭop* in v. 5b as "their life ebbed from them" claiming a similarity to the phrase "but my fury will subside from me" (*kî rûaḥ millĕpānay ya'ăṭôp*) in Isa 57:16. He noted that *bāhem* means "from them" in UT, I Aqht:145-46 ("and he took Aqhat from them" – *wyqḥ bhm aqht*). Both the traditional translation and Dahood's translation convey the idea of the imminent demise of the travelers.

prayer we read about God leading the people to a habitable city (v. 7) and providing them with sustenance (v. 9).[41] The pithy account gives a sense of an extraordinarily quick reversal of fortunes caused by God's powerful intervention. The psalmist interprets this change as an example of God's *ḥeseḏ*, as one of God's "wonderful works" (*nip̄le'ôṯāw*) for which the recipients should be thankful (v. 8).[42]

Verses 10-16

The same pattern is found in verses 10-16. In these verses we read first about the extreme dilemma of the prisoners. There are two hendiadyses which strengthen the sense of their trouble: they dwell in "darkness and in gloom" (*ḥōšeq wĕṣalmāweṯ*), and they are prisoners "in misery and in irons" (*'ănî ûḇarzel*).[43] The term *ṣalmāweṯ*, translated as "gloom," is, in fact, a much more severe term than "gloom", being a compound of *ṣal* ("shadow") and *māweṯ* ("death"). *Ṣalmāweṯ* is the "death-shadow."[44] The repetition of dark images by the use of the terms *ḥōšeq wĕṣalmāweṯ* ("darkness and the death-shadow") appears to indicate that they are prisoners confined in dungeons.

[41] According to v. 9 God satisfies the "thirsty" (*nep̄eš šōqēqāh*) and fills the soul of the hungry with good. *Šōqēqāh* is difficult to interpret. J. Alexander, *Psalms*, 445, suggested "craving."

[42] M. Dahood, *Psalms III*, 82, 83, translates *yôḏû* at the beginning of vv. 8, 15, 21, 31 as "Let these confess" rather than "Let them thank;" this means, however, that *yôḏû* is used in two different senses in the same verse, as Dahood himself notes. His interpretation of this verse could be paraphrased as "Let them confess to the Lord his steadfast love, and let them confess to people his wonderful works." The traditional translation of thanking God for God's steadfast love and works for people seems more likely.

[43] Literally "trouble and iron." This use of two sets of two terms to depict the dire situation is similar to the use of *miḏbār* and *yĕšîmôn* in the same way in v. 4. Besides "prisoner of trouble" other examples of reification occur in this psalm in v. 18b ("the gates of death") and in v. 20a ("He sent his word and healed them.").

[44] For the translation of *ṣalmāweṯ* as "a deathly shadow" and the understanding of it as a superlative referring to a dense, deep darkness, see D.W. Thomas, "*ṣalmāweṯ* in the Old Testament," *JSS* 7 (1962) 191-200; W. Holladay, *Psalms Through Three Thousand Years*, 11.

In verse 11 we read that the source of the prisoners' problems was their rebellion against God. Two sets of sound connections present this opposition in a striking manner. In verse 11a the psalmist wrote "they rebelled against the words of God." In Hebrew both "they rebelled against" (*himrû*) and "words" (*'imrê*) begin with gutturals with the short *ḥîreq* vowel followed by the letters *mêm* and *rêš*. In verse 11b ("and they spurned the counsel of the Most High") the medial consonants of *wa'ăṣaṯ* ("and the counsel") are picked up by the comparable consonants of *nā'āṣû* ("they spurned").[45]

Verse 12 continues the description of the prisoners predicament by describing their weakened state.[46] Not only are they securely bound in the bowels of the earth, but there appears to be no hope of rising from this situation. According to verse 12 they are actually falling down in this depressed state. They are both dispirited ("Their hearts were bowed down with labor -" v. 12a)[47] and enervated ("they fell down, with no one to help" – v. 12b). There is neither will nor vigor to extricate themselves from their Erebus, and the utmost of each is needed for such a release.

It is at this desperate point when both their spirits and bodies have been sapped of their energy that the prisoners cry out to God and we read about their deliverance. Verses 13b, 14, 16 emphasize the power of God for salvation. There are two "liberation" verbs found next to each other at the end of verse 13 (*yôšî'ēm*) and at the beginning of verse 14 (*yôṣî'ēm*). In verse 14 the words "darkness" and "death-shadow" are repeated, to describe the situation from which God has saved them. There are three impediments to their emancipation mentioned in verses 14, 16: "fetters" (*môsĕrôṯêhem* – v. 14), "doors of bronze" (*dalṯôṯ neḥōšeṯ* – v. 16a) and "bars of

[45] The second and third letters of each word are gutturals followed by a *ṣāḏê*.

[46] A connection between vv. 11-12 appears to be that because the people have "spurned the counsel of the Most High" (*'elyôn*) they are "humbled" (*wayyakna'*).

[47] While *'āmāl* may mean "labor," it can also denote "distress, trouble" or "disaster" (*HAL*, 276). Thus, it may be that Ps 107:12a is saying that their incarceration brought about their dejection.

iron" (*ḇěrîḥê ḇarzel* – v. 16b). They emphasize the difficulty of rescuing the prisoners while the three corresponding *piel* (intensive active) "breaking" verbs which are used with them (*yěnattēq*, v. 14b – *šibbar*, v. 16a – *giddēa'* , v. 16b) highlight God's surpassing power over such seemingly unbreakable instruments of confinement.

Verses 17-22

Verses 17-22 are about those who were sick because of their sinful ways.[48] They "endured affliction" (v. 17b). Their bodies, moreover, were not able to fight the disease because "they loathed any kind of food" (v. 18a) so that "they drew near to the gates of death" (v. 18b). Once again, a serious problem is followed by images showing the diminution of the people's energy and their consequent inability to free themselves. At this point the cry to God comes and with it God's help.[49]

Verses 23-32

Verses 23-32 constitute the longest subsection in the first part of the body of the psalm, comprising nine distiches compared to six for verses 4-9, seven for 10-16 and six for 17-22. It exhibits the same basic structure as the other three units but goes beyond them in both length and content. These verses are a segment of high dramatic tension in which the psalmist placed the most complete description of a group's being swallowed up by their problems and of God's presence in these difficulties: of their loss of identity in the turmoil which their lives have become and of God's presence in this maelstrom. Before verses 23-32 we read of God saving

[48] The NRSV editors suggest the reading "sick" (*'umlālîm*) in v. 17a but the Hebrew is "fools" (*'ewilîm*). That these people are sick comes through clearly in v. 18. The LXX of v. 17a is "he helped them out of the way of their iniquity" (*Antelabeto autōn ex hodou anomias autōn*). This anticipates God's deliverance and breaks the pattern of first describing the seriousness of the problem and the people's inability to help themselves before describing God's salvific act.
[49] More will be said on vv. 17-22. See below, pp. 144-145.

from the distress (*sar*): God leads them from the desert to a city (v. 7), shatters the bronze doors and the bars of iron (v. 16), and sends the word to heal them (v. 20). In verses 23-32, however, God not only saves from without, but also from within: God's salvific presence is within the storm.

Verses 23-32 begin with an introduction not found in the previous three sections which commence with the statement of the plight of a group of people. The prologue in verses 23-24 provides background material which makes understandable the situation described in the following verses. In verse 23 we read that some went to sea on a business trip. "They saw the deeds of the Lord, his wondrous works in the deep" (v. 24). These verses explain why some are at sea in the first place (v. 24), and they establish witnesses for God's work in nature (v. 25). Such a setup is needed for a stanza which treats God's rescue at sea because the Israelites were not by and large a seafaring people.[50]

The statement of the difficulty itself is found in verses 25-26a. The mariners encounter a tempestuous wind and God's waves (v. 25).[51] In verse 26a we read that these godly waves carry them up to the heavens (*šāmayim*) before they are dropped back down to the depths (*tĕhômôṯ*). Only those who have been out on the open sea and have experienced seasickness will be able to understand fully the misery which it brings. All can appreciate, however, the intensity with which the psalmist describes this nausea. The boat is not rolling with just any crests or troughs, but it is going up to the heavens and down to the primeval depths (v. 26a). As in the corresponding sections in the three preceding strophes, the situation is depicted as desperate.

The account continues in verses 26b-27 by showing the apparent absence of a way out of their problem because of a lack of vital force. This is shown by the following considerations.

[50] This may also be the reason for the positioning of *hēmmāh* ("they") in v. 24. It is highlighted by its placement as the first word in this sentence. Some did experience God's salvation on the open sea!

[51] See supra, pp. 120-122, for my arguments for referring to these waves as God's waves.

Verse 26b reads "their lives melted away because of the evil."[52] This refers to a great fear. As we have seen, *mûg* ("to melt") is used metaphorically to portray a transfixing fear in Exod 15:15; Jos 2:9, 24; 1 Sam 14:16; Ps 75:4; Isa 14:31; Nah 2:7.[53] This is probably similar to the modern expression of one's "joints becoming unhinged"; both portray a powerlessness to act, a cessation of the body's response to impulses from the brain. If this were not bad enough, verse 27 ("they reeled and staggered like drunkards, and were at their wits' end") proceeds to depict how their brains are no longer able to oversee and coordinate the bodies of the mariners.

The image which ties both parts of this verse together is that of drunkenness. This figure of speech is present not only in the word *kaššikôr* ("like drunkards"), but is also found throughout the line. Verse 27a reads "they reeled (*ḥāgag*) and staggered like drunkards." The verb which the NRSV translated as "reeled" usually means to make a pilgrimage or to celebrate a pilgrimage feast, and in 1 Sam 30:16 the verb *ḥāgag* is used of Amalekites who are celebrating. Thus, *BDB* suggests interpreting *ḥāgag* in verse 27 as "reeling in giddiness" and *HAL* proposes "make leaps (like a drunk)."[54] The words "like drunkards" (*kaššikôr*) and "reeled" (*ḥāgag*) in verse 27a go together. The seafarers are like drunkards at feasts; they have imbibed too much during the celebration and so have lost control of their motor skills. It is in this context that "they reeled (*yāḥôgû*) and staggered (*wĕyānûʿû*)" should be viewed. The image is not simply that "they reeled and staggered like drunkards"; it is the more complex and intertwined one of reeling and staggering because of imbibing too much (*kaššikôr*) at a party (*yāḥôgû*).

Verse 27b continues this line of thought. The NRSV translates it as "they were at wits' end." In the Massoretic Text (Hebrew) the subject is "all their wisdom" and the predicate is the *hithpael* of

[52] The NRSV translates *napšām*, literally "their lives," as "their courage."
[53] Supra, pp. 122-127.
[54] *BDB*, 290-91; *HAL*, 95.

bāla', which is the only example of this derived form of *bāla'* in the Massoretic Text (Hebrew). One of the meanings of the *piel* of this verb is "to confuse." To many commentators it appears that this is the meaning of the *hithpael* form in verse 27b.[55] It should be remembered, however, that the root, and the most common meaning of *bāla'* is to swallow or to be swallowed up, to engulf.[56] Later in this section arguments will be provided that this meaning is also a part of the image conveyed by this term in verse 27b. For now, it should be noted that in essence verse 27b expresses the idea that those who have swallowed too much (*kaššikôr* – "like drunkards") are having their reasoning capacities swallowed (*bāla'*). The intake has subsumed those who have consumed it.

If we emerge from this detailed look at the images in verses 26b-27 to an overview of how they express the incapacity of the mariners to deal with their great danger, various features stand out. First, verse 26b ("their life melted away because of the evil") expresses not simply a lack of courage as is the case in the translations of the RSV ("their courage melted away in their evil plight") and the NRSV ("their courage melted away in their calamity"). As I have previously argued, when used metaphorically, *mûg* expresses something close to a physical paralysis caused by intense emotional anguish. In verse 26b *mûg* refers to a great fear that transfixes the mariners: "their lives melted away" (i.e., "their joints became unhinged").

It is important to distinguish these ideas in order to appreciate the extent of the mariners' helplessness. According to verse 27, what movement is possible for the mariners is uncontrolled because their brains are in a stupor. Thus, the seafarers have no ability to coordinate an effective response to the threatening situation in which they find themselves; their mental capacities have been swallowed up by incoherence and their bodies are ineffectual tools to the matter at hand because of this intellectual disintegra-

[55] A. Anderson, *The Book of Psalms*, 2:755, said it may refer to the failure of their navigational skill.
[56] *BDB*, 118 *HAL*, 41.

tion (v. 27) and because of life-binding fear (v. 26). They have been taken in and been taken over by abulic spirits.

Another way in which the psalmist emphasizes the desperateness of their situation is by melding them and the chaotic depths. This is done in the following ways.

The first attempt at admixture comes in verse 26a. In verse 25 we read "he commanded the tempestuous wind and he raised his waves." This is followed in verse 26a by the words "They mounted up to heaven, they went down to the depths," and in verse 26b by the clause "their souls melted away in their calamity." Verse 25 obviously refers to the elements and verse 26b just as surely to the mariners. What is the referent of verse 26a? There are two rising verbs (*'āmaḏ* and *rûm*) used in conjunction with the wind and waves in verse 25 and another rising verb (*'ālāh*) used in verse 26a. Reading about the waves rising at the end of verse 25 leads us to think that it is the waves which rise to the heavens and sink to the depths (v. 26a).[57] The second half of verse 26 refers, however, to people: "their souls melted away in their calamity." The lack of a clear change of subjects merges the action of the elements and the people who appear to be at their mercy. The winds whip both waves and people on the ship up to the heavens and down to the depths.[58] Verse 26a is an equivoque.

There are several other ways in verses 26b, 27 in which the psalmist indicates the mariners' immersion in the situation. The *hithpolel* of the verb *mûg* is used in verse 26b and at times *mûg* is used to mean "to melt," or to convey similar liquid images (e.g., "to flow," or "to drip" etc...): "their souls melted because of the evil" (Ps 107:26b).[59] Coming after the account of the waves rising

[57] M. Dahood, *Psalms III*, 87, wrote that v. 26a referred to the waves and not to the people aboard the ship.

[58] J. Alexander, *The Psalms*, 448, said that v. 26a refers to the mariners and not to the waves because v. 26b refers to those at sea.

[59] *BDB*, 556; *HAL*, 185. P. Raabe, *Psalm Structures: A Study of Psalms with Refrains* (JSOTSS, 104; Sheffield: JSOT, 1990) 50, claimed that *mûg* conveys more a sense of trembling and shaking than of melting. He cited Exod 15:15;1 Sam 14:16; Nah 1:5; Job 30:22 and Ps 107:26 in support. Such a sense of *mûg* is certainly conveyed by the first four of these passages because other shaking

heavenward and plummeting to the depths (v. 26a), the portrayal of their souls' melting because of this situation both continues the water imagery and graphically depicts their being taken over by the sea's swells and troughs. This is also the effect of the description of their reeling and staggering "like drunkards" (v. 27a). Here the liquid imagery is used to evoke the sense of the sea-storm's possession of their faculties.

In verse 27b the mariners are "at their wits' end" (NRSV), and this also conveys the idea that they are confused because they are engulfed by the surrounding deluge. The following considerations indicate that *bāla'* in verse 27b is used in such a polysemous manner. First, the basic and most common meaning of *bāla'* is to swallow or to be swallowed. Second, liquid images are found in each of the other hemistiches in verses 26-27 in order to relate the inundation to their participation in, and experience of it. The mariners are going up and down on the waves (v. 26a); their lives are melting (v. 26b). They are taking in and taking on water to such a degree that they are swallowing (indicated by their comparison to a *šikôr* in v. 27a) and being swallowed up by (*bāla'* – v. 27b) the chaos.

The final features which demonstrate the identification which the psalmist creates between the mariners and their plight are found in verses 29-30a. Twice in verse 29 there is a reference to God turning the winds and waves to silence (*dĕmāmāh* – v. 29a and *ḥāšāh* – v. 29b). The NRSV translates verse 30a as "Then they were glad because they had quiet."[60] The rejoicing refers to those on board the ships (v. 30a). The verb *šātaq* ("to be or become quiet

imagery is used in conjunction with *mûg* in these places. On the other hand, *mûg* is clearly used to convey liquid images in Amos 9:13; Nah 2:7 and Ps 65:11 as is shown by the other liquid images used in these contexts. In Amos 9:5 and in Ps 46:6 *mûg* is found in conjunction with both seismic and liquid images, and it should be remembered that the Exod 15:15 passage which Raabe cites is in the Song of the Sea with its emphasis on God's power over the waters (Exod 15:1, 4-5, 8, 10, 19, 21). Thus, *mûg* conveys either a shaking or a liquid image. In Ps 107:26b the latter clearly predominates as is obvious from its context of the storm at sea. The previous word study (see supra, pp. 122-127) has indicated that both types of uses allude to an incapacitating fear.

[60] There is a rhyme established by the words *wayyiśmeqû* ("they rejoiced") and *yištōqû* ("they were quiet").

or calm") in verse 30b could refer either to the wind and the waves or to the mariners.

There are arguments for each. In support of the first option, the following evidence may be adduced. *Šātaq* is used with the waves of the sea as its subject in Jon 1:11. Further, in Ps 107:29 it is the wind and the waves which are said to be quieted. On the other hand, the fact that the first verb in verse 30a (*śāmaḥ* – "to be glad") refers to people leads one to interpret the second verb (*šātaq*) in this short, three-word clause in the same way. Thus, once again the wording causes us to link the storm and the people in it.

Finally, the Massoretic Text (Hebrew) of verse 29b reads "their waves (*gallêhem*) were quieted." The NRSV translation is "and the waves of the sea were hushed." This requires emending the text to *gallê hayyām* ("waves of the sea"). While this is possible, it is not the best reading. It has been argued that *gallāw* in verse 25b is best translated as "his waves," referring to God.[61] This attribution of the waves to God makes it likely that there is also a linkage of the waves to the people (v. 29) who are described in verses 26-27 by the use of liquid images and who are blended with the sea in these verses and in verse 30 by textual ambiguities. The description of the storm begins with a description of God's waves (v. 25b) and ends with the voyagers' rescue from waves which had unfortunately become their own (v. 29b).[62]

Thus, the formless, chaotic depths (*tĕhômôṯ* – v. 25a) have for all intents and purposes swallowed the mariners alive.[63] Apparently

[61] See supra, pp. 120-122.

[62] M. Dahood, *Psalms III*, 88, proposed *gallē hāmû* ("roaring waves") for the MT *gallêhem* in v. 29b. This thesis has a certain attractiveness, not the least of which is that it fits well in the context of the quiet which God brings about (v. 29). I prefer the Massoretic pointing because it accords with the tendency to present the mariners as having been engulfed by the waves and because there is another example of identifying the waves in a similar way (*gallāw* – v. 25b) in this subsection.

[63] It is not the case, as it is in Ps 124, that had God not acted the people would have been swallowed (*bāla'* – Ps 124:3) by their enemies as by the waters (Ps 124:3-5– the swallowing in v. 2 being in a parallel construction to the one used in v. 4 to express the waters sweeping the people away). In Ps 107:23-32 the seafarers are treated as if they have already been swallowed by the waters.

the sea has been victorious; the finishing blow is all but assured. In verses 23-32, as in the three previous subsections, the cry for help (v. 28) comes when the situation is bleakest.

According to the psalmist, God is present in the chaos to save those who have all but succumbed to it. The chaos which they have taken into themselves is itself taken up in God's salvation. If the agony is in them, there is no need to fear because God is in it. The tempestuous wind (*rûaḥ sĕʿārāh* – v. 25) is raised (*wayyaʿămēḏ* – v. 25) by God who also raises (*yāqēm* – v. 29) the tempest (*sĕʿārāh* – v. 29) into quietness (*dĕmāmāh* – v. 29).

The NRSV translates *yāqēm* in verse 29 as "he made." The word is a *hiphil* of *qûm*, and sometimes this form means "to do, to perform";[64] the *hiphil* of this verb can also mean "to raise." In the light of the fact that verses 25 and 29 treat the tempest and the waves, and that in verse 25a it is God who raises the tempest, it may be that the psalmist uses *qûm* in verse 29a, – instead of *ʿāsāh* (which was used in v. 23) or some other such verb – to continue the image of God raising these elements. The wind and waves which were lifted (v. 25), and in the process lifted and dropped the storm-tossed mariners (vv. 26-27), are themselves raised to the higher reality of calmness (*dĕmāmāh . . . ḥāšāh* – v. 29).[65]

The chaos itself is used by God for salvation.[66] "Their waves" (*gallêhem* – v. 29b) are God's waves ("his waves," *gallāw* – v. 25). God's steadfast love engulfs the waters which have engulfed them ("and all their wisdom was swallowed up" – v. 27b). All the seemingly overwhelming power of the waters ("They mounted up to heaven, they went down to the depths" –

[64] See e.g., Deut 9:5; 1 King 2:4.

[65] The raising of the tempestuous wind and the tall waves (v. 25) are God's works (*maʿăśê* – v. 24) and wondrous deeds (*niplĕʾôṯāw* – v. 24) because they participate in the salvation of God which is raised (v. 29). This is why we read about these *niplĕʾôṯāw* right before God's lifting up of the tempest and the waves (vv. 25-26a) and right after God's quieting them (vv. 29-31).

[66] In Job 30:21-23 we read that God has lifted Job up on the wind and tossed him about in the storm (v. 22), but there is no immersion in the storm expressed in these verses. Further, the storm is not a force for salvation but only a destructive force which causes death (Job 30:21, 23).

v. 26a) is itself raised by God to the higher realm of quiet salvation ("He raised the tempest to silence" – v. 29a).[67] The chaos that threatens to overwhelm them is not the overarching reality. The tumult is itself a small manifestation of God's power ("He spoke and raised the tempestuous wind and raised his waves." – v. 25) which God uses and lifts until it meets God's quiet salvation (v. 29).[68] What could cause despair is now a reason for hope; there is an ordering and saving principle in, and controlling, the disorder.[69]

In response to the deliverance, the psalmist exhorts this group to extol God (*wîrōmĕmûhû* – v. 32a). The verb *rûm* means "to rise, to exalt, to be high or to be exalted."[70] Its use, instead of another verb such as *šbḥ* ("to praise"), reminds one of God's raising (*yāqēm*) of the tempest to silence (v. 29). God has controlled and towered over the chaos (v. 29), and we should acknowledge this quality of God in our praise (v. 32).

[67] J. Alexander, *The Psalms*, 447, notes that the use of *wayyō'mer* at the beginning of v. 25 is an allusion to the first creation account in Gen 1:1-2:4a. There may be an attempt in Ps 107:23-24 to evoke this account. In the first three verses of the Book of Genesis, we read about a primal chaos described by the use of the words *ṯehôm*, *tohû* and *mayim* (v. 2). The *rûaḥ 'elōhîm* (v. 2) is in contact with the chaos and from this meeting proceeds the divine command (*wayyō'mer* – v. 3) that brings order out of chaos. In Ps 107:23b we read about the *mayim rabbîm*, and in v. 25 we read about God's command (*wayyō'mer*) in conjunction with *rûaḥ* and with the waves (*gallîm*). The word *ṯehôm* is used in v. 26. These similarities to the beginning of the first creation account may suggest God's bringing order out of the chaos.

[68] D. Freedman suggested translating the inseparable preposition *b* in the word *bimṣûlāh* as "against" because the relation between God and the abyss is a combative one. See M. Dahood, *Psalms III*, 87. H. Kraus, *Psalms 60-150*, 329, said that such a struggle is found in these verses; he offers, however, no arguments for the view. L. Sabourin, *Le livre des Psaumes*, 480, said that the verses following v. 24 deal with God's mastery over the sea. While this idea is certainly clear from these verses, there is no adversarial tone in vv. 25-27 which would justify Freedman's translation in v. 24; rather, the abyss is an instrument moved by God.

[69] The mention of God's works in "the deep," (*mĕṣôlāh*) emphasizes God's presence in what has become a destructive force.

[70] *BDB*, 942; *HAL*, 341.

Summing Up

The four strophes in verses 4-32 provide examples of God's *ḥeseḏ* to those who experienced life threatening dangers because of the inability to procure sustenance and to find a habitable place (vv. 4-9), or because of societal separation (vv. 10-16), sickness (vv. 17-22), troubles with nature or with their own occupations (vv. 23-32).[71] In each stanza it is clear that far from being able to save themselves the people are incapacitated and on the verge of death. They cry to God and are delivered from these extreme situations. Within this type of context, the accounts of God's deliverance provide hope that no situation is beyond repair or can halt the ongoing love *(ḥeseḏ)* of God for us.

It is not only the depiction of various groups' predicaments and the positioning of their cry for help that lends encouragement, but also the downward movement towards the underworld as we progress from one section to the next in verses 4-32. This is manifest in the following aspects of the text.

In verses 4-9 some are fainting in the desert (vv. 4-5). In verses 10-16 some are falling down in dark dungeons under the earth.[72]

In verses 17-22 one is drawing close to the gates of death (*ša'arê māweṯ* - v. 18). The image of *Sheol* which is conveyed by the phrase in verse 18 is again put into focus by the expression "from their pit" (*miššĕḥîṯôṯām*) or by the textual emendation "their life from the pit" (*miššaḥaṯ hayyāṯām*), which some prefer.[73]

[71] Recall that the reason some went to sea is to do business "on the great waters" (v. 23).
[72] N. Tromp, *Primitive Conceptions of Death and the Netherworld in the Old Testament* (Rome: Pontifical Biblical Institute, 1969) 144, 155, noted places in the OT where darkness and prison imagery is expressive of the underworld, and he said that these images in vv. 10-16 allude to Sheol. So too J. Kroll, *Gott und Hölle: Der Mythos von Descensuskampf* (Leipzig: B. G. Teubner, 1932) 343. There may be an allusion to Sheol in vv. 10-16, but it is not as clear as the image of Sheol in vv. 18, 20. References to darkness and prison do not always refer to the underworld, and it may be that the primary image in vv. 10-16 is that of the dungeon and not of Hades.
[73] E.g., L. Jacquet, *Les Psaumes*, 3.165. There is less support for the view of M. Dahood, *Psalms III*, 86, that the root is *šhn* and for his translation "from their boils."

Whether we are dealing with *miššĕḥîṯôṯām* or with *miššaḥaṯ hayyāṯām* the psalmist has created a crossed rhyme by the use of this expression and the term *mimmĕṣuqôṯêhem* ("their distress") in verse 19.[74] The similarity of sound between the consonants *mššḥṯṯm* and *msqṯhm* establishes such a rhyme. The connection between these terms is part of the linkage between them and the construct phrase "gates of death" in verse 18. Each stands as the last, or as the second to last word, in three consecutive lines and each function so as to describe the dangers in which those who are ill find themselves. The net result is that the idea expressed in the construct phrase "gates of death" (v. 18) is intensified by the reference to people in pits (v. 20). Both describe the realm of the underworld; "pit" (*šaḥat*) is used most frequently in the OT as a metaphor for *Sheol*.[75]

Thus, the downward movement continues in verses 17-22. By the use of the words "they drew near the gates of death" (v. 18b), and "he delivered them from their pits" (v. 20b), the psalmist portrays people as being on the doorstep of the underworld.

Finally, in verses 23-32 we read about some who are practically enveloped in the chaotic depths. The mariners descend into the chaos (*ṯĕhômôṯ* – "depths" [v. 26]). They have apparently been swallowed up by (*tiṯballa'*, translated by the NRSV as "at wits' end" – v. 27b), and become a part of ("melted away," *tiṯmôgāg*– v. 26) the ocean's depths.[76]

[74] A crossed rhyme is where a word in the middle of one line is rhymed with one in a similar position in the following line. *Mimmĕṣuqôṯêhem* is in the middle of v. 19, and *miššĕḥîṯôṯām* is the last word of v. 20, but in terms of line length both terms are in the same position, the second appearing right under the first. This positioning is found both in the BHK[3] and in the BHS.

Another crossed rhyme is found in this strophe in the uses of *piš'ām* and *napšām* as the last words of vv. 17a,18a respectively.

[75] *Šaḥaṯ* is found twenty-three times in the MT and at least fourteen of these times it refers to Sheol. (Pss 9:16; 16:10; 30:10; 49:10; Job 17:14; 33:18, 22, 24, 28, 30; Isa 38:17; 51:14; Ezek 28:8; Jon 2:7.) This is shown by the use of *šaḥaṯ* in conjunction with the term "Sheol" or by its use with imagery of the underworld. In addition *šaḥaṯ* in Ps 103:4 may also refer to Sheol, but I find the evidence less clear in this case.

[76] The use of these *hithpael* and *hithpolel* verbs, with their reflexive significance, may also be a way of melding the watery chaos and the seafarers. The *qal* of both

The accounts in verses 4-32 of God's salvation from areas that are closer and closer to the chaotic vortex give hope to those whose lives appear on the verge of being engulfed. At the center of the submerging whirlpool is a more powerful, emerging waterspout.[77]

To recapitulate, in verses 4-32 the psalmist begins describing the distresses of people by stating the problems in desperate terms. This is followed by an elucidation of the incapacitation which the difficulties cause. The people cannot save themselves; rather, they have been so weakened by the distress, their life-force so depleted, that they are on the brink of death. The cry to God for help comes at the nadir of each of the four sections, following the descriptions both of the serious problems and of the enervation which makes people unable to deal with them. As we move through these four strophes, each group is drawn successively closer to the underworld. This, together with the positioning of the cry to God for help and the accounts of God's salvation, highlights God's salvific power as we move through verses 4-32.

Verses 33-42

Verses 33-42 are an abstraction from the specific examples of God's *ḥesed̲* written about in verses 4-32; the point of verses 33-42 is that this is the way God acts at all times in the areas of life treated in verses 4-32.[78] In verses 33-42, moreover, the psalmist claims that God not only delivers people from problems with sustenance, shelter, society, sickness, nature and occupation, but that

verbs conveys the same meaning that the *hithpael* and *hithpolel* of them do. Recall that this is the only use of the *hithpael* of *bāla'* in the MT.

[77] Ps. 107:4-32 demonstrates the pattern of intensification "in a narrative continuum" that R. Alter has seen in much of biblical poetry. Alter also defines this feature as "a dynamic process moving toward some culmination." See *The World of Biblical Literature*, 182-186.

[78] Cf. J. Eaton, *Psalms*, 257 who wrote that vv. 33-43 generalize the previous teaching.

God also blesses and transforms the righteous in these areas.[79] Verses 4-32 are about God's deliverance of people from narrow straits; in verses 33-43 the *ḥesed* broadens out to include the transformation of the environment (vv. 33-37, 38b) and an increase of the people (vv. 38a, 41). God's *ḥesed* from the past continues in the expansion of shalom in the present and future.

In verses 33-42 there are two subsections. Verses 33-38 treat the problems of sustenance and shelter, dealt with also in verses 4-9; verses 39-42 treat the three difficulties written about in verses 10-32.[80] The image of water, found in verses 23-32 and in verses 33-35, creates a transition between verses 4-32 and verses 33-42.

In verses 4-7a, 33-35 one reads about people in a desert.[81] God leads both groups to "an inhabited town" (*ʿîr môšāḇ*) according to verses 7b, 36b. The people who benefit from God's actions are the "hungry" (*rĕʿēḇîm*- vv. 7a, 36a). Finally, in both passages God provides sustenance to those who have been delivered (vv. 9, 36-38). Thus, verses 33-38 point back to verses 4-9; they also go beyond these verses.

In verses 33-38 the psalmist portrays not only a salvation from problems of sustenance and shelter, but also a transformation of both the people and their environment so that they enjoy a fullness in these areas. The desert has been transfigured; it has become a well-watered land (v. 35) so that the hungry sow fields and vineyards and have a fruitful yield (v. 37). God's humectant work has sustained their herds of cattle (v. 38). Further, God has made the

[79] C.& E. Briggs, *The Book of Psalms*, 2:358, wrote that the function of vv. 33-43 is to increase "the number of exhibitions" of God's steadfast love. They claimed (p.362) that vv. 33-43 are different from vv. 4-32 in that the latter are about the difficulties people experienced and the former are about the land. This distinction cannot be upheld because people are clearly the focus of vv. 36, 38a and their difficulties are written about in vv. 39-41.

[80] L. Allen, *Psalms 101-150*, 63, noted that six words are found both in vv. 33-43 and in vv. 4-22, five in both vv. 33-43 and in vv. 23-32 and one in both vv. 33-43 and vv. 10-16 and in vv. 33-43 and vv. 17-22.

[81] In both strophes there is a stress on the arid land by the use of several terms denoting this concept. Thus, *miḏbār* and *yĕšîmôn* are found in v. 4 and *miḏbār* (twice), *ṣimmāʾôn*, *mĕlēḥāh*, and *ʾereṣ ṣîyāh* in vv. 33-35.

desert habitable ("And there he lets the hungry live, and they establish a town to live in" - v. 36). Finally, the people have grown numerous (v. 38a)[82]

Thus, whereas verses 4-9 are about the people's salvation from starvation and the ravages of the desert, verses 33-38 are about an abundance of provisions and a multitude of people. God's steadfast love is not only a freeing, but also an expansive force.

The second subsection of verses 33-42 comprises verses 39-42. Verses 39-42 refer to the problems treated in verses 10-32, just as verses 33-38 point back to the difficulties written about in verses 4-9. The linkage between verses 33-38 and verses 39-42 is the hook word *mā'aṭ* ("to diminish, to decrease") which is the last word in verse 38 and the first in verse 39. Verse 38 is the conclusion of the subsection dealing with the desert experiences (vv. 33-38). God does not let the people's cattle decrease (*mā'aṭ* – v. 38). Verses 39-42 treat other problems: the diminishment of the people (*mā'aṭ* – v. 39) through "oppression, trouble and sorrow."[83]

This threefold designation corresponds to the three problems written about in verses 10-32. The first problem mentioned in verse 39 – and the second written about in verses 33-42 – is the people's experience of "oppression." The word is *'ōṣer*, and it comes from the verb *'āṣar* which means "to restrain, to imprison,

[82] God's blessing (*waybārăkēm*- v. 38) and the people's increase (*wayyirbû*) are linked to each other by a "chiasmus of sound."

[83] M. Dahood, *Psalms III*, 90, wrote that "oppression, trouble and sorrow" are the subject of this verse; it is these which are diminishing and not the people because of these problems, according to Dahood. He argued this on the basis of a proposed chiastic structure in vv. 38b-39a. As has been noted, the verb *mā'aṭ* ("to diminish") is found at the end of v. 38b and at the beginning of v. 39a, and a substantive is found at the beginning of v. 38b and three of them are at the end of v. 39a. Dahood saw this as representing an abb'a' chiasm where the substantives are the a elements and the predicates the b elements. His implied argument is that because the first substantive is a subject of a sentence, the same is the case for the three substantives "oppression, trouble and sorrow"; it is they which are diminished. This argument is made more tenuous by the observation that the presence of *lō'*("not") in v. 38b and, more importantly, a second predicate (*wayyašōḥû*- "to bring low") in v. 39a break the proposed chiastic structure.

to detain."[84] As such it links up to the description in verses 10-16 of the imprisonment of a group of people. This is the second problem written about in verses 4-32. Thus, there is a thematic and sequential correspondence between *ʿōṣer* in verse 39 and verses 10-16.

There are also verbal connections between the two. In verse 12 we read about the prisoners stumbling and there being no one to help (*ʿōzēr*). This is the only use of *ʿōzēr* in this psalm, and the similarity of sound between it and *ʿōṣer* ("oppression-" v. 39b) is obvious. That this is not simply a haphazard connection is indicated by the terms that are used in connection with *ʿōṣer* and *ʿōzēr*.

In verse 12b the psalmist writes "they fell down with no one to help" (*kāšĕlû wĕʾên ʿōzēr*). In verse 39 the psalmist writes about some being "diminished and brought low (*wayyāšōḥû*) through oppression (*mēʿōṣer*), trouble and sorrow ...." Both "oppression" (*ʿōṣer*) and "help" (*ʿōzēr*) are brought into a close connection with a term that denotes a downward movement. In both cases the reference is to people being brought lower. Moreover, there is a chiasmic alliteration in the "downward" verbs used with "oppression" (*ʿōṣer*) and "help" (*ʿōzēr*): in Hebrew "they fell down" (*kāšĕlû*) in verse 12b and "they are brought low" (*wayyāšōḥû*) in verse 39a have a *kāš-šāḥ* similarity of sound at the beginning of the root of each verb. In verse 39 there are two verbs and three nouns and *ʿōṣer* and *wayyāšōḥû* appear right next to each other. In these ways the psalmist, with the use of *ʿōṣer* in verse 39b, leads us back to verses 10-16.

There is not as clear of a connection between the two other terms in verse 39 for the afflictions of the people, "trouble and sorrow" (*rāʿāh wĕyāgôn*), and the two strophes in verses 17-32; the following considerations make it probable, however, that "trouble" (*rāʿāh*) alludes to the sickness treated in verses 17-22 and "sorrow" (*yāgôn*) to the storm at sea written about in verses 23-32. First, verses 33-38 clearly refer back to the problems in the

[84] *BDB*, 783; *HAL*, 281.

desert (*miḏbār*) described in verses 4-9. Second, the naming in verse 39 of three other types of troubles brings the number of difficulties dealt with in verses 33-42 to four. This is the amount covered in verses 4-32. Third, the thematic connection between "oppression" (*'ōṣer* in v. 39b) and verses 10-16, the similarity in sound between *'ōṣer* ("oppression," v. 39b) and *'ōzēr* ("help," v. 12b), and the similar contexts in which these terms are placed ("they are brought low" [*wayyāšōḥû* – v. 39] and "they fell down" [*kāšělû* – v. 12b]) show that "oppression" (*'ōṣer*) in verse 39b alludes to verses 10-16. These considerations make it probable that verse 39 is a recapitulation of the three strophes in verses 10-32. The remaining two terms for adversity ("trouble and sorrow," *rā'āh and yāgôn*) allude to the problems with sickness and with nature which were treated in verses 17-32. In this light it would not be strange for the psalmist to designate verses 23-32 by the word "sorrow" (*yāgôn*) because the first reaction of the seafarers upon being saved is to be glad (*śāmaḥ*- v. 30a).

Verses 39-42, like verses 33-38, not only summarize the deliverances written about in earlier parts of the psalm, but also treat the transformation of people. In verse 41 the psalmist again takes up the idea about God's actions on behalf of the needy. This takes the form of both a deliverance and an increase of the people: "He raises the poor from trouble, and he makes their families like flocks." As in verses 33-38, God's *ḥeseḏ* is both a freeing and an expansive power.

Verses 33-42 function to restate the problems covered in verses 4-32, but without the specificity found in the earlier verses. Thus freed from particularity, verses 33-42 are a claim that God's steadfast love, manifested in the areas of life mentioned in the four strophes in verses 4-32, is present at all times both to save and to enrich in the different facets of our existence.

Verse 43 is the concluding verse of this psalm: "Let those who are wise give heed to these things, and consider the steadfast love of the Lord." This verse continues the stress on God's steadfast love, which is the leitmotif of this psalm. It does so by forming a *ḥeseḏ inclusio* with verse 1 ("O give thanks to the Lord for he is good; for his steadfast love endures forever"). This literary stress on the Lord's steadfast love has been reinforced in the first part of the body of the psalm by the summons, found in verses 8a, 15a, 21a, 31a, to be thankful for this divine quality which was expressed in deliverance from various problems (vv. 4-32).

In verse 43 the psalmist also plays variations on this thematic continuity. Twice in this verse people are encouraged to give attention to the actions which manifest God's steadfast love. There is a change from thanking the Lord for his steadfast love (vv. 1, 8a, 15a, 21a, 31a) to considering this divine attribute. As we have seen, the psalmist uses both parts (vv. 4-32 and vv. 33-42) of the body of the psalm to present God's steadfast love as demonstrated in saving people from problems of sustenance and shelter (vv. 4-9, 33-38), societal difficulties (vv. 10-16, 39-42), sickness (vv. 17-22, 39-42) and problems with nature and business (vv. 23-32, 39-42). Thus, in verse 43 the psalmist is saying that by attending to how God delivered some (vv. 4-32) and by reflecting that God always delivers and blesses (vv. 33-42) the righteous (v. 42a) one will be able to perceive the Lord's steadfast love.

The thankfulness of the first part of the psalm gives way to the meditation encouraged by the last verse.[85] Whereas the singular *ḥeseḏ* is used in verses 1, 8a, 15a, 21a, 31a, the plural construct *ḥasḏê* is used in verse 43, where it refers to the prior examples of God's *ḥeseḏ*.[86] By attending to these examples one will be able to

[85] W. Bellinger, Jr., *Psalms* (Peabody, MA: Hendrickson, 1990) 78, wrote that vv. 33-43 "have a 'wisdom' tone;" they are an exhortation to learn about God's *ḥeseḏ* from the experience of God's salvation. In response, it should be noted that certainly this encouragement is found in the last verse (v. 43) of the psalm. As we have seen, vv. 33-42 is a recapitulation of the description of God's salvation, and the *ḥeseḏ* which is the basis for it, as recounted in vv. 4-32. Repetition reinforces ideas previously treated and by so doing invites reflection (v. 43) on them. In this nuanced sense we may say that vv. 33-43 inculcates the value of learning of God's *ḥeseḏ* from the experiences of God's salvation.

[86] Cf. L. Allen, *Psalms 101-150*, 63. H. J. Stoebe, "Bedeutung und Geschichte des Begriffes häsäd," (Munster: Unpublished Doctoral dissertation, 1951) 18-34, argued that when the plural of *ḥeseḏ* is used it refers to specific acts.

The plural construct *ḥasḏê* may also function as an intensive plural stressing God's steadfast love: a stress that previous verses in the psalm have established.

turn to the Lord in prayer in difficult times and by so doing be open to God's *ḥeseḏ* ("Then they cried to the Lord in their trouble, and he delivered them from their distress-" vv. 6, 13, 19, 28).

In verse 43 reflection on God's *ḥeseḏ* as written about in verses 4-42 is advocated twice. The verbs *šāmar* and *bîn* ("to discern") are used to reinforce the value of this type of meditation. At times *šāmar* is used to mean "to observe."[87] The psalmist has been providing readers with mental images which manifest God's steadfast love and he concludes the psalm with the exhortation to attend to these phantasms. The usual meanings of *šāmar* are "to keep, watch or guard." Thus, it usually expresses a phylactic intent. It is difficult to say whether this larger semantic field was intended by the psalmist, but it is good to keep the usual meanings of this term in mind. There is a possibility that *šāmar* in this verse connotes a protecting of the lesson (God's *ḥeseḏ*) to be learned by these mental representations through a consideration of them. In any case, the value of such a preservation is achieved through the double prompting found in verse 43.

The value of the twofold exhortation in verse 43 comes through when we reflect on the following observation by Robert Penn Warren.

> Certainly there is a significant distinction to be made, to say the least, between *fact inert* and *fact operative*, and how does a fact become operative except by the mind's recognition of its relation to a pattern?[88]

In verses 4-32 the psalmist has presented a pattern of God's deliverance to those who call upon him when there appears to be no hope. In verses 33-42 this model is both alluded to, and expanded to include the bountiful, transformative blessings which God gives in such situations. Verse 43 stresses reflection on this pattern.

On this use of the plural see A. Ember, "The Pluralis intensivus in Hebrew," *AJSL* (1905) 195. and *GKC*, 397.

The use of *lĕʿôlām* ("forever") with *ḥeseḏ* in v.1 shows that God's specific acts of salvation in the past (vv. 4-32) apply to all times.

[87] See, e.g., 1 Sam 1:12; Isa 42:20; Jer 8:7; Pss 37:7; 130:3.

[88] R.P. Warren, *A Place to Come to* (N.Y.: Random House, 1977) 19.

Only through such consideration will the experience of some live again in the lives of a new generation.

Our very perception occurs by organizing sensations into patterns.[89] Without such structure, stimuli are meaningless. In Psalm 107 the psalmist provides a pattern designed to open people to the transgenerational *ḥesed* of God.[90] The final words of the psalm, the last words to reach the readers' ears, are the repeated admonition to make this pattern one's own through reflection on it. In such a way "*fact inert*" can become "*fact operative*" in a new generation's calling on God in the experience of serious problems.[91]

"Continuity, That Great Nutritive Element"

In her novel, *Hudson River Bracketed*, Edith Wharton writes about a young man in the nineteenth century who moves from a

[89] See e.g., S. Chatman, *A Theory of Meter* (The Hague: Mouton, 1965) 25; E. Greenstein, "How Does Parallelism Mean?" 41.

[90] In his analysis of the Historical Psalms (Pss 78, 105, 106, 136) W. Brueggemann, *Abiding Astonishment: Psalms, Modernity and the Making of History* (Louisville: Westminter/ John Knox, 1991) 13, 14, 83, n. 102, noted the distinction between what actually happened and what the psalmists present as happening. In these psalms the psalmists shape history by choosing some events and rejecting others. Such reconstructions provide a model for the present. See also Y. H. Yerushalmi, *Zakhor: Jewish History and Jewish Memory* (Seattle: U. of Washington, 1982).

I note that there is a progression in the canonical remembering found in Psalms 105-107. By placing these psalms next to each other there is a movement from viewing God's actions for Israel as a whole (Psalms 105, 106) to focusing on God's works for unspecified groups (Psalm 107). In Psalm 107 the history of the unnamed is taken seriously as a focus of God's *ḥesed*. This feature encourages the readers of Psalm 107 to believe that their lives too are the loci for the expression of this divine faithfulness: that their "little stories" and the "large story" of God's salvific care for the people as a whole (Psalms 105, 106) are congruous. Viewed in this context, the exhortations in vv. 22, 32 to go public with the thanksgiving and praise is a call to enable the "little stories" to be joined communally to the "large story" so as to create both a deepening and an expanding realm of trust and praise.

[91] Unlike Psalm 136, where the refrain "for his steadfast love endures forever" is preceded by colons treating different aspects of God's being (vv. 2-3), creative work (vv. 4-9) and salvific activities for Israel (vv. 10-25), Psalm 107 focuses on the experiences of select groups (vv. 4-32) as representative of the different types of problems that everyone experiences in life. This type of concentration helps the ancient doctrine be revalued and reexperienced.

small midwestern town to New York. He discovers a rich library in an old house and he is allowed to delve into this resource which was not available to him in his former home. He spends his days reading in the house and he discovers, in his words,

> a sense of continuity that we folks have missed out of our lives – out where I live anyway – and it gave me the idea of a different rhythm, a different time-beat: a movement without jerks and breaks, flowing down from ever so far off in the hills, bearing ships to the sea.

It is both the oldness of his New York surroundings – in contrast to the new, and so unstoried, town in the Midwest – and the fresh contact in the books with previous generations that places him in touch with larger currents in the life of humanity.

> His mind struck root deep down in accumulated layers of experience, in centuries of struggle, passion and aspiration...
>
> For him the place had symbolized continuity, that great nutritive element of which no one had ever told him...[92]

The psalmist of Psalm 107 reflects on a larger rhythm and continuity throughout life: God's steadfast love which is expressed by delivering people from problems with shelter, sustenance, persons, sickness, nature and business, and by blessing them in these areas.

The literary dynamic in verses 4-32 shows that no matter how bad the situation gets and how few the resources are for dealing with it, God's steadfast love saves[93] and transforms. The double encouragement in verse 43 to reflect on this dynamic places meditation at the service of hopeful living.

Reflection on Psalm 107 can strengthen parental trust in God's abiding love in every aspect of life. Such a perspective fosters a rich emotional life by building up layer upon layer of historical reserves of care. It also helps us not to be overwhelmed by present

[92] E. Wharton, *Hudson River Bracketed* (New York: D. Appleton, 1929) 354, 360, 498.

[93] E. Beaucamp, *Le Psautier: Pss.73-150*, 176, noted that God is presented as being the only chance for the salvation of each group, but he did not explain his reasons for this assertion. Independently, I arrived at the same conclusion and I have provided arguments for it.

troubles by setting them in the context of the larger pattern of steadfast love which binds together periods of our life. This nourishment of the emotional lives of parents will help the phatic ambience which they create for their children.[94]

Psalm 107 can produce an exergonic emotional reaction. This liberated energy can be refocused and reconcentrated towards the establishment of the types of familial phatic relations which children need for psychosocial health and growth. Emotional stability and social development are byproducts of continual concern. "With continuity comes emotional support."[95]

In his essay entitled "Vom Sinn der Geschichte" (On the Meaning of History), Oswald Spengler wrote the following.

> As little as one can know about the events of the future, nevertheless it is certain that the powers which move the future are none other than those which moved the past: the will of the stronger, healthy instincts, race, the desire for property and power. And over them the dreams, which will always remain dreams, swing ineffectually: justice, happiness and peace.[96]

[94] E. Leslie, *The Psalms*, 305, notes a calmer tone in vv. 33-43. Certainly the shift from a concern about specific instances of distress to an abstraction of how God works effects a reduction of the poem's tension. The pressure valve is opened further by the accounts not only of release from danger but also of safety and well-being (vv. 36-38, 41). This decrease in narrative tension coincides with the confidence which is the point the psalmist is trying to inculcate in this psalm.

Remember that R. Alter noted that narrativity is an important element in biblical poetry because of the concern with a process or a movement in these poems. Alter wrote about an intensification in which the drama is heightened and which leads to a climax. (*The World of Biblical Literature*, pp. 178, 183-84, 189.)

The tone of Ps. 107:33-43 shows that it is an emotional decrescendo; the drama is deintensified, the tension is diffused through the manner in which the psalmist writes in vv. 33-43 about God's relation to problems. A shift in focus from vv. 4-32 – which culminates in the emotionally charged pericope of the mariners' apparent engulfment by the raging waters (vv. 23-32) – to vv. 33-43 aids in the emotional assimilation of the psalmist's message of the assurance of God's salvation.

[95] P. Molitor in a television interview in Milwaukee, WI, USA in 1992.

[96] Spengler, "Vom Sinn der Geschichte," *Gedanken* (Munchen: C.H. Beck, 1941). The original German is as follows.

> So wenig man von den Ereignissen der Zukunft weiss... so sicher ist es, daß die bewegenden Mächte der Zukunft keine anderen sind als die der Vergan-

The psalmist of Psalm 107 would certainly reject the idea that human power is the governing force of history. It is not human force which is the decisive factor, but God's *ḥesed̲* which delivers even when believers are at their weakest (vv. 4-7, 10, 12-14, 17-20, 25-29). When people are afflicted (v. 39), God deals with the powerful (v. 40) and blesses the needy (v. 41). Thus, the message of Psalm 107 is at odds with Spengler's ideas on the moving powers in history.

Both are in agreement, however, that "As little as one can know about the events of the future, nevertheless it is certain that the powers which move the future are none other than those which moved the past." The psalmist inculcates the message that it is God's steadfast love which is the determinative and transperiodic power that moves the history of believers. The twofold exhortation to reflect on this reality (v. 43), if heeded, can provide an emotional bedrock underlying the fluctuations parents encounter in all aspects of our lives.[97]

Psalm 107 contains a literary dynamic that encourages a psychic resiliency in the reader: one that is very helpful to parents. The situations are desperate and the people are helpless; the situations become worse. Yet, God's steadfast love is always present to effect salvation for those who call to him ("Then they called to the Lord in their trouble, and He delivered them from their distress –" vv. 6, 13, 19, 28).

genheit: der Wille des Stärkeren, die gesunden Instinkte, die Rasse, der Wille zu Besitz und Macht. Und darüber hin schwanken wirkungslos die Träume, die immer Träume bleiben werden: Gerechtigkeit, Glück und Friede.

[97] The French word *adoucissement* comes from the verb *adoucir* which means to soften, to smooth, to soothe; to sweeten; to assuage, to alleviate. Psalm 107 is an *adoucissement* that can smooth the rough edges of parental anxieties and, by so doing, enable parents to sooth and assuage the pains of children and make their lives emotionally smoother at home.

CHAPTER 7

PSALM 92
WHERE IS GOD'S STEADFAST LOVE AND FAITHFULNESS DURING DIFFICULT TIMES?

For most of us, there is only the unattended
Moment, the moment in and out of time.
T.S. Eliot, "The Dry Salvages," *Four Quartets*

The most important thing we
can give our children is time. *Anonymous*

The Reading[1]

Psalm 92

A Psalm. A Song for the Day of the Sabbath

1 It is good to give thanks to the Lord,
to sing praises to your name, O Most High–
2 to declare your steadfast love in the morning
and your faithfulness by nights–
3 upon the ten and upon the stringed instrument,
upon the sounding of the harp.
4 For you, O Lord, have made me glad by your work;
at the works of your hands I sing for joy.

5 How great are your works, O Lord!
Your thoughts are very deep!
6 The dullard cannot know,
and the stupid cannot understand this:
7 that though the wicked sprout like grass
and all evildoers blossom,
they are doomed to destruction forever.

[1] The translation provided is my modification of the NRSV translation. The reasons for the changes will become clear in the course of this chapter.

8 But you, O Lord, are on high forever.
9 For behold, your enemies, O Lord,
for behold, you enemies are perishing;
all evildoers are being scattered.

10 But you have raised my horn like that of the
wild ox;
you have poured fresh oil over me.
11 My eye has seen my enemies, my ears have heard.

12 The righteous flourish like the palm tree,
and grow like a cedar in Lebanon.
13 They are planted in the house of the Lord;
they flourish in the courts of our God.
14 They still bring forth fruit in old age;
they are ever full of sap and green,
15 to declare that the Lord is upright;
my rock, there is not unrighteousness in him.

The Thesis

Psalm 92 is a protreptic designed to free one from the concern over the present success of the wicked and to establish, both by a set of contrasting images and by an expansive, expatiating style, a different, less demanding temporal perspective.[2] This is significant for the parental care of children because when time is too much with us we are too little with others. When the concerns of the present are pressing, we spend too little time with those who need us. Although the Sabbath superscription may be secondary,[3] insofar as the Sabbath is viewed as a release from the constrictions

[2] Both the interpretation of the psalm's poetry and genre considerations support this thesis. At the conclusion of the second subsection I will offer my proposal, based on the analysis in the body of this chapter, of how the various genre features found in this psalm are fused.

[3] So e.g., M. Tate, *Psalms 51-100* (WBC, 20; Dallas: Word, 1990) 465, 470-71; N. Sarna, "The Psalm for the Sabbath Day (Ps 92)," *JBL* 81 (1962) 155-168, pp.158-59. According to H. Plantin, "Leviternas Veckodagspsalmer i templet," *SEA* 48 (1983) 48-76, Psalm 92 was first used for the sabbath temple service in 165 B.C.

of time, this heading encapsulates an important dimension of Psalm 92. Time was meant for people, and not people for time. With Psalm 92 time has again become a homey, livable matrix instead of a domineering taskmaster. This psalm introduces a new clock with longer, less hurried hours. It accomplishes this first by the message which it inculcates and second by the tenor established by the author's choice of words and syntactical constructions. As a propaedeutic to this endeavor, problems of translation, lineation and literary parallels will be treated in the next section.

Text Considerations

Five elements of the psalm will be dealt with in their order of occurrence in Psalm 92. An understanding of them enables an exegesis of the psalm to proceed on solid ground. The first consideration is the joining of God's "name" *(šēm)* to day and night imagery in verses 1-2 and a similar phenomenon in one of the Amarna letters.

In EA 288:6-7, *Ir-Heba*, the ruler of Jerusalem, wrote of Pharaoh that "The king, my Lord, has set his name at the rising of the sun, and at the setting of the sun!"[4] Rudolph Hess noted that this refers to the scope of Pharaoh's authority, expressed either in geographical or temporal terms. While relating this text to Pss 20:8-9; 80:19; 83:19; 113:3, Hess made no reference to Ps 92:1-2 which may be the strongest similarity to the use of these images in EA 288:6-7.[5]

Hess did not provide arguments for his interpretation. In what follows, support is provided both for his view on EA 288:6-7 and for considering this idea of power over the enemies to be an aspect of the meaning of Ps 92:1-2.

[4] This translation is by W. Albright, "The Amarna Letters," *Ancient Near Eastern Texts*, ed. J. Pritchard (Princeton: Princeton University Press, 1950).
[5] R. Hess, "Hebrew Psalms and Amarna Correspondence from Jerusalem: Some Comparisons and Implications," *ZAW* 101 (1989) 249-265, pp. 253-54.

Both EA 288:1 and the overall structure of this letter corroborate Hess' thesis. The image of Pharaoh's name being set "at the rising of the sun, and at the setting of the sun" (288:6-7) links up to the appellation "Sun-God" given to Pharaoh in 288:1. Thus, "sun" is used in reference to Pharaoh's power. The form of this letter would also lead us to expect mention of Pharaoh's might at this point in the letter.

EA 288 is organized roughly as a chiasm. In the A sections (1-4, 62-65), *Ir-Heba* calls himself Pharaoh's servant and writes about falling at Pharaoh's feet. The central C material (EA 288:8-48) is about the problems *Ir-Heba* is experiencing from enemies who are taking the land of Pharaoh which *Ir-Heba* administers. This section begins by stating *Ir-Heba's* plight ("[It is] vile what they have done to me" - 288:8), and proceeds to describe *Ir-Heba's* faithfulness to Pharaoh (288:9-12) before writing about the threat to Pharaoh's land (288:23-48). The call for Pharaoh to take care of his land forms an inclusio (288:23, 48) to this latter group of lines.

The B sections (288:6-7, 49-61) comprise references to Pharaoh's power to save. This is clear in 288:49-61 which follows the call for the king to protect his land (288:48) by the request that the king send archers. This leads me to interpret the first B section, 288:6-7 ("Behold, the king, my lord, has set his name at the rising of the sun, and at the setting of the sun!"), as also a reference to the Pharaoh's power. Thus, both the sun imagery in 288:1 and the overall structure of EA 288 support the interpretation that the reference to Pharaoh's setting "his name at the rising of the sun and at the setting of the sun" denotes Pharaoh's power.

Although EA 288 is in prose, and Psalm 92 is a poem, both are addressed to a master (Pharaoh–God).[6] Moreover, both are concerned with the master's power over the enemies (EA 288:8-48; Ps. 92:7, 9, 11). In Psalm 92 this power is associated with God's

[6] R. Hess, "Hebrew Psalms and Amarna Correspondence," 264. Hess notes this in reference to other psalms in which he found similar imagery to EA 288:6-7; he did not mention Psalm 92.

being "on high." In between the verses about God's destroying enemies (vv. 7, 9), we read "But you, O Lord, are on high forever" (v. 8). Thus, the claim that it is good to sing to God's name *(šēm)*, "Most High," *('elyôn)* in verse 1 indicates power over the enemies; a theme which is more fully treated in verses 7-9.[7] Finally, there is either an explicit (EA 288:9-22) or an implicit (Ps. 92:10-15) contrast between the faithful or righteous author and the enemies.

This is not to claim that there is any direct literary connection between EA 288 and Psalm 92, not even by means of a common Jerusalem scribal tradition. What is being proposed is that the connection of name and sun imagery in EA 288:6-7 helps to clarify the function of this same type of linkage in Ps 92:1-2. While the primary meaning of Ps 92:1-2 is that it is good to thank and praise God in the morning and in the evening because of God's steadfast love and faithfulness, there is an overtone right from the outset of this psalm that this steadfast care is expressed in the use of God's power against the psalmist's enemies. The day and night imagery describes both when the exaltation should occur and also when God's exalted power ("Most High," *'elyôn*) is expressed.

The second aspect of this psalm treated in this section is the lineation of verses 7-9. This psalm is composed mainly of bicola with three notable exceptions. Tricola appear in verses 7, 9 and a monocolon in between them in verse 8. It is obvious that verse 9 is a tricolon ("For behold, your enemies, O Lord, for behold, your enemies are perishing; all evildoers are being scattered"). A. Anderson construes verse 7a ("that though the wicked sprout like grass, and all evildoers flourish") as a bicolon and verses 7b, 8 ("they are doomed to destruction forever. But You, Lord are on high forever") as another bicolon. This does not appear to be the case. Verse 7 is a tricolon and verse 8, just as the Tiberian Masoretes presented it, is a monocolon.

[7] M. Tate, *Psalms 51-100*), 461, has noted other uses of *'elyon* in the Psalms to indicate God's power. T. Mettinger, *In Search of God: The Meaning and Message of the Everlasting Names* (Philadelphia: Fortress, 1988) 122, has argued that *'elyôn* is an "epithet for kingship."

The value of distinguishing between monocola, bicola and tricola is that the correct assessment gives us the primary matrix within which a colon should be interpreted. Various criteria may be used, with a cautious valuation as to the degree of success possible, to determine the demarcation of individual cola;[8] it is difficult to determine, however, if these cola are monocola or parts of larger bicola or tricola. None of the criteria which have been proposed are helpful in the adjudication of every case.[9]

Individual specific rules must be applied in order to arrive at an informed decision on this matter. It is the poet's own manner of constructing cola throughout the psalm that must be taken as the standard by which individual cola are appraised. Patterns of line construction throughout the poem establish the proper matrix within which to determine the lineation of questionable cola. It is a critical circularity that is needed: one in which cola whose versification is clear on semantic, grammatical, morphologic and/or phonic grounds serve as a check, based on the poet's style, of disputed cola.

In Ps 92 one encounters limited semantic parallelism in which the same or a similar reality is treated in two different ways in contiguous cola, before another, but closely related, topic is treated

[8] E.g., O. Loretz, "Die Analyse der ugaritischen und hebräischen Poesie mittels Stichometrie und Konsonantenerzählung," *UF* 7 [1975] 265-69) counts consonants; D. Pardee, "Ugaritic and Hebrew Metrics," in G. Young, ed., *Ugarit in Retrospect: Fifty Years of Ugarit and Ugaritic* (Winona Lake, IN: Eisenbrauns, 1981) 113-30, counts words; D.N. Freedman,"Acrostic Poems in the Hebrew Bible: Alphabetic and Otherwise," *CBQ* 48 (1986) 408-31, counts stresses and syllables, and P. Raabe, *Psalmic Structures*, 20, 21, follows Freedman, but modifies the syllable enumeration on the basis of what we know about classical Hebrew. All of the preceding attempts involve a search for a stylistic regularity as the basis for establishing individual cola.

The last parts of vv. 7, 9 ("they are doomed to destruction for ever," "... all evildoers will be scattered") cannot fit in with the previous sections of these verses in a way that is consistent with the number of stresses, consonants, syllables or words found in other verses of this psalm. This means that they can be viewed as monocola or as parts of bicola or tricola. It will be argued that both are best seen as the last cola in two separate tricola.

[9] See, e.g., the different versifications of Ps 7:15 given by N. Ridderbos, *Die Psalmen: Stilistische Verfahren und Aufbau mit besonderer Berücksichtigung von Ps 1-41* (Berlin: Walter De Gruyter, 1972) 86-87.

in the same manner. This type of parallelism can be described as "limited" to indicate the "what's moreness" that is also operative. Thus, the two cola in verse 1 treat how good it is to acclaim God, and the two in verse 2 provide qualities of God and temporal factors which should be considered in this praise. The cola in verse 3 deal with the accompanying musical instruments. Verse 4 is about the joy caused by God's work, and each of the two parts of verse 5 is about the greatness of the divine activity and plans. In verse 6 we read twice about the inability of the foolish to fathom God's planned activity.

Verse 7 is an exception. Here we read about the enemies in three distinct clauses. It is the wicked who are the focus of concern in each of these clauses. The shift from dealing with their lives (the first two cola) to treating their destruction (the third colon) does not indicate that the third colon is linked primarily to verse 8. The same pattern occurs in verse 9 where the first colon holds the enemies up for inspection and the last two treat their demise; yet, no one would see the first colon of verse 9 ("For behold, your enemies, O Lord...") as linked primarily to the one in verse 8 ("But you, O Lord are on high forever"). The "forever" *(ʿaḏê-ʿaḏ-lĕʿōlām)* connection in verses 7-8 connects a tricolon (v. 7) with a monocolon (v. 8). Contrary to the style of the rest of the psalm, the topic of the enemies is treated three times in each of verses 7, 9 and in verse 8 the topic of God's exaltation is dealt with but once.

Verses 10-15 resume the type of limited semantic parallelism found prior to verse 7; in verses 10-15 two cola treat a topic before they are succeeded by two others which treat a related but distinct concern. The two cola in verse 10 are about the success of the psalmist, and those in verse 11 are about the psalmist's perception of the enemies. In verse 12 there are two similes to describe the righteous, and in verse 13 the just are situated twice in the temple precincts. The psalmist treats the longevity of the just in both parts of verse 14, and the righteousness of God in both parts of verse 15.

Thus, a consideration of the stylistics of Psalm 92 shows that the psalmist has cultivated a twofold way of writing about a subject that is not found in verses 7-9. These verses break the pattern, and are best described as two tricola (vv. 7, 9) treating the topic of the enemies, on either side of a monocolon (v. 8) which is about God's exaltation.

The third feature treated in this section is the similarity between verse 9 and the following piece of Ugaritic literature.

> Behold, your enemies, O Baal,
> behold, your enemies you will smite,
> behold, you will crush your foes.

> *ht 'ibk b'lm*
> *ht 'ibk tmḫṣ*
> *ht tṣmt ṣrtk*[10]

This may refer to Baal's defeat of the sea god. We cannot speak of any direct borrowing on the basis of the available evidence.[11] Thus, Dahood's thesis that the enemies of Ps 92:9 refer to the Canaanite deities is not likely.

The fourth matter for consideration is the choice of the reading for the second clause in verse 10, which the NRSV translates as "you have poured fresh oil over me." In the Massoretic Text (Hebrew) the words are *ballōṯî běšemen ra'ănān* ("I anoint with fresh oil"). This reading is problematic. Verse 10a is about God exalting the psalmist and this leads one to suspect that once again in verse 10b God would be the subject of this favorable action.[12]

There have been several modern and ancient attempts to solve this problem. Booij suggested "I shine" (the *Qal* perfect form *bālagtî*). In Arabic *balaja* means "to shine, to dawn," and although the Hebrew *blg* is only found in the *hiphil* and means "to be glad" or "to look cheerful," Booij proposed that the Arabic

[10] *CTA* 2, IV 8-9. See W. Baumgartner, "Ras Schamra und das Alte Testament," *ThR* 13 (1941) 3-31, p. 8; W. Albright, "The Old Testament and Canaanite Language and Literature," *CBQ* 7 (1945) 5-31.

[11] So D. Pardee, "Un héritage poétique commun," *MDB* 48 (March-April, 1987) 45-46; H. Donner, "Ugaritismen in der Psalmenforschung," *ZAW* 79 (1967) 322-350, pp. 345-46; A. Anderson, *The Psalms*, 663.

[12] There are no examples of the Qal of *bll* expressing the passive so the reading "I am anointed..." is improbable.

meaning can be assumed for the *Qal*. He translated verse 10b as "I shine with fresh oil."[13] The combination of deriving the meaning from the Arabic term with no other examples of this meaning in Hebrew and suggesting an unattested form of the verb gives one pause.

Loewenstamm opted for the translation "my old age is like a fresh olive tree." He viewed "oil" (*šemen*) in this verse as "oil tree" (*šemen ʿēṣ*) referring to the olive tree. In support, he noted that "olive" or "olive tree" (*zayiṯ*) is frequently used with *šemen*.[14] According to Booij, with whom I concur, this view is not likely given the general use of *šemen* to mean "oil."[15]

Much more probable are either one of two ancient textual readings. First, the Syriac version and the Targum suggest "You have anointed me" (*ballōṯanî*).[16] This would mean that only one letter (a *nûn*) had not been copied. The LXX and Symmachus indicate that the reading was "my old age" (*bělōṯî*).[17] This requires only a reconstrual of the consonantal text as containing only one *lāmeḏ* (i.e. the *lāmeḏ* as having no *daghēš forte* in it) and a different vocalization of this word. It is a slightly simpler emendation than the one proposed by the Syriac text, although either is quite possible.[18] The LXX translation of verse 10 ("My horn will be exalted as a unicorn, and my old age with rich mercy") requires that we view this verse as elliptical; interpreting *blty* as *bělōṯî* ("my old age") means there is no verb in verse 10b and that *tārem* ("you

[13] T. Booij, "The Hebrew Text of Psalm XCII, 11," *VT* 38 (1988) 210-213, pp. 212-13.

[14] S. Loewenstamm, "Ballōtî běšāmān raʿănān," *UF* 10 (1978) 111-13; Idem, "An Additional Remark upon Ps. 92:11b," *UF* 13 (1981) 302.

[15] Booij, "Hebrew Text of Psalm XCII, 11," 212.

[16] The retroversion of the Syriac to *ballōṯanî* was suggested by J. Olshausen, *Die Psalmen* (Leipzig: S. Hirzel, 1853) 376.

[17] The LXX reads *kai to gēras mou én éleō pioni* ("and my old age with rich mercy") and Symmachus has *hē palaiōsis mou* ("my old age").

[18] The LXX "my old age with rich mercy" is interesting. The MT parallel to the words "with rich mercy" *(én éleō pioni)* are the words *běšemen raʿănān*, which are commonly translated a "fresh oil." As we have seen, (supra, 87-88), *šemen* can be a sign of happiness. Perhaps *éleos* ("mercy") is the LXX view of the significance of *šemen* used in this way with *bělōṯî* ("my old age").

raise" – *hypsoō*, "to exalt" [LXX]) in verse 10a must serve double duty.

The readings "you have anointed me" and "my old age" are strong ones. They are to be preferred both to those of Booij and Loewenstamm and to the MT *ballōṯî* ("I anoint with fresh oil") which has no object for this transitive verb and which shifts the subject of the action from God (v. 10a) to the psalmist (v. 10b). God is the actor in both of the other ancient, textual options.

While no consensus may be able to be reached on the precise pointing of *blt*, the preceding textual considerations have culled the more likely options. These observations, as well as a study of the other terms used in verse 10b, are the basis for the analysis in the next part of this chapter of the meaning of this verse.

The final feature to consider in this preliminary is a Ugaritic passage which is similar to Ps 92:10.

> *qrn dbàtk btlt ʿnt*
> *grn dbàtk bʿl ymšḥ*
> *bʿl ymšḥ hm bʿp*
>
> Your powerful horn, girl Anat,
> your powerful horn will Baal anoint.
> Baal will anoint them in flight.[19]

The anointing is the preparation of Anat to fight. Taking his clue from the preceding passage, Pardee translated Ps 92:10 as "You have raised my horn like that of a wild bull; I have smeared (my horn) with fresh oil."[20] The image would refer to the preparation of the psalmist for battle. This interpretation of verse 10 is unlikely because, as we will see, the fight has already been completed by God (v. 9).

These reflections on parts of the text, on versification and on literary similarities solidify the basis for the subsequent interpretation.

[19] UM 76. 22-23.
[20] D. Pardee, "The Preposition in Ugaritic," *UF* 8 (1976) 215-322, p. 252.

The Poetics of Deferred Success

Psalm 92 is a poem about the righteous divine response to all. The joy over God's works (vv. 1-4) leads to acclaim for their greatness (vv. 5-6) and then to their specification as God's just actions to both the wicked and the righteous (vv. 7-15). In the process three sets of contrasting images are used for the dissimilar fates of each group: lowliness and height, quick prosperity with an equally quick destruction on the one hand and long-term success on the other, and desiccation and verdure. It is (1) the opening note of joy, (2) the imagery of verses 7-15 and (3) the retrospective quality imparted by certain verses to the rest of the psalm which lead the reader to be comfortable – in the light of the present good fortune of the wicked – both with the idea of the deferred success of the righteous, and with the slow movement of time toward such an end.

The first four verses set the joyful tone of the psalm and begin the description of the reason for this mood. The happiness signals the fulfillment of the psalmist's hopes. When these hopes are later specified as the destruction of the wicked and the ascendancy of the righteous, the initial unspecified anticipation shades to an expectation of divine retribution. Optimism prevails in the major key played in verses 1-4. This prelude causes confidence when the psalmist sings in a minor key about the enemies in verses 7, 9, 11 and again in its relative major about the future of the righteous in verses 10, 12-14.

The psalm begins with resounding outbursts of joy. The psalmist writes both about giving thanks (v. 1a) and about singing (v. 1b). The singing is to be accompanied by musical instruments (v. 3), and the reason for the song is twice said to be because of the psalmist's joy; "For you, O Lord, have made me glad by your work;/ at the works of your hands I sing for joy" (v. 4). We are being prepared for good news, the nature of which is already adumbrated in the first four verses.

The steadfast love of God, actively expressed for the benefit of the just, is the reason for the psalmist's exuberance. In between the music imagery of verses 1, 3-4 are the words "to declare your steadfast love in the morning and your faithfulness by night" (v. 2). This position shows that verse 2 does not describe an action which is unrelated to the joyful songs; rather, verse 2 describes what these songs are about. The thanks (v. 1a) and the hymns (vv. 1b, 3, 4b) are the result of God's "steadfast love" and "faithfulness." These abstract concepts have been historically expressed, and they have been experienced by the psalmist who writes twice about rejoicing in God's "works" (v. 4).[21] The psalmist's joy is anchored in, and caused by, the manifestation of God's enduring care. This stay supports the reader's appropriation of this joy by providing a guy from the psalmist's experience to the reader's own life: what has happened to one may happen to another.

As has been noted, verse 2 – viewed in conjunction with verse 1b – alludes to God's power, but it primarily expresses the idea that it is good[22] to proclaim God's steadfast care both in the morning and in the evening. This begins the process of helping the reader to consider the divine faithfulness in long spans of time. This tincture is imparted in greater degrees as the psalms progresses.

Verses 5-6 acclaim the greatness of the divine deeds which have caused the paean of the previous verses. The hook word is "deed" (*ma'ăśeh*), found in both verse 4b and verse 5a. As we have seen, the works of God in verses 1-4 involve the active expression of the divine steadfast love and faithfulness. Thus, the panegyric of verses 5-6 is about God's expressed concern. The description of how wonderful it is (vv. 5-6) heightens the reader's appreciation of it.

The encomium proceeds. God's deeds are great (v. 5a), God's thoughts are deep (*'āmĕqû* – v. 5b). The word "deep" (*'āmĕqû*) conveys the sense of the mysteriousness of God's plans as is

[21] The singular *pā'ălekā* is found in v. 4a and the plural construct *ma'ăśê* in v. 4b. In the next section of this chapter, I give a possible reason for this change from the singular to the plural.

[22] V. 2 is elliptical: the *ṭôḇ* ("[It is] good") of v. 1a applies to all six bicola in vv. 1-3.

shown both by other uses of this term,[23] and by the following verse: "The dullard cannot know,/and the stupid cannot understand this" (v. 6).[24] God's works of steadfast care are so superlative (v. 5) that their underlying design is unintelligible to the dullard (v. 6). The obscurity of verse 6 emphasizes, by way of contrast, the radiant divine activity.

The reader has had a secure base of powerful divine concern erected for him or her by verses 1-6. It is with this type of emotional buildup that the psalmist leads one to the specific ways in which the godly activity is expressed: the *zō'ṯ* ("this") of verse 6b ("and the stupid man cannot understand this").[25] In the following verses the psalmist writes about the precise acts of God.

Verses 7 and 9 treat the fate of the wicked in such a way as to acknowledge the unease which their prosperity may cause and to replace this ailment with a confident calmness. The anxiety is conveyed both by the content of part of these verses and by their form as tricola. The stress is only incipient because of the high and optimistic spirits evoked by verses 1-6. Relief comes both through the type of tricola which we have in verses 7 and 9 and through their relation to the intervening verse 8.

Subject matter and form dovetail to produce a vague dissatisfaction in verses 7 and 9. As has been noted, Psalm 92 is composed

[23] See, e.g., Ps 64:7; Job 11:8; Isa 33:19; Ez 3:5. Some (e.g., M. Tate, *Psalms 51-100*, 461) note that *'āmōq* may mean "strength/violence," as in the comparable Ugaritic term, and that this interpretation of *'āmōq* would cause it to parallel the word *gāḏělû* ("great") found in the first part of this verse. While this sense may also be conveyed by *'āmōq*, the translation "deep," with the meaning "mysterious," is justified as a setup for the following verse, as we will see.

[24] The words *ba'ar* ("brutish person") and *kesîl* ("stupid person") are also used together in Pss 49:12; 94:8.

[25] E. Greenstein, "How Does Parallelism Mean?" 55-56, wrote that Ps 92:9 ("For behold, your enemies, O Lord, / for behold, your enemies are perishing; / all evildoers are being scattered") is a "pivotal point" because before this verse the enemies "proliferate" and after it the psalmist "flourishes." This attempt to get at the structure of Psalm 92 is unsuccessful because it does not adequately account for vv. 1-6. In these verses there is no mention of the increase of the enemies. The joyfulness and acclaim expressed in vv. 1-6 anticipates the destruction of the enemies. It is only v. 7 which treats the flourishing of the wicked, and this verse also mentions their destruction. There is no peripeteia (reversal of fortunes) in this psalm.

of bicola except at two points in the psalm where the enemies are written about. When the psalmist is singing to, and thanking and praising God (vv. 1-6), there are a series of bicola. In verse 7 the success and then the downfall of the enemies is treated: "that though the wicked sprout like grass, / and all evildoers blossom, they are doomed to destruction forever." This is a tricolon.

There are a number of ways in which tricola can be used.[26] Two of these are appropriate to what we find in Ps. 92:7, 9. Alter noted that, at times, tricola are used by the biblical poets to convey "tension or instability" and that, in such cases, the third colon may contrast with the other two or even reverse them.[27] I would add that both of these aspects appear to be present in Ps 92:7, 9.

The first two cola of verse 7 are about the prospering of the wicked. In the first we read about how quickly they have attained their good fortune ("that though the wicked sprout like grass"); in the second we read about the extent of their success ("and all evildoers blossom"). Not only has their ascent been rapid, but it has also reached a certain fruition: the grass has sprouted and blossomed.[28]

The mounting depiction of the ascendancy of the wicked in the first two cola of verse 7 is at a point where we expect a certain tension in the poem. Psalm 92 is not an ivory-towered discourse on the problem of evil. The wicked (*rĕšāʿîm*) and evildoers (*pōʿălê ʾāwen*) of these two cola are the psalmist's enemies (*šôrĕrāy* – v.11).[29] In Ps 92:7 the longer verse corresponds to the excess attention caused by the problem of the wicked.[30]

[26] N. H. Ridderbos, *Die Psalmen*, 86-87, finds the tricolon to be very flexible. He proposes that among its uses are the expression of a divine response to situations, the conveyance of a certain nostalgic quality (e.g., Ps 39:3-7) and the movement of verse at a good pace (e.g., Ps 24:7-10).
[27] Alter, *The World of Biblical Literature*, 177.
[28] The *hiphil* of the verb *ṣûṣ* ("to blossom") is used in the second colon of v. 7.
[29] Most scholars emend the MT *bĕšûrāy* ("my watchers") to *bĕšôrĕrāy* ("my enemies"). M. Tate, *Psalms 51-100*, 463, keeps the MT reading. In either case, the context (vv. 7, 9-10) shows that the reference is to enemies. The MT reading adds more irony to this verse: to paraphrase the MT version of the first part of this verse, "My eyes have seen those who were on the look out (for my downfall)."
[30] It is not the case, as H. Fisch, *Poetry with a Purpose*, 131, argues, that the enemies of God (vv. 7, 9) are a different group than the enemies of the psalmist (v. 11).

Verse 9 is also about enemies, and it is also a tricolon. Once again subject matter and form dovetail: a tension-inducing topic is treated in a verse whose length conveys the degree of concern the matter causes. Thus, the length and content of verses 7 and 9 create a slight uneasiness; this feeling, attenuated by the emotional state produced by verses 1-6, is quickly dissipated both by the type of tricolon found in verses 7 and 9 and by the relation of these verses to verse 8.

The tricola of verses 7 and 9 treat not only the presence and prosperity of the enemies, but also the divine response which reverses their pattern of success. In the third colon of verse 7 ("they are doomed to destruction forever") we find a radical reversal of the fortunes of the wicked. A rapid, resounding success becomes an equally swift annihilation.

The sense of a definitive reversal of fortunes also comes through the placement of the verbs in the last two cola of verse 9; the words "they are perishing" (*yō'ḇēḏû*) and "they are scattered" (*yiṯporḏû*) are placed right next to each other at the end of the second colon and the beginning of the third colon respectively. This positioning accentuates their destruction. This type of emphasis may also be conveyed by the lack of a *wāw* ("and") preceding the second verb. Although the *wāw* is found in some manuscripts, this appears to be a scribal insertion to smooth the text. As a result of there being no *wāw*, the two verbs which convey the idea of the demise of the enemies are brought into a very close connection, the effect being similar to a one-two punch.[31]

The repetitive pattern found in verse 9 highlights God's destruction of the enemies. Repetition, both narrowly conceived of as the use of a word, or two or more stem-related words, in a certain con-

If this is so then one cannot as easily expect anxiety on the psalmist's part in v.9. For my arguments against Fisch's view, see infra, pp. 181-182, n. 57.

[31] The third colon of v. 9 begins with the word *yiṯporḏû*. This is a *hithpael* form of the verb *pāraḏ*, and this form means "to be separated or scattered" (*BDB*, 825; *HAL*, 297). The use of this term in the final colon of v. 9 forms a phonic inclusion in vv. 7-9, one which deals with the enemies. The first word in v. 7 is *biprōaḥ*; there is a *pr* sound in both verbs. Those wicked who have blossomed lushly (*biprōaḥ* –v. 7) are doomed to become strewn about (*yiṯporḏû* –v. 9)

text, and in the larger sense of the *parallelismus membrorum*, is a very important feature of biblical poetry. While the full meaning of any repetitive passage must be derived from its relation to its context, generally repetition in biblical poetry functions to hammer home the message a poet wants to make.[32] This is the case in Ps 92:9 where we have an anaphora: the words "For behold, your enemies" (*kî hinnēh 'ōyĕḇekā*) are repeated at the beginning of two successive clauses.

What has occasioned the paean in the initial verses of this psalm is God's destruction of the enemies. In verse 9 the psalmist brings the two poles of his attention together: God and the enemies. *YHWH* follows the first part of the anaphora and "they are perishing" (*yō'ḇēḏû*) follows the second. The repeated clause ("for behold, your enemies") concentrates the reader's attention on the two major participants in the drama: God and the enemies. The anaphora also acts as a literary background for the words which immediately follow it. These words, *YHWH* and *yō'ḇēḏû* ("they are perishing") are forgrounded against the anaphoric stylistic backdrop. They present what is taking place between the actors who have been called to our attention: God is destroying the enemies. By means of anaphora the psalmist stresses God's definitive action against the enemies.

Each of the tricola in verses 7 and 9 move from tension to divine response: each begin with statements about the lives of the enemies and conclude with comments about their demise. Thus, in verse 7 the first two cola are about the prosperity of the wicked ("that though the wicked sprout like grass and all evildoers flourish") and the first colon of verse 9 holds up the reality of the enemies for attention ("for behold, your enemies, O Lord"). The last colon in verse 7 is "they are doomed to destruction forever,"[33] and

[32] N. H. Ridderbos, *Die Psalmen*, 43-45; M. Buber, *Good and Evil: Two Interpretations* (New York: Scribners, 1953) 52.

[33] J. Magonet, "Some Concentric Structures in Psalms," *HJ* 23 (1982) 365-376, p. 371, has claimed that by writing first in v. 7 about the wicked portrayed as grass, the psalmist has created the dull, stupid person of v. 6: the one who sees the power of the wicked and does not understand God's ways. According to Magonet, it is

the last two cola of verse 9 read 'for behold, your enemies are perishing;/all evildoers are being scattered.[34]

If the move in each of these tricola is from the instability caused by the enemies to the psalmist's stability caused by their destruction, the relative stress on each of these elements in verses 7 and 9 also conveys this direction. Verse 7 begins with two cola on the prosperity of the enemies and ends with one on their annihilation; whereas verse 9 leads off with just one colon that is not about their prosperity, but simply their existence, and concludes with two on their deaths.[35]

What brings about both the intraverse and interverse shifts is the exalted presence of God, mentioned simply, with no elaboration in verse 8 ("But you, O Lord, are on high forever").[36] This eternal divine exaltation renders the paltry flourishing of the wicked insignificant and transmogrifies it to death.[37]

Verse 8 is a majestic monocolon, highlighted by its position between the two tricola (vv. 7, 9) which punctuate the regular bicola in this psalm. The verse possesses a stately dignity by its simple and regal assertion "But you, O Lord, are on high forever."[38] It is the stable point in the middle of the tense fluctuations

not until we read about the "success of the righteous" (presumably he is referring to v. 11, 12 or 13) that the contrasting fates of each become clear. This last idea is true, but it does not imply that the reader expects the success of the wicked before the conclusion of the psalm. The tone of joy in vv. 1-4, the praise for God's works in v. 5 and the third colon in v. 7 lead the reader from the outset to expect the downfall of the wicked.

[34] For a similar use of tricola indicating the tension caused by enemies and the divine response, see Ps 11:2, 4.

[35] The Codex Vaticanus version of the Septuagint and the Old Latin version do not have the first colon in v. 9 ("For behold, your enemies, O Lord"). This creates a bicolon as is found throughout most of this psalm, but it does so at the expense of the pattern of a movement from instability to stability found both in v. 7 and in v. 9.

[36] L. Jacquet, *Les Psaumes*, 2:755, opts for *môrām* ("their terror"), but *mārôm* ("on high") is consistent with the other height imagery (vv. 1, 10, 12) in this psalm.

[37] Cf. Ps 93:4b (*'addîr bammārôm YHWH* – "the Lord on high is mighty") for a similar use of the tetragrammaton and *mārôm* to convey divine power.

[38] In the psalms monocola are the exception; bicola and tricola are the rule. P. Raabe, *Psalm Structures*, 14, found only two monocola in the 247 cola he studied.

of the fortunes of the enemies (vv. 7, 9), and the power that effects their reversal and ultimate demise.[39]

The image in verse 8 of God being "on high"[40] shows God's power over the enemies. It sets up a contrast between God's exalted state and the lowliness of the enemies, presented in verse 7 as grass. In Psalm 57 there is a similar use of high and low imagery to signify divine power over one's enemies. Those who persecute the psalmist trample him and dig a pit for him (57:3, 6). God the "Most High ... fulfills his purpose for me" (v. 2) and sends "from heaven and saves me" (v. 3). The following refrain is found in Ps 57:5,11. "Be exalted, O God, above the heavens!/ Let your glory be over all the earth." This exaltation language is linked to God's deliverance because in verse 10 we have a similar type of height imagery used for God's salvific power: "For your steadfast love is great to the heavens,/your faithfulness to the clouds"(v. 10).

Thus, the psalmist of Psalm 92 anticipates the tension caused by the existence and prosperity of the wicked, and obviates it by the particular presentation of God and the enemies found in verses 7-9.

In verse 10 God's exaltation and power are bestowed somewhat upon the psalmist. As we have seen in the treatment of verse 8, the exaltation imagery itself is used to express the idea of a victorious power over the enemies. The expression "you have raised" (*tārem*) of verse 10 links up to "on high" (*mārôm*) in verse 8 because each comes from the Hebrew root *rûm* ("to raise"). It is God who is "on high" (*mārôm* - v. 8). From this height God raises (*tārem* – v. 10) the psalmist. This elevation is kept in the reader's

[39] The importance of v. 8 is also indicated by its central position in the psalm. J. Bazak, "Numerical Devices in Biblical Poetry, *VT* 38 (3, 1988) 333-337, p.335, has noted that there are fifty-two words before and fifty-two words after this verse. Less convincing is the attempt to discern a concentric pattern in the whole psalm, with v. 8 at its center. Thus, H. Fisch's proposal of such a pattern does not take vv. 4-6 into account. See H. Fisch, *Poetry with a Purpose*, 134-35. In another attempt at discerning a concentric pattern J. Magonet, "Some Concentric Structures in Psalms,"368-72, noted that it is difficult to see how vv. 5-6 could fit into it.

[40] The LXX, Syriac version and the Targum have "Most High" (*hypsistos*).

mind by the words “like a wild ox my horn” (*kir’êm qarnî*) which follow *tārem* in verse 10. These words are a simile explaining how God has exalted the psalmist. Not only do they reinforce this idea by visually concretizing it, but they also do so by repeating the *rm* (*kir’êm*, “like a wild ox”) consonants – or by using the similar *rn* (*qarnî*, “my horn”) ones – found in *tārem* (“you raise,” v. 10) and *mārôm* (“on high,” v. 8).

There are several other devices in verse 10 which communicate the power which God has given the psalmist. In the OT the image of the wild ox (*rĕ’ēm*) is one of strength;[41] when applied to Israel in relation to its enemies it is used in conjunction with other images which together present a power that is victorious over the opposition.[42] The enemies and their downfall are mentioned in the verses immediately preceding Ps 92:10 and so here too the image is probably one of a victorious power which God gives to the psalmist.[43]

The same point, with a different referent and consequently with different nuances, is made by the phrase “exalt the horn” (*tārem ... qarnî* – v. 10). We find this phrase in 1 Sam 2:1, 10; Pss 75:4, 5, 10 (twice); 89:17, 24; 92:10; 112:9. Some have claimed that it signifies vitality.[44] The point I would like to stress, which I have not seen noted before, is that all of these uses appear in the context of victory over one’s enemies.

In 1 Sam 2:1 Hannah says “my horn is exalted in the Lord.” This is followed immediately by the words “My mouth derides my enemies, because I rejoice in your salvation.” Similarly, in verse 10 Hannah claims that the Lord will judge the earth, “give strength to his king, and exalt the horn of his anointed.” Before

[41] See e.g., Num 23:22; 24:8; Deut 33:17; Isa 34:7; Ps 22:21; Job 39:9, 10. The imagery about the wild ox in Job 39:9-11 shows both its inability to be domesticated and its great strength.

[42] This is the case in Num 23:22; 24:8; Deut 33:17.

[43] So, too, Kraus, *Psalms 60-150*, 229, who, however, does not note OT examples of *rĕ’ēm* applied to Israel in the context of the treatment of Israel’s enemies.

[44] Booij, “The Hebrew Text of Psalm XCII,” 210; Weiser, *The Psalms*, 616; A. Anderson, *The Psalms*, 663. Anderson (p.663) notes that the LXX reading of *monokeros* (“unicorn”) for *rĕ’ēm* in Ps 92:10 is unlikely given the reference in Deut 33:17 to the horns (plural) of a *rĕ’ēm*.

this, she says "The adversaries of the Lord will be broken to pieces; against them he will thunder in heaven" (2:10).

The destruction of the wicked is also the setting for the raising of the horn sayings found in Psalms 112, 75. The reference to the horn of the righteous being exalted in honor (Ps 112:9) is continued with the description of the progressive frustration, and ultimate death, of the wicked.

> The wicked see it and are angry;
> they gnash their teeth and melt away;
> the desire of the wicked comes to nothing
> (Ps 112:10).

In Psalm 75 there are four such horn sayings (vv. 4, 5, 10 [twice]) and they all appear in the context of God's defeat of the wicked (vv. 2, 4, 7, 8, 10). The clear and pithy connection between the image of exalting one's horn and that of the downfall of evil people is found in verse 10: "All the horns of the wicked I will cut off, but the horns of the righteous will be exalted."

Finally, the words "exalt the horn" are found twice in Psalm 89:17-24.

> 17 For you are the glory of their strength;
> by your favor our horn is exalted.
> 18 For our shield belongs to the Lord,
> our king to the holy one of Israel.
> 19 Then you spoke in a vision
> to your faithful one and said:
> "I have set the crown upon one who is mighty.
> I have exalted one chosen from the people.
> 20 I have found David, my servant;
> with my holy oil I have anointed him
> 21 so that my hand will ever abide with him,
> my arm will strengthen him.
> 22 The enemy will not outwit him;
> the wicked will not humble him.
> 23 I will crush his foes before him
> and strike down those who hate him.
> 24 My faithfulness and my steadfast love will be with him,
> and in my name his horn will be exalted."

We read about a horn being exalted in verses 17 and 24 and verses 22-23 set this in the context of God's defeat of the enemies.

Ps 89:17-24 and 1 Sam 2:10 may shed light on the two primary images found in Ps 92:10: the exalting of the psalmist's horn and "you anoint me" or "my old age" (*blty*) used in reference to the psalmist.[45] The combination of these two elements indicate the conferral both upon the psalmist and upon all who are righteous of God's special victorious power which was exercised for the Davidic king.

Both the passage from First Samuel and the one from Psalm 89 link the exalting of the horn to the anointing of the king (1 Sam 2:10; Ps 89:20, 24). Both present the king as a divinely appointed instrument of power through whom God will act to destroy the wicked. Thus, the beginning of 1 Sam 2:10 reads "The adversaries of the Lord will be broken to pieces; against them he will thunder in heaven." So too, in Psalm 89, between the mention of David's anointing (v. 20) and that of the raising of his horn (v. 24), are three verses that treat the power of God which enables David to always be victorious over the enemies (Ps 89:21-23).

It is interesting that in both the First Samuel passage and the one from Psalm 89 we have the beginnings of the democratization of the image of the raising the king's horn. Thus, while the Song of Hannah concludes with this image (*wĕyārēm qeren mĕšîḥû* – v. 10), it commences with the raising of Hannah's horn (*rāmāh qarnî bYHWH* –v. 1). According to Ps 89:17 God is "the glory of their strength; by your favor our horn is exalted" (*ḇirṣōnĕkā tārîm qarnēnu*).

In Psalm 92 this figure of speech is used in a completely egalitarian way. Even if, as Dahood has argued,[46] this is a royal psalm – and, in addition to the difficulty in determining a royal psalm,[47]

[45] As we have seen, there is a question as to whether the MT *blty* in v. 10b refers to an anointing or to old age. The considerations which will be presented – in addition to the fact that oil (*šemen*) and an anointing word are commonly found together in the MT (see, e.g., Exod 30:25, 31; 37:29; Lev 8:2, 10; 21:10; Pss 45:8; 89:21) – tip the scales in the direction of the former option.
[46] M. Dahood, *Psalms 51-100*, 336-38.
[47] See supra, p. 22.

I note that there are no specific references to the Davidic king in this psalm – the psalmist is portrayed as representative of the righteous. Both are elevated. The horn of the psalmist is raised (v. 10), and the righteous grow as lofty palms and cedars (vv. 12-13).[48] Thus, even if the psalm is a royal psalm, the images in it represent the fortune of both the psalmist and the righteous.

Both the image in verse 10 of raising the psalmist's horn and the use of "you anoint me" or "my old age" (*blty*) convey God's special powerful and victorious presence over the enemies;[49] as God acted in such a way for the anointed king so God will act for the psalmist (v. 10) and for the righteous (vv. 12-13).[50] The images together convey the surety of the psalmist's victory over the enemies by means of images which evoke God's special, powerful commitment to an individual.

The preceding observations show that verse 10 is about a divine bestowal of exaltation and power upon the psalmist. It does not appear to refer to a military dominance, however, as is the case in the other OT passages where "wild ox" (*rĕ'ēm*) is applied to Israel in relation to its enemies.

The psalmist of Psalm 92 is referring to a staying and fructifying power – lacking in the enemies – as is shown from the following observations. According to verse 10b "fresh oil" is given to the psalmist. The word which the RSV editors translate as "fresh" is *ra'ănān*. This term means "luxuriant, full of leaves."[51] In all but one of its eighteen uses in the Massoretic Text (Hebrew), it refers to trees, and, in the one exception (Cant 1:16), cedar and pine trees (Cant 1:17) are mentioned in close association. This leads

[48] Although v. 12 uses the singular, v. 13 shifts to the plural in the depiction of the righteous.

[49] A study of the use of *rûm* ("to raise") with *qeren* ("horn") shows that it is much more than the formulaic pairing which H. Fisch, *Poetry with a Purpose*, 130, claimed it to be.

[50] Tate, *Psalms 51-100*, 467, and Anderson, *The Psalms*, 663, note correctly that v. 10 does not refer to any ceremony in which the psalmist was anointed; the position presented above is that it does refer, however, to the anointing of the king as a metaphor for how God is acting for the psalmist and for all who are righteous. The metaphorical interpretation is to be preferred to J. H. Eaton's view, *The Psalms*, 226, that the anointing of a leader in v. 10 is to be interpreted literally.

one to see a connection between verse 10b and the depiction of the righteous by the use of tree imagery in verses 12-14. This linkage is reinforced by the fact that the plural of this term (*ra'ănannîm*) is employed with the tree imagery in verse 14.[52] These trees "bring forth fruit in old age; they are ever full of sap and green" (v. 14). In contrast, the wicked perish as quickly as does grass (v. 7).

To sum up, in verse 10 we read that the psalmist receives somewhat the divine victorious power over the enemies; the psalmist will last and be productive in contrast to the transitory achievements of the wicked.

Verse 11 refers to the summary defeat of the enemies as a result of the presence of the divine, exalted power (vv. 8, 10). This content coincides with the pithiness of this verse. A shortened version of the Massoretic Text, one which succinctly expresses the swift overthrow of the enemies, is in my opinion, the original reading.

The Hebrew (Massoretic Text) of verse 11 is *wattabbēt 'ênî bĕšûrāy baqqāmîm 'ālay mĕrē'îm tišma'nāh 'āzĕnāy* ("My eye has seen my enemies; my ears have heard the wicked rising up against me").[53] The editors of *BHS* suggest that the words "the wicked rising up against me" (*baqqāmîm 'ālay mĕrē'îm*) be deleted, creating the reading "My eye has seen my enemies; my ears have heard." This deletion, and consequent new reading, appear to be warranted for the following reasons.

Verses 7-12 are arranged according to an *a b a b a b* pattern in which the "*a*'s" refer primarily to the enemies, the "*b*'s" primar-

[51] *BDB*, 947; *HAL*, 343.

[52] Another element of v. 10b which may link up to the tree imagery at the end of this psalm is *blty*. The reading was probably "you anoint me" (*ballōṯanî*) or, less likely, "my old age" (*bĕlōṯî*). If *bĕlōṯî* is the original reading then it links up clearly to *śêḇāh* ("old age") in v. 14. If it is *ballōṯanî* it may still be close enough in sound to *bĕlōṯî* ("my old age") to at least evoke this meaning, especially retrospectively after reading or hearing the psalm which ends with God's actions in one's old age as revelatory of God (vv. 14-15).

[53] The translation of the MT which is provided is based on the BHS lineation; however, there is no *athnaq* in this verse in the Leningrad codex. Thus, the words could also be read "My eye has seen my enemies rising up against me; my ears have heard the wicked." The word order of the accusative in relation to the verb is fluid in the Hebrew poetry. See B. Waltke and M. O'Connor, *Biblical Hebrew Syntax*, p. 162.

ily to the exaltation of God or the psalmist, and the two together are about the relation of God and the psalmist on the one hand, to their enemies on the other.[54] To take the *b* elements first, in verse 8 we read about God being on high forever (*mārôm lĕʿōlām*). In verse 10(b) the psalmist is lifted up (*wattārem*)[55] Verse 12 (b) reads: "The righteous flourish like the palm tree, and grow like a cedar in Lebanon." This verse also uses height imagery. Moreover, as we have seen, verse 10b with its use of *blty* and "luxuriant" (*raʿănān*) refers to the long-term fruitfulness of the psalmist. Thus, both verse 8 (*lĕʿolām*) and verse 10 (*blty*, *raʿănān*) talk about great sweeps of time. This is also the case with verse 12 because the image of trees found in it is extended through verse 14, where we read "they bring forth fruit in old age, they are ever full of sap and green."

The first two "*a*" elements (vv. 7, 9) refer to the reversal of the fortunes of the wicked or the enemies so that they are being destroyed. This argues that the third "*a*" section, verse 11, which refers to the enemies of the psalmist, is also about their demise. That this is the case is also indicated by the relation of the "*a*" and "*b*" elements to each other.

Both verse 8 and verse 10 are about an exaltation; both are followed respectively in verses 9, 11 by a twofold notice of an inspection of the enemies. God is on high (v. 8), and the enemies are

The NRSV use of the words "downfall" and "doom" are an interpretation of this verse.

[54] It is important to realize that no claim is being made that vv. 7-12 constitutes a distinct strophe or are part of a single strophe. It is difficult to determine strophic parameters in this psalm where one thought flows smoothly into another. Thus, the singing of vv. 1-3 is because of the joy over God's works (vv. 4-6), which are the destruction of the wicked and the exaltation of the psalmist by giving this one power over the enemies (vv. 7-11). The NRSV editors place vv. 10-11 as a distinct strophe, but the reference to exaltation and to the enemies in v. 10 and v. 11 respectively, link these verses to the same type of elements in vv. 7-9. While vv. 12-15 appear to comprise a distinct strophe, yet they are linked to vv. 7-11 by means of the height imagery and the *raʿănān* terms in vv. 10, 14.

Thus, there is a concern to link together major sections of this psalm, and the presence of an *a b a b a b* pattern in vv. 7-12 is another example of this tendency.

[55] The root of the "exaltation" words both in v. 8 and in v. 10 is *rûm*.

twice called to God's attention ("For behold, your enemies, O Lord,/ for behold, your enemies are perishing – v. 9). In verse 10 the horn of the psalmist is raised, and in verse 11 the enemies appear for a twofold perception ("My eye has seen my enemies, my ears have heard"). This similarity between verses 8-9 on the one hand and verses 10-11 on the other points to verse 11 as indicating the downfall of the enemies as does verse 9.

The parallelism of verses 7-12 suggests that what the psalmist sees (v. 11) is the destruction of the enemies (vv. 7, 9). The preceding interpretation of verse 11 suggests that the words "the wicked rising upon me" (*baqqāmîm ʿālay mĕrēʿîm*) were not originally found in the text. They seem to refer to the psalmist's realization of, or preparation for, the enemies' attack and not to their destruction.[56]

The phrase "the wicked rising upon me" (*baqqāmîm ʿālay mĕrēʿîm*) suggests the power of the enemies. In Ps 93:3 we read about the lifting up (*nāśā'*) of the floods. In 93:4 this is interpreted as an act of power ("... mighty the waves of the sea " – *'addîrîm mišbĕrê-yām*). Again, Ps 92:11, including the phrase "the wicked rising upon me" (*baqqāmîm ʿālay mĕrēʿîm*), suggests the psalmist's perception of a concerted, powerful attack by the wicked. Such force is, however, precisely what the progression of the poem makes improbable. The enemies have already been defeated (vv. 7, 9) and the psalmist has already been given dominion over them (v. 10).[57]

[56] Some propose that the verb *nbṭ* ("to see") in v. 11 indicates a perception of the downfall of the enemies. They base this on the fact that *nbṭ* is used several times in conjunction with *rā'āh* ("to see") and *rā'āh* refers to such a perception in Pss 37:34; 54:7; 59:10; 112:8; 118:7. See M. Tate, *Psalms 51-100*, 463; Booij, "The Hebrew Text of Psalm XCII,II," 210. In these verses, however, *nbṭ* does not appear with *rā'āh*.

A stronger case for this argument can be made by noting that in the previous psalm these two verbs are used as parallel components in a bicolon and there *rā'āh* clearly refers to the destruction of the wicked: "You will only look (*ṯabbîṭ*) with your eyes and see (*tir'eh*) the recompense of the wicked" (Ps. 91:8)

[57] H. Fisch, *Poetry with a Purpose*, 131, states that according to v. 11 the outcome of the confrontation with the enemies is undecided because the enemies have achieved a certain height (*baqqāmîm ʿālay*) as has the psalmist. According to

The choice of the reading "My eye has seen my enemies, my ears have heard" also more closely parallels the words "for behold, your enemies, O Lord, for behold, your enemies are perishing," the prior "a" element in verse 9. In each case one clause is completed by another. If we keep the words "the wicked rising upon me" (*baqqāmîm 'ālay mĕrē'îm*) then there are two complete clauses and verse 11 would not approximate its sister feature in verse 9 as closely. As I have shown, parallelism characterizes verses 7-12.[58]

The brevity of the reading "My eye has seen my enemies, my ears have heard," and the consequent lack of specification as to what precisely the psalmist has witnessed concerning the enemies, is not an obstacle to the acceptance of this reading. In Ps 59:10b we have an equally abrupt and ill-defined construction using *rā'āh* and *bĕšôrĕrāy* ("God lets me look on my enemies"), but the larger context (59:8, 11-13) shows that it is the demise of the enemies to which the terse sentence refers.

Fisch, God's enemies are clearly destroyed, but the matter of the psalmist's enemies is not so unambiguously determined.

This thesis contradicts the tenor of Psalm 92, which is one of joy over what has happened to the wicked (vv. 1-7). These "wicked" *rĕšā'îm* – v. 7) are designated first as God's enemies in v. 9, and then as the psalmist's enemies in v. 11. According to vv. 1-7, the wicked unambiguously suffer defeat. There is no radical separation in v. 9 that causes us to conceive of God's enemies as a disparate group. (So, too, H. Donner, "Ugaritismen in der Psalmenforschung," 345, sees the enemies of God and of the psalmist in this psalm as one and the same group.) God's actions affect the psalmist. As a result of what is done to God's enemies (v. 9) the psalmist's horn has been raised (v. 10): the defeat of God's enemies is the defeat of the psalmist's foes, an interpretation for which I have given support in the text. These considerations argue both against the retention of the phrase *baqqāmîm 'ālay*, and against the subsequent interpretation that the psalmist's enemies "are not so unambiguously defeated."

Fisch, *Poetry with a Purpose*, 130, did not note, as I have previously (supra, p. 175), that when the image of the wild ox (*rĕ'ēm* – Ps 92:10) is applied to Israel in relation to its enemies, it conveys a sense of victorious power over them. This argues against Fisch's theory on v. 11.

[58] In the Leningrad Codex v. 11 is a monocolon; there is no *athnaq*. This is exceptionally long for a monocolon; it is much longer than the monocolon found in v. 8 and longer than all the bicoloa found in this psalm. (Cf. Kraus, *Psalms 60-150*, 227, who eliminates *mere'im* on the grounds that this verse is overcrowded.) The BHS treats it as a bicolon. Could the Massoretic treatment of it as a monocolon reflect a certain unease about the words *baqqāmîm 'ālay mĕrē'îm*?

Thus, the message of the defeat of the psalmist's enemies is, in verse 11, treated with a conciseness that mirrors the reference to the divine presence ("But you, O Lord, are on high forever" - v. 8) which defeats the wicked (vv. 7-9). This terseness reflects the absolute power of God over the psalmist's foes.

In verses 12-14 the psalmist presents the righteous by means of words and images which show how their future differs favorably from that of the wicked. In verse 12 this is achieved by the use of "flourish" (*pāraḥ*) and by height imagery.

The righteous are compared to trees in verse 12, and according to verse 12a they "flourish" (*pāraḥ*). The last thing said about the enemies, presented as grass (vv. 7, 9), is that they are being "scattered" (*pāraḏ* – v. 9b). In Hebrew the sound linkage between the two verbs is apparent. This connection is reinforced by a second use of *pāraḥ* ("to flourish") in verse 13b to describe the righteous.

The contrast to the wicked is also effected by means of vegetative and height imagery in this verse. The righteous are compared to a palm tree and to a cedar.[59] Both are stately trees. The cedars of Lebanon were especially noted in the OT. According to verse 12b, the righteous "grow like a cedar in Lebanon"; they grow where this type of tree grows well. Thus, both verse 12a ("the righteous flourish like the palm") and verse 12b are images of growing greatly. As such, the height of the righteous is contrasted with the height of the wicked who are presented as grass (v. 7). The righteous grow closer to the God who is on high (*mārôm*– v. 8) and who raises (*tārem*) the righteous (v. 10).

This closeness to God is the concern of the next verse (v. 13) which continues the image of the trees. Both parts of verse 13 are about the righteous, presented as trees, being in the temple precincts: "They are planted in the house of the Lord, they flourish in the courts of our God." They grow greatly (v. 12) because of their proximity to the source of such height and greatness (v. 13 – again recall the image of the exalted God in v. 8).

[59] The *tāmār* is the date palm: *Phoenix dactylifera*.

Verse 14a ("They still bring forth fruit in old age") is about the longevity and the prosperity of the righteous, and this is implicitly contrasted with the short-term success of the wicked. The cedar (*'erez*) may live as long as two thousand years;[60] thus, it is a good symbol for the continued success of the just. Verse 14 says that the righteous participate to a certain degree in the eternity of the divine, just as verse 12 says that they participate to a degree in the divine exaltation. God is on high "forever" (*lĕʿōlām* – v. 8) and the righteous bear fruit in old age (v. 14).

The contrast is with the wicked who perish as quickly as grass. In various parts of the OT grass is used as a figure of speech for a fleeting transience.[61] Just two psalms prior to Psalm 92 we read the following.

> You sweep people away; they are like a dream,
> like grass which is renewed in the morning;
> in the morning it flourishes and is renewed;
> in the evening it withers and fades. (Ps 90:5-6)

So too in Psalm 37, which is about the fate of the wicked, grass is used in this way.

> Do not fret because of the wicked;
> do not be envious of wrongdoers!
> For they will soon fade like the grass,
> and wither like the green herb. (Ps 37:1-2)

> But the wicked perish;
> the enemies of the Lord are like
> the glories of the pastures.[62] (Ps 37:20)

This transience is indicated in Ps 92:7 where we read that "though the wicked sprout like grass and all evildoers flourish, they are doomed to destruction forever." The contrast in verses 7, 14 is between the quick, but ephemeral, success of the wicked

[60] P. Crawford, "Cedar," P. Achtemeier, ed., *Harper's Bible Commentary* (San Francisco: Harper & Row, 1985) 159.
[61] See e.g., Isa 40:6-8; Pss 90:5-6; 102:4,11; 103:15-16.
[62] In Ps 37:2, however, the term *deše'* is used and in Ps 90:5 and Isa 40:6-8 the word *ḥāṣîr*.

and the slow, but steady and lengthy, prosperity of the righteous.[63]

Another way the opposition is conveyed is by the first two terms used in verse 14b. The claim that the just are as trees which are always "luxuriant" (*ra'ănannîm*) alludes to their continued health, and this is set against the destruction of the wicked, who are presented as grass which will be destroyed (v. 7). The implied destruction in verse 7 is a desiccation, as is mentioned in Isa 40:6-8; Pss 37:2; 90:6, verses which, as we have seen, use the image of grass to express the idea of transience.[64]

The term *děšenîm* in verse 14b is often translated as "full of sap"[65]. This appears to be its meaning in Ps 92:14. This also contrasts with withered grass.

It is possible that this particular term was used to lead the reader back phonically to the grass image in verse 7. *Děšenîm* ("full of sap"), the plural of the adjective *dāšēn*, is an unusual word for the context of v. 14. *Dāšēn* means "fat." In Jdg 9:9 it is used of the olive tree: "But the olive tree said to them. 'Shall I leave my fatness, by which gods and men are honored, and go to sway over the trees'?" This occurrence is understandable in a land where olive oil was the only type of oil produced. The appearance of "fat" (*dāšēn*) in a section about the palm and the cedar is problematic. It

[63] Cf. Ezek 47 where the water proceeds from the temple to water the land. In Ezek 47:12b we read the following about trees by the banks of a river created by this water. "Their leaves will not wither nor their fruit fail, but they will bear fresh fruit every month, because the water for them flows from the sanctuary." In Ps 92:13-14 we have a similar idea of the divine presence in the temple as being the source of life. Jacquet, *Les Psaumes*, 2:760, does not note the passage from Ezekiel, but he also interpreted the image in Ps 92:14 as one of a drawing upon the divine force which enables a flourishing transformation of the nature of the righteous.

The use of the images of grass and trees to present the contrast between the wicked and the righteous makes it probable that vv. 12-14 refer to living trees and not, as H. Fisch, *Poetry with a Purpose*, 132, maintained, to the cedar timbers which formed part of the temple structure, nor to the palm designs which were said to have adorned it.

[64] Both the palm and the cedar have deep roots which enable them to search for water. See P. Crawford, "Cedar," "Palm," *Harper's Bible Commentary*, 159, 746.

[65] E.g., in both the RSV and the NRSV.

may be that *děšenîm* ("full of fat") was used so that it would provoke the similar sounding *deše'* ("grass") and the grass imagery in verse 7.[66]

After this look of verses 12-14 individually, a review of them as a unit is in order. The primary idea of these verses is that the righteous flourish for a long time because of their proximity to God, the eternal source of life. A similar idea, with similar imagery, is found in Ezek 17:22-24 where the Lord takes a sprig of a cedar and plants it on "the mountain height of Israel." There it will "bring forth boughs and bear fruit." This section of Ezekiel ends as follows: "I, the Lord, bring low the high tree, and make high the low tree, dry up the green tree, and make the dry tree flourish..." The resemblances between Ps 92:12-14 and Ezek 17:22-24, involving the planting of the cedar, the mountain of Israel (Zion), the flourishing, fruitful tree and the withering one, are apparent, but I have not seen them noted before.

To recapitulate, in verses 12-14 the righteous are presented in ways which remind one of the wicked[67] and which show how dissimilar are their lots. A long, productive existence belongs to the former, and a fleeting and deceptive one to the latter. This look into the grace-filled future places the present in an appropriate and manageable matrix.

The psalm concludes with the words "to declare that the Lord is upright;/ my rock, there is no unrighteousness in him" (v. 15). What shows this moral integrity of God? The preceding verses and the wording of verse 15 suggest that it is the manner in which God has dealt with both the wicked (vv. 7-9, 11) and the just (vv. 10, 12-14).

[66] This argument would be stronger if *deše'* had been used in v. 7, but *'ēśeḇ*, another term for "grass," was used there. Still, the presence of *ra'ănannîm* ("luxuriant") after *děšenîm* shows that the possibility that this latter term was intended to allude phonically to the grass imagery in v. 7 should not be casually dismissed.
[67] Another connection between the images in vv. 12-14 and v. 7 is the term *šāṯal* in v. 13. In at least nine out of the ten other times the verb appears in the MT it is used in conjunction with the ideas of flourishing or withering. The tree that is planted (*šāṯal*) in dry ground withers (Ez 17:10; 19:13) while the one planted (*šāṯal*) by water thrives (Ps 1:3; Jer 17:8; Ezek 17:8, 22-23;19:10). In Ps 128:3 this verb refers to the frutiful wife. The reading in Hos 9:13 is a difficult one.

God's actions for the righteous manifest this quality in God (v. 15a). God's actions against evildoers manifest that there is no unrighteousness in God (v. 15b).[68] Both sets of actions prove that God is just, that God acts justly, and that history is governed by such rectitude.

Thus, the imagery of verses 7-15 is finely honed to reveal the underlying pattern of the otherwise unforeseeable future: one in which the reversal of the fortunes of the wicked and the upright is assured by God's placement of the latter into proximity to God as the source of life. Such a repositioning is expressed in terms of an elevation (v. 10), a temple transplantation (v. 13) and a fructification (v. 14).

The comfort with the future as the time for the divine retribution is strengthened by the point of view of this psalm which is a retrospective one. The element of thanksgiving (v. 1), which itself implies such a standpoint, and the joy and acclaim of verses 1-6, are the result of what God has done to the enemies (vv. 7, 9, 11) and for the psalmist (v. 10). The psalmist is writing from the perspective of one who has been delivered by God from the wicked;[69] the psalmist's horn has been raised (v. 10), and the psalmist has witnessed the destruction of the wicked (v. 11). Thus, the verses about the righteous being like trees (vv. 12-14) are buttressed by the tone of experience just expressed in verses 10-11. The idea about God's long-term faithfulness in making the righteous productive (vv. 12-14) is entered into by the reader with this authoritative tone leading and preparing the way for its reception. Throughout the psalm, the perspective is of one who has lived through the slow but sure movement of which he writes. This imparts an assurance to the reader. We can now look at the manner in which the psalm engages the reader in the slow movement itself.

[68] H. Fisch, *Poetry with a Purpose*, 133-34, claimed that the subject of *lĕhaggîḏ* ("to declare") in v. 15 is Psalm 92 itself; the poem reveals God's righteousness by showing the just ways of God. This would be unusual because nowhere else in this psalm is the psalm its own referent. It seems more likely that it is God's actions toward the wicked (vv. 7-9, 11) and the just (vv. 10, 12-14) that declares God's absolute rectitude.

[69] So too H. Kraus, *Psalms 60-150*, 230.

Psalm 92: The Song Played Adagio

The psalm accustoms the reader to the gradual fulfillment of God's just designs by means of the slow articulation of its message. A meandering, protracted and unhurried discourse creates a leisurely experience of reality in the light of the surety of God's deliberate response. Although it may be later than the rest of the psalm, the superscription itself commences this protracted writing pattern.

The superscription is "A psalm. A song for the Day of the Sabbath" (*mizmôr šîr lĕyôm haššēbāṯ*).[70] It has been noted that this is a rather full description.[71] Most psalms with superscriptions use one of four terms, in addition to any accompanying information on the proposed setting, to designate a psalm: *šîr* ("a song"), *mizmôr* ("a song"), *maśkîl* ("an insightful psalm" or perhaps "a didactic poem" or "a skillful poem")[72] or *miktam*, whose meaning is uncertain. Sixteen, or roughly one out of every ten canonical psalms, has a double designation. Of these, thirteen use the words *mizmôr* and *šîr* together.[73] Thus, while not found frequently, this twofold preface is by no means uncommon.

The preface does, however, have a certain repetitive quality because both *šîr* and *mizmôr* mean "song." Heightening the iterative quality is the positioning of these two terms right next to each other without other words intervening. This is the case in ten psalms,[74] including Psalm 92. A still further reiteration comes from the fact that the verb *zmr* ("to sing") in verse 1b echoes the noun *mizmôr* in the superscription. This type of reverberation occurs in only three of the thirteen psalms which use *mizmôr* and *šîr*: Psalms 66, 92 and 108. Thus, there is a certain reiteration in

[70] The tradition for using Psalm 92 on the Sabbath is a very old one, found not only in the MT but also in *M.Tamid* 7.4 and in the LXX.
[71] H. Fisch, *Poetry with a Purpose*, 128.
[72] *Maśkîl* comes from *śākal* which means "to understand," or "to give attention to," or "to ponder." See *HAL*, 352; *BDB*, 968.
[73] The thirteen are Pss 30, 48, 65-68, 75-76, 83, 87-88, 92, 108.
[74] Pss 30, 48, 66-68, 83, 87-88, 92, 108.

the superscription of Psalm 92 and this contributes to the sense of the psalm's extension.

The words *lĕyôm haššēbāṯ* ("for the Day of the Sabbath") in the superscription put the reader into a relaxed frame of mind by setting the day of rest as the proper matrix for this psalm. This embedment moves the reader emotionally out of the realm of the pressing exigencies within which we normally operate and into the restful, atemporal sabbath. Time is less pressing, less urgent, from the outset of this psalm. For the person responsible for the superscription, the sabbath provided an opportunity for standing back from immediate concerns and for reflecting on the long view of Psalm 92.

There are four basic complexes of ideas in this psalm. Each is expressed in a protracted manner which contributes to the unhurried and relaxed feeling of Psalm 92: (1) the praise of God (vv. 1-3), (2) the work(s) of the Lord (vv. 4-6), (3) the exaltation of God and the psalmist over the enemies (vv. 8-11) and (4) the long lasting productivity of the righteous (vv. 12-15).

The first aspect of verses 1-3 to be noted is the prevalence of the "l" sound which creates a lulling, soothing mood. There are five *lāmeḏs* (the Hebrew letter which has the "l" sound) in verse 1, four in verse 2 and another four in verse 3. In verse 1 "l" is the dominant sound, appearing as the first or second sound in every word of the verse with the exception of the initial *ṭôḇ* ("[It is] good"). Moreover, as will be seen, one of the "l" sounds in v.3 is certainly unnecessary for the clear expression of the idea found in this verse.

The Massoretic Text (Hebrew) of verse 3 is *'ălê-'āśôr wa'ălê-nāḇel 'ălê higgāyôn bĕkinnôr*. The NRSV translates this: "to the music of the lute and the harp, to the melody of the lyre." A *nēḇel* is a stringed instrument. In Ps 33:2 we read of a *nēḇel 'āśôr*, and there the numeral *'āśôr* ("ten") assumes its normal adjectival place following the noun. In Ps 92:3 the two words are broken up into the phrase "upon the ten and upon the stringed instrument" (*'ălê-'āśôr wa'ălê-nāḇel*). The effects of such an unusual configuration is the prolongation of the time it takes for the message to be expressed. This sense of temporal elongation is also conveyed both by the addition of an extra *'ălê* ("upon") which this construction affords,[75] and by writing "upon the sounding (*higgāyôn*) of the harp" rather than simply "upon the harp."

Verse 2 ("to declare your steadfast love in the morning and your faithfulness by night") also contributes to the psalm's prolonged and unhurried feeling. This parenthetical verse breaks up the music imagery of verses 1, 3 in order to tell the content of the psalmist's song. The words "to sing praises to your name, Most High" (v. 1b) are logically continued by "upon the ten and upon the stringed instrument,/ upon the sounding of the harp" (v. 3).[76] Further, as Fisch has noted, the verb which governs verse 2 is a peculiar one to use in the context of singing.[77] This verb (ngḏ) means "to declare, to expound" or "to inform."[78] Thus, both the positioning of verse 2 and the use of *ngḏ* in this verse, break up the flow of verses 1b, 3 and give the reader pause.[79]

To sum up, the song to God in the morning and in the evenings (vv. 1-3) is a rhythmic activity, with measures designed to help one participate in the larger and slower lines of time in which God acts: the "forever's" of verses 7-8 and the long-term view of verses 12-15. The way in which verses 1-3 invite the reader to sing, enables one to adjust his or her tempo of expectations to the pace of God's conducting.

The repetitions found in verses 4-6 and in verses 7-11 also add a temporal breadth to the psalm. In verses 4-6 there are six bicola dealing with the work(s) of God. They slowly succeed each other without specifying the work(s). The reader must wait as he or she

[75] The Septuagint and the Syriac version delete this *'ălê* but this truncates the phonic repetitiveness of the "l" sound which the psalmist has created.

[76] This is why I set v. 2 apart by dashes in my translation rather than using the NRSV placement of a semicolon after v.1 and a comma after v. 2.

[77] H. Fisch, *Poetry with a Purpose*, 128.

[78] *BDB*, 616-17; *HAL*, 226. *HAL* also notes that in Jer 20:10 it means "to denounce."

[79] Weiser, *The Psalms*, 614, wrote that this praise by day and night is best explained by envisioning the psalmist remaining at the temple for a few days during a feast. While some such situation may have inspired the psalmist, the image also functions to accustom the reader to lengthier spans of time.

reads over and over again directly (vv. 4a, 4b, 5a) or indirectly (vv. 6a, 6b) about God's works.[80] In verses 1-3 the psalmist rejoices but it is not until verses 4-6 that the general reason for the joy is given (God's work[s]), and not until verse 7 that the specific one is given (the destruction of the wicked).

There are also verbal and phonic reiterations in verses 9-10. As we have seen, the clause "for behold, your enemies, O Lord" (*kî hinnēh 'ōyĕbekā*) in verse 9 is repeated twice, and the verbs "to perish" (*yō'ḇēḏû*) and "to scatter" (*yiṯporḏû*) appear right next to each other.[81] Moreover, the word *yō'ḇēḏû* immediately follows the

[80] There is not only repetition, but also variation, caused by a number of morphological or syntactic shifts between half-lines or lines, in this psalm. In v. 1a God is addressed in the third person and in v. 1b in the second. The singular "day" of v. 2a is followed by the plural "nights" in v. 2b, and the psalmist is the object in the first part of v. 4 and the subject in the second. The singular "work" (*pā'alekā*) of v. 4a becomes the plural "works" (*ma'asê*) of v. 4b. Finally, there is the shift from the singular to the plural in v. 11 ("my eye" – "my ears"), and in vv. 12-14 where the righteous person (singular) is presented as a palm and cedar (v.12), and then the righteous as a group are compared to trees (vv. 13-14).

One reason for these changes may be to avoid monotony: a very real danger given both the parallelistic character of biblical poetry and the prolonged treatment of each idea in this psalm. Cf. A. Berlin, "Grammatical Aspects of Biblical Parallelism," *HUCA* [50, 1979] 17-43, pp. 20, 40-41) who cites most of these well-recognized features in this psalm and proposes that one reason for these types of shifts in the Hebrew Bible is to avoid monotony. She does not, however, suggest any reason for these features in Psalm 92.

Beaucamp, *Le Psautier: Pss.73-150*, 105, has noted that 4QPsb and the ancient versions have tended to unify the number (singular or plural) in the text. Berlin, "Grammatical Aspects of Biblical Parallelism," 42, has written about such a unifying tendency by modern commentators.

[81] The significance of the perfect and the imperfect conjugations is one of the most difficult and widely discussed aspects of Hebrew grammar. See B. Waltke & M. O'Connor, *Biblical Hebrew Syntax*, 455-78 for an overview of the critical scholarly discussion on this matter. A major theory (sometimes termed the Aspectual Theory or the *Aktionsart* Theory) is that the imperfect conveys a sense of an ongoing situation: of one that is extended or continued over a period of time, be that past or present time. See e.g., Waltke & O'Connor, *Biblical Hebrew Syntax*, 502-06; *GKC*, 313-16; J. Weingreen, *A Practical Grammar of Classical Hebrew* (2nd ed.; Oxford: Clarendon, 1959) 56, 75-76.

It is interesting to view the uses of the two verbs in the second and third cola of v. 9 from this perspective. *Yō'ḇēḏû* ("they are perishing") and *yiṯporḏû* ("they are being scattered") are both imperfect verbs. As such, they may present the destruction of the enemies as an ongoing one and by so doing highlight the longer temporal perspective which the psalmist is inculcating in this psalm.

two *kî hinnēh 'ōyĕbekā* clauses and by so doing the *y'b* sound of *yō'ḇēḏû* echoes the *'yb* sound of the last word in these clauses. The phonic echoes continue in verse 10a where the final *rm* sound is found both in the first word, *wattārem* ("you have raised") and in the second word, *kir'ēm* ("like a wild ox"). The initial *kr* sound of this latter term is picked up in the same initial sound in the next term, *qarnî* ("my horn").

The repetitiveness found in Ps 92:4-11 requires and invokes a certain patience. This iterative style accustoms one to waiting for the message: a message which integrally involves just such a waiting for God's "steadfast love" (*ḥeseḏ*) and "faithfulness" (*'emûnāh*) ("faithfulness") to become manifest.[82] This stylistic feature inculcates a longheadedness for the long run.

That the prolongation of the message puts the reader in touch with longer spans of time is indicated by the fact that in verse 2 the psalmist begins such expansiveness with "to declare" (*lĕhaggîḏ*). (Recall that this breaks up the music imagery of vv. 1, 3b.) This word also appears at the beginning of the last verse of the psalm (v. 15). According to verse 14 the righteous "still bring forth fruit in old age, they are ever full of sap and green." In verse 15a the psalmist says that this shows God's righteousness ("to declare [*lĕhaggîḏ*] the Lord is upright"). The employment of the second *lĕhaggîḏ*, in the same linear position as the first one and in the context of the proof of God's righteousness over a lengthy stretch of time leads one to see the first use of this term as indicating God's long-term actions ("to declare [*lĕhaggîḏ*] your steadfast love in the morning and your faithfulness by nights"– v. 2).[83]

[82] See the seventh and the eighth Sabbath songs from Qumran cave 4 for a repetition of ideas and images as one moves through these psalms. C. Newsom, *Songs of the Sabbath Sacrifice: A Critical Edition* (Atlanta: Scholars Press, 1985) 15, said that the repetitiveness of these psalms has an "almost hypnotic quality" which contributes to a "change of mood." Similarly, it is being argued in this section that the prolongation and reiteration in Psalm 92 enables one to experience life more slowly and, in light of the psalm's message, more securely.

[83] The two declarations (*lĕhaggîḏ* – vv. 2, 15) link up with each other. The proclamation of God's steadfast love and faithfulness in the morning and in the evening (v. 2) is consonant with God's long-term actions (vv. 12-14) which also proclaim the righteousness of God operative in these ways. Our regular, rhythmic procla-

The style of Psalm 92 helps create, if only while reading this psalm, a resonance in the reader's life with the all-inclusive song of godly retribution. Form and content combine to stress a rhythmic articulation– foreign to our hurried and impatient perceptions– which is in time with the divine decrees.[84] By so doing, the reader is empowered both to affirm the divine rectitude, and to readjust his or her expectations as to when it will be expressed. The imagery and style of Psalm 92 combine to encourage a patience and peacefulness in the reader.

The particular type of mixture of elements which are proper to different genres suggests an exhortatory function for this psalm.

This is a composite psalm with thanksgiving, hymnic and wisdom characteristics. The initial words are "It is good to give thanks to the Lord" (v. 1a), and these are followed by a short hymn of praise (vv. 1b-4).[85] The wisdom elements begin in verse 5. In verses 5-6 there is the assertion of how the stupid cannot understand God's works and thoughts. This is followed in verses 7-15 by the wisdom motif of the contrast between the wicked and the righteous.[86]

It has been common for scholars to take for their lead those tendencies which come first. Thus, while noting the other types of elements, commentators classify Psalm 92 as either an individual

mation of these divine attributes at the beginning and close of each day creates a consistent spatic-temporal fabric – individual (v. 2) and ecumenical (vv. 12-15), microchronic (v. 2) and macrochronic (vv. 12-15).

[84] Because of human impatience, the message of God's *ḥesed̠* as expressed over the long term reaches us in a fringe area. The danger is that this human tendency will cause the signal to be weak and distorted. A basic sociolinguistic insight is that repetition is necessary in order to overcome the static, the numerous factors which impede communication. The psalmist presents just such a repetition of terms and ideas in the four stanzas of Psalm 92. This has the effect both of breaking through the psychic barrier of opposition to delay and of introducing an alternate manner of attending to God's *ḥesed̠*: viewing it from a longitudinal perspective.

[85] The *kî* (because") followed by the reason for praise common to hymns is found in v. 4.

[86] The shift to a didactic tone argues against the asertion of E. Beaucamp, *Le Psautier: Pss.73-150*, 106, that the repetition has no part in instructing anyone. According to Beaucamp, the psalmist is not interested in teaching others but only in savoring what God did for him. This is not the case as is shown by the shift from treating the life of the psalmist in vv. 10-11 to talking about the righteous person in v. 12 and about righteous people (plural) in vv. 13-14.

thanksgiving,[87] or a hymn.[88] I would like to change the emphasis and propose that the primary functions of the psalm are to instruct and exhort, and that the thanksgiving and hymnic elements are at the service of these ends.

There are several features whch justify this type of reprioritization of genre characteristics. First, not only does the psalm end with a focus on the future of the righteous, but the very treatment of God's work which has made the psalmist glad, the destruction of the psalmist's enemies, is presented in the context of God's doing away with all who are wicked. Thus, the psalmist writes first about the overthrow of the wicked (*rešāʿîm* – v. 7), next about the defeat of God's enemies (v. 11) and finally about the fate of his own enemies (v. 11). It is the larger actions of God against all evildoers that are the focus, and the psalmist's own experience is an example of this type of divine activity.[89]

Secondly, the works of God which have made the psalmist glad (v. 4) are unintelligible to the stupid (v. 6). Again, the psalmist's life functions in the larger context of instruction or the inability to benefit from teaching. These features of the psalm indicate that a greater emphasis needs to be put on the wisdom elements in Psalm 92 than has traditionally been the case in its genre classification.

Psalm 92 is exhortation, but its effectiveness is achieved in part through the thanksgiving elements which give a retrospective quality to this poem. The psalmist has already experienced the equally long-term destruction of the wicked and salvation of the righteous. As such, the words come from beyond the constraints of the alluring, yet transient, present and offer the indirect and compelling advice of success rather than more direct words of admonishment. The tone of thanksgiving with which the psalm begins

[87] E.g., L. Sabourin, *Le livre des Psaumes*, 424; M. Tate, *Psalms 51-100*, 464.
[88] L. Jacquet, *Les Psaumes*, 2.753. E. Beaucamp, *Le Psautier: Pss.73-150*, 106, notes the thanksgiving, hymnic and wisdom features, but he claims that this psalm defies classification.
[89] The treatment of the psalmist's enemies (v. 11) only after the prior discussion on the wicked in general (vv. 7, 9) and on the exaltation of the psalmist (v. 10) invites the reader not to be impatient and hope for a quick fix, but rather to be in touch with the larger and longer rhythms of life in which God is rectifying the situation.

gradually leads to the instructive voice of experience; and the voice is slow and measured, and the message is that the slowness itself is the abundantly producing instrument of God's faithful love.[90]

Living in the Interim Between Promise and Fulfillment

Psalm 92 boldly asserts the victorious power of God's steadfast love and faithfulness, and even more daringly claims that the apparent delay in its fulfillment is the stuff out of which this divine faithfulness achieves its end. The message is that time is an ally, not an enemy of the righteous; that time too is under the control of the God who uses it to achieve a rich fruitfulness for the righteous. "They still bring forth fruit in old age; they are ever full of sap and green" (v. 14).

The implications of such a view are not only a patience with the delays in the fruition of our plans, but also a restfulness during these postponements. With the perspective inculcated by Psalm 92, time is no longer the unvanquishable opponent against whom we foolishly flail, but God's servant for our own good.

It was perhaps this perspective of the psalm which contributed most to its use in the sabbath worship. When time becomes an ally, the border between it and our concerns need not be attended to so rigorously and sabbath becomes a reality. The sense of sabbath (the superscription) in Psalm 92 is grounded in the slow-moving, experienced surety of God's good designs (vv. 1-15).

Children thrive on the sabbath; they need to have both time to grow and parents who are present to sensitively allow such a

[90] L. Jacquet, *Les Psaumes*, 2:753, noted that while the theme of moral retribution is treated in Pss 37, 49, 73 and 92, there is in Psalm 92 no complaint and no questioning, no sense of troubled thoughts which precede a solution, as is the case in these other psalms. In their place is a peaceful affirmation of God's justice. I note that the psalmist's experience of success due to the righteousness of God also appears to contribute to this irenic quality.

process to proceed at its own pace.[91] Youth should neither be scheduled nor hurried. At times, parents' lives are so busy that making time is difficult, and it is easier to schedule the lives of children.[92] A reordering of our priorities may be required if we are to have time for our children. The perspective of Psalm 92 makes such a reprioritization possible. In this psalm we see the ways in which God's steadfast love and faithfulness are manifested, and this perception gives us hope when we cannot see their effects in the present. The Sabbath is possible in the midst of difficult day to day life given the brushwork of God's steadfast care with which our lives are being colored.

If we were not so constrained by time, we would live healthier lives and have more time to give to our children. Psalm 92 states the certainty of the heritage of the righteous in ways which enable the reader to escape the tyranny of time. We need not be overly-concerned about the difficulties of the present in the light of the certainties of the future. The faith inspired by Psalm 92 recreates a sabbath for parents with their children.

[91] See the following books by D. Elkind for the terrible effects of asking too much of children too soon. *The Hurried Child: Growing Up Too Fast Too Soon* (rev. ed.; Reading, MA: Addison-Wesley, 1988); *Miseducation: Preschoolers at Risk* (New York: Alfred Knopf, 1987); *All Grown Up and No Place to Go: Teenagers in Crisis* (Reading, MA: Addison-Wesley,1984).

[92] Perhaps impatience in parents may lead to an impatience with youth, which is an incomplete, formative time.

PART IV

SUSTAINING HEALTHY RELATIONSHIPS

CHAPTER 8

PSALM 62: GOD AND VERBAL VIOLENCE

> A cruel story runs on wheels, and every hand oils the wheels as they run.
>
> Ouida, *Moths*

> Calumnies are answered best with silence.
>
> Ben Johnson, *Volpone*

Relationships: A Casualty of Verbal Violence

Remaining in authentic, caring relations is contingent upon the ability not to be excessively concerned with the effects of what people say about us. Slander hurts, and it can cause both parents and children to turn in upon themselves rather than to seek to establish and maintain relationships. After dealing with how Psalm 62 responds to the problem of verbal violence, I will present insights on the strength of other people's views of ourselves when these views become accepted by the group. These come from the "organizational culture" approach to analyzing organizations, and they help to clarify why we are so concerned about what others say about us. Psalm 62 can both break the stranglehold of excessive self-concern which slander often causes, and free parents and children to refocus their attention on relationships with others.

Psalm 62: The Restorative Word

The Reading

To the choirmaster: according to Jeduthun.
A Psalm of David.

1 For God alone my soul waits in silence;
from him comes my salvation.
2 He only is my rock and my salvation,
my fortress; I will not be greatly moved.

3 How long will you assail a person,
will you batter your victim, all of you,
like a leaning wall,
a tottering fence?
4 Their only plan is to bring down a person
of prominence.
They take pleasure in falsehood.
They bless with their mouths,
but inwardly they curse. Selah
5 For God alone be silent, my soul,
for my hope is from him.
6 He only is my rock and my salvation,
my fortress; I will not be moved.
7 On God rests my deliverance and my honor;
my mighty rock, my refuge is God.

8 Trust in him at all times, O people
pour out your heart before him;
God is a refuge for us. Selah
9 Those of low estate are but a breath,
those of high estate are a delusion;
in the balances they go up;
they are together lighter than a breath.
10 Put no confidence in extortion,
set no vain hope on robbery;
if riches increase, set not your heart on
them.

11 Once God has spoken; twice have I heard this:
that power belongs to God;
12 and that to you, Lord, belongs steadfast
love.
For you repay to all, according to their
work.

Highlighting the Nuances of the Hebrew Text

The NRSV translation of this psalm has been changed in several places. First, in verse 5a the NRSV has "For God alone my soul waits in silence..." This has been changed to "For God alone be silent, my soul..." because the imperative verb *dômmî* ("be silent") is used here instead of the substantive "silence" (*dûmîyyāh*), as is found in verse 1.[1] Secondly, the second part of the only line in verse 6 has been translated as "I will not be moved" instead of "I will not be shaken." The rationale was to show the connection between the second part of verse 2 ("I will not be greatly moved") and the second part of verse 6. The same Hebrew verb (*môṭ*) is used in both verses.

Verse 1 – Dahood has proposed that *dûmîyyāh* in verse 1 and *dômmî* in verse 5 do not mean "silence" and "be silent." They think that these words come from *dûmāh* ("bastion"), which itself comes not from the verb *dmm* ("to be silent"), but rather from *dmt* which in Ugaritic and Akkadian means "fortress."[2]

In conjunction with this view, Dahood and Sabourin also translate *'l* not as *'ēl* ("in") as did the Massoretes, but rather as *'el* ("God"). Their reading of the first part of verse 1 is "The God of Gods is my castle (strong bastion [Sabourin])." Correspondingly, they read the first part of verse 5 as "God himself alone is

[1] There is no Hebrew verb in this clause in v. 1; the present tense of the "to be" verb is not expressed in Hebrew. The NRSV translators have supplied the verb "wait" in v. 1 as part of their interpretation of this verse. This seems justified because v. 3 begins with "*how long* (*'aḏ-'ānāh*) will you set upon a man to shatter him, all of you..." Thus, the psalmist's self-exhortation to silence is placed in the context of the enemies' present persecution of the psalmist. Such a state would require the psalmist *to wait* for God. It should be noted that although the psalmist is recounting the persecution of the enemies as if it is presently happening, this does not mean that the persecution is a current reality for the psalmist. Later, we will see why the problem of the time in which the psalmist of Ps 62 is experiencing trouble is a vexing one.

[2] Dahood, *Psalms II – 51-100* (AB, 17; Garden City, NY: Doubleday, 1968) 90-91; L. Sabourin, *Le livre des Psaumes*, 287-288. Dahood explains the *yāh* suffix as an intensifying element

my castle (bastion)." To date, the majority of scholars prefer the readings "For God alone my soul waits in silence" (v. 1) and "For God alone be silent my soul" (v. 5). If Dahood and Sabourin are correct, then verse 1 reinforces the ideas of God as the psalmist's security found in verses 2, 6 and 7.

The word *'ak* ("only/ surely") is used six times in this psalm. It appears at the beginnings of verses 1, 2, 4, 5, 6 and 9. This term can be used affirmatively ("surely") or restrictively ("only"). There is considerable disagreement as to which of these uses the term has in Ps 62.[3] *'ak* is used in reference both to God (vv. 1, 2, 5, 6) and to the enemies (vv. 4, 9).[4] Although we may not be certain if the term is used affirmatively or restrictively, the two types of uses of *'ak* convey a fixity of intent on the part both of the psalmist and of the enemies. The psalmist focuses himself ("surely/only") on God (vv. 1, 2, 5, 6) and the enemies are concentrating ("surely/only") on the psalmist's destruction (v. 4).

Verses 1, 2, 5 and 6 – Another focus worthy of attention has to do with the similarities and the differences found in vv. 1, 2, 5 and 6. These verses form a refrain, but there are also some differences between verses 1 and 2 on the one hand and verses 5 and 6 on the other.

1 For God alone my soul waits in silence;
    from him comes my salvation.
2 He only is my rock and my salvation,
    my fortress; I will not be greatly moved.

5 For God alone be silent my soul,
    for my hope is from him.
6 He only is my rock and my salvation,
    my fortress; I will not be moved.

As we have seen, the beginning of verse 1 reads "For God alone my soul waits in silence (*dûmîyyāh*)," and the beginning of verse

[3] See e.g., C.& E. Briggs, *Psalms*, 2:71 for how nineteenth century scholars were divided on how to translate this term. The same problem confronts modern scholars.

[4] Below arguments will be presented for my proposal that v. 9 alludes to the enemies of the psalmist.

5 is a self-exhortation: "For God alone be silent (*dômmî*) my soul." In verse 1 we read that from God comes "my salvation" (*yĕšû'āṯî*), whereas in verse 5 we read that from God comes "my hope" (*tiqwāṯî*). In verse 2 we find the words "I will not be greatly moved," whereas in verse 6 the word "greatly" (*rabbāh*) is not found ("I will not be moved").

Some scholars wish to harmonize both sets of verses by claiming that verse 1 originally had "my hope," as does verse 5, and that this was later altered to "my salvation" because of the influence of "my salvation" found in verse 2: "he only is my rock and my salvation."[5] In addition, some claim that the adverb "greatly" (*rabbāh*) in verse 2 is also an insertion.[6] If this is the case then the reading "I will not be moved" is found both in verse 2 and in verse 6. Both of these assertions are highly speculative. It seems safer to accept "my salvation" in verse 1 and "greatly" in verse 2 as being the original readings because of the strong textual support for them. Further, Raabe has noted that both the spelling and the words vary frequently in refrains in the same psalm, and that this fact makes one question harmonizations of psalmic refrains.[7] Like the change from "silence" (*dûmîyyāh*) in verse 1 to "be silent" (*dômmî*) in verse 5, these other changes in verses 5-6 must be accounted for as part of the psalmist's poem.

Scholars have explained these differences from the perspectives of 1) the situation of the psalmist vis-a-vis his enemies and 2) the mood of the psalmist.

Various proposals have been made to attempt to understand the changes in verses 1 and 2 and verses 5 and 6 from the perspective of the psalmist's situation vis-a-vis his enemies. Thus, Elmer Leslie interprets verses 1 and 2 as expressive of the psalmist's

[5] See, e.g., L. Jacquet, *Les Psaumes*, 281, 282.

[6] E.g., C. Westermann, *The Living Psalms* (Grand Rapids: Eerdmans, 1989); E. Beaucamp, *Le Psautier: Pss.1-72* (Paris: Gabalda, 1976) 257; L. Jacquet, *Les Psaumes*, 2:281-282; H. J. Kraus, *Psalmen 2: Psalmen 60-150* (Neukirchen-Vluyn: Neukirchener, 1978) 595.

[7] P. Raabe, *Psalm Structures*, 168. See also J. Goldingay, "Repetition and Variation in the Psalms," *JQR* 68 (1978) 146-51.

experience of God during a time of suffering in the past; he claims that verses 3 and 4 witness to the experience of present suffering. The experience of God's presence during times of suffering in the past (vv. 1, 2) helps the psalmist wait quietly for God (vv. 5-7) in the midst of the present crisis (vv. 3, 4).[8]

In contrast to Leslie's view, Jacquet and Westermann think that this psalm was written after the liberation of the psalmist. Westermann claims that the fact that in verses 8-12 the psalmist turns to exhorting others to trust, and the fact that "refuge" (*maḥseh*) is found in verses 7, 8 linking the psalmist's experience of trust to his exhortation to others to trust in God, show that this encouragement is based on his own experience of God as security.[9] This appears to be correct; there are, however, no indicators in the psalm as to whether this security was experienced in the past (i.e., he is no longer being attacked by his enemies [Jacquet, Westermann]) or in the present (i.e., his enemies are still attacking him [Leslie] but to no effect). There is too little evidence in the psalm to recover the precise situation of the psalmist and the enemies at the time of the psalm's composition.[10]

Others explain the differences between verses 1 and 2 and verses 5 and 6 as reflective of a change of the psalmist's mood.[11] Thus, Cox writes that verse 1 shows that the psalmist is at peace. He says that "the indicative form" used in verse 1 shows that the psalmist's "actual state" is one of peace. It is difficult to determine whether this is the meaning of verse 1. The words are "For God alone, silence, my soul..." This can mean either that the psalmist is currently at peace, as Cox maintains, or it could be an exhortation to wait peacefully for God.

Cox claims that the mood changes from peace to a turmoil in the psalmist's heart: a turmoil which is expressed in frustration and doubt (vv. 3, 4, 9, 10).

[8] E. Leslie, *The Psalms* (Nashville, TN: Abingdon, 1959), 395, 396. So, too, A. Anderson, *The Book of Psalms*, 1:450, and E. Blaiklock, *Commentary on the Psalms* (Philadelphia: Holmgren, 1971) 138.

[9] C. Westermann, *Living Psalms*, 152, 153.

[10] So, too, H. Kraus, *Psalmen* 2, 597, 598.

[11] See e.g., A. Weiser, *The Psalms*, 449, 450, who wrote that the psalm represents the inner struggle "which the poet has mastered."

Verses 3 and 4 are neither an expression of frustration and doubt, as Cox maintains, nor of the psalmist's fear, as Beaucamp claims.[12] Verses 3 and 4a deal with the enemies' plans and verse 4b with how the enemies put these plans into effect; they are not about the psalmist's reactions to them.

As has been noted, Cox thinks that verses 9 and 10 are an expression of the turmoil within the psalmist. Later, it will be argued that the primary referent in verse 9 is the enemies, and that verse 10 is the psalmist's teaching based upon his experience; it does not express any frustration and doubt.

The psalm does not give us a clear picture of the precise situation in the psalmist's life.[13] We get a much more focused picture when we look at the psalm as a literary portrait than we do when we look through the psalm as a lens to view the psalmist's life. For example, although we may not arrive at certainty as to what the differences between verses 1 and 2 and 5-7 show about the life of the psalmist, we are on firmer ground when we ask what effect these differences have on the reader of Psalm 62. In the latter case we have the context of the psalm itself to help us with the meaning of these differences, whereas we do not have knowledge of the psalmist's life as an interpretive matrix. A focus on the psalmist's situation when writing the psalm could obscure both the dramatic movement in the psalm, and the effects which the psalm has on the reader. The differences between verses 1 and 2 and verses 5-7 create a dramatic movement in the psalm through which the psalmist's theopoetic is conveyed. For this reason the changes in the psalm will be approached from the perspective of the dynamics of the psalm itself instead of from the perspective of a hypothetical reconstruction of the psalmist's life.

[12] D. Cox, *The Psalms in the Life of God's People* (St. Paul: Slough, 1984) 90-93, 95; E. Beaucamp, *Le Psautier: Pss.1-72*, 259.

[13] Anderson and Kraus wrote that vv. 2, 6, 7 indicate that the psalmist has taken refuge in the sanctuary. This interpretation of the rock, fortress and refuge images is a possible one, but more proof needs to be brought forth before it can be accepted. In this light, Kraus wrote that vv. 11b, 12c could be a salvation oracle which the psalmist received in the sanctuary; Kraus recognized, however, that this thesis has not been proven. See Anderson, *Psalms* 1.450; Kraus, *Psalmen 2*, 596.

From Reflection Back to Relation: The Interpretation of Psalm 62

There are two major parts to this psalm: (1) verses 1-7 are the psalmist's meditation on his own experience and (2) verses 8-12 are the psalmist's exhortation to others based on this experience.

Ps.62:1-7

The first part is divided into three strophes: (1) verses 1 and 2, (2) verses 3 and 4, (3) verses 5-7. As has been noted, vv.1 and 2 have a parallel in vv.5 and 6. These verses are a refrain which are about waiting in silence for God's salvation.

The verses in between the refrain, that is, verses 3 and 4, are both about the enemies' intent to harm the psalmist (v. 3 and the first part of v. 4), and about their attempt to do this by means of what they are saying about the psalmist: "They take pleasure in falsehood./ They bless with their mouths,/ but inwardly they curse."[14] They are spreading lies about the psalmist in the hope that these lies will shatter him:[15] that they will "thrust him down from his eminence."

[14] That the enemies are verbally trying to hurt the psalmist is also indicated by the first line in v. 3: "How long will you set upon a man..." Anderson, *Psalms*, 1:452, notes that the verb in this line which is translated as "set upon," *tĕhôṯĕṯû*, may come from *hwt* ("to shout"– so *BDB*, 223) or from *htt* ("to speak continually"– so *LVL*, 243). *Tĕhôṯĕṯû* is the intensive (*polel*) form of the verb. Thus, it indicates an intense verbal attack on the psalmist.

E. Gerstenberger, *Psalms: Part I* (FOTL, 14; Grand Rapids: Eerdmans, 1988) 84, has suggested that *'aḏ-'ānāh* and *'aḏ-mātay*, both of which mean "how long," express "reproachful speech, apparently after repeated attempts to amend a situation have failed... The undertone in all these passages is that a change is overdue." Gerstenberger says this on the basis of the use of these words in Ps 6:4; Job 8:2;18:2;19:2, 3; Exod 10:3;16:28; Num 14:11, 27; Jos 18:3; 1 Sam 1:14. If he is correct, then perhaps *'aḏ-'ānāh* in Ps 62:3 is used to indicate a verbal attack of some duration.

[15] L. Sabourin, *Le livre des Psaumes*, 287, 288, and others suggest reading *tarusu* ("you run") instead of *tĕrāṣṣĕḥû* ("you batter") in v. 3. So too, e.g., Westermann, *Living Psalms*, 151. Sabourin says that "you batter" does not fit the context of the verse, but then he proceeds to add "*comme pour le démolir*" ("so as to destroy him") to the text in order to complete its sense. Thus, the context does support the reading "you batter" (*tĕrāṣṣĕḥû*).

The Hebrew verb translated in verse 3 as "batter" (*Tĕrāṣṣĕḥû*) is the *piel* form of the verb "to kill" (*rṣḥ*). Clearly the psalmist is not dead yet; he is still "like a leaning wall, a pushed-in fence" (v. 3cd). Thus, this verb is to be interpreted figuratively. Nevertheless, it is a strong word to use and so the psalmist thinks that the result of the enemies' maledictions could be disastrous. "You batter" (*tĕrāṣṣĕḥû*) links up with "they take pleasure in falsehood" (*yirṣû kāzāḇ* – v. 4a) by means of alliteration: the root of each verb beginning with *rs*. The wordplay links the destructive goal of the enemies to their verbal attempt at accomplishing it.

As a response to this verbal violence the psalmist writes in verse 1 "For God alone my soul waits in silence" (*dûmîyyāh*), and again in verse 5, "For God alone be silent (*dômmî*) my soul." It is an amazing contrast between the verbal violence done by one's enemies and waiting for God in silence.

Why can the psalmist advocate waiting in silence for God in the midst of this verbal violence? The answer is found in the imagery of verses 1-7. The enemies attempt to "batter" the psalmist "like a leaning wall, a tottering fence." They plan to "thrust him down" (vv. 3, 4a).[16] Corresponding to these images are the images of God as secure refuge in verses 1, 2, 5-7. Six times God is referred to as rock, fortress or refuge, and three times God is referred to as the psalmist's salvation. The result is that the psalmist will not be (greatly) moved (vv. 2, 6). Thus, the psalmist can advocate silence in the midst of verbal violence because he realizes that the enemies cannot make him "like a leaning wall, a tottering fence."[17]

[16] The NRSV editors have translated Ps 62:4a as "Their only plan is to bring down a person of prominence." Kraus, *Psalmen 2*, 595, Sabourin, *Le livre des Psaumes*, 288, Jacquet, *Les Psaumes*, 2:282, Westermann, *The Living Psalms*, 151, et al. read "falsehoods" (*maššû'ôt*) in the place of "prominence" (*miśśĕ'ēṯô*), and they translate v. 4a as "They plan falsehoods." They note that rendering *mss't* as "prominence" makes for a clumsy grammatical construction. Thus, v. 4a refers either to the casting down of the psalmist ((*miśśĕ'ēṯô* – "prominence"), as does v. 3b, or it refers to the means by which the enemies attempt to hurt the psalmist (*maššû'ôt* – "falsehoods"), as does v. 4b.

[17] The word translated "tottering" is the participle of *dāḥāh* which means "to push, to thrust." Thus, the image is of a fence which has been pushed in.

They cannot bring him down from his eminence (vv. 3, 4) because for the psalmist, God is rock, refuge, fortress so that the psalmist will not be moved; God is unshakeable security for the psalmist.[18] Thus, verses 1, 2, 5-7 present great faith in God in times of verbal violence, regardless of whether the psalmist is currently experiencing this violence or whether he experienced it in the past.

There is a beautiful feeling-idea going on in the progression of Ps 62:1-7. The psalmist states his quiet confidence in the security of God (vv. 1, 2), goes on to express how the enemies are plotting against him (vv. 3, 4), and then proceeds to repeat a stronger expression of trust, and more encouragement to trust, in order to show what should be the response to the recognition that verbal violence is being done to one's self. The expression of trust is stronger in verses 5-7 because in these verses the psalmist says he will not be moved (at all) and because verse 7 repeats the idea of God as security found in the refrain in verses 1, 2, 5 and 6.[19] The expression "my hope is from him" in v. 5 encourages the psalmist.[20]

In verses 1-7 the psalmist brings to the readers' attention a situation which could cause debilitating fear in order to counter the tendency of fear. Reference to the verbal violence being done to the psalmist by enemies (vv. 3, 4) is surrounded by references to the psalmist's security in God (vv. 1, 2, 5-7). It is this divine security which is the all-encompassing reality and not the enemies' verbal attacks. In order to help convey this aspect of God's presence to the reader, the psalmist refers over and over to God as

[18] The attempt of the enemies to cast down the psalmist from his "eminence" (v. 4) will be unsuccessful because "On God rests" the psalmist's "honor" (v. 7).
[19] J. Alexander, *The Psalms*, 269, and E. Blaiklock, *Commentary on the Psalms*, 1:139, also wrote that vv.5-7 present a stronger faith response then do vv. 1, 2.
[20] J. Eaton, *The Psalms* (London: SCM, 1967) 158, 159, also noted that v. 5, brings "an element of self-encouragement to the psalm." I note that this concern to encourage his soul may also account for the presence of "because" (*kî*) in v. 5: "For God alone be silent my soul because (*kî*) my hope is from him." There is no such linkage in v. 1: "For God alone my soul waits in silence; from him comes my salvation." The "because" (*kî*) in v. 5 may make more explicit the reason to be silent in the face of the actions of the enemies (vv. 3, 4).

rock, fortress, refuge: as the unshakeable one. This repetition has a mantra-like effect: it functions to draw us into the experience of profound security in God's presence like the repetition of a mantra is meant to draw one into a certain type of experience.

Ps 62:8-12

In vv 8-12 the psalmist brings the fruits of his reflection (vv. 1-7) to bear on the experiences of his community. He encourages others to trust in God when they find themselves in the situation in which he found himself.

The psalmist advises people to pour out their hearts before God because "God is a refuge (*maḥseh*) for us" (v. 8).[21] "Refuge" (*Maḥseh*) is a hook word. It is used twice in Psalm 62: in verses 7 and 8. In verse 7 the psalmist uses it as the final image in his description of God as unshakeable security (vv. 1, 2, 5-7). Thus, when, in verse 8, the psalmist advises people to pour out their hearts before God because "God is a refuge (*maḥseh*) for us," he is appealing to his own experience of God as a refuge as a basis for his entreaty.[22]

Verse 9 is the obverse side of the coin, so to speak. Verse 8 expresses the reason for trust in God, and verse 9 gives the reason to not worry about what people say about one. Verse 9 reads as follows. "Those of low estate are but a breath,/ those of high estate are a delusion;/ in the balances they go up;/ they are together lighter than a breath." This verse has been interpreted in

[21] J. Alexander, *The Psalms*, 269, wrote that the *selāh* which follows v. 8 is a "solemn pause" which shows the earnestness of the psalmist's exhortation to "trust in him at all times, O people; pour out your heart before him" (v. 8). V. 8 is the core of the message which the psalmist gives to others and so Alexander may have a point about the effect of *selāh* after v. 8. Of course, the interpretation of *selāh* is problematic, and its use after v. 4 would also have to be treated.

[22] As Cox, *The Psalms*, 92, 94, has said, at this point the psalmist becomes a sign for the people: "a sacrament of God's presence for others." If we define a sacrament as a sign which effects what it signifies then it is interesting to note that the mantra-like repetition of images of God as immovable safety has just been completed in vv. 1-2, 5-7, and, as I noted, this draws the reader into experiencing God in such a way.

numerous ways. The interpretations revolve around the issues of who are these people and what is the meaning of the images which are associated with them.

There have been three major interpretations of the phrases "Those of low estate... those of high estate" (*bĕnê-'āḏām...bĕnê-'îš*) in verse 9. First, they may refer to the wealthy and powerful on the one hand and to the poor on the other because in Ps 49:2 these same words are used to designate the rich and the poor.[23] Second, the two phrases may be synonymous, each referring to all people.[24] Finally, they may refer to the psalmist's enemies.[25] The images of verse 9 show that it is the psalmist's enemies who are the primary referent of this psalm.

The people of verse 9 are presented as a "breath" (*heḇel*) and as a "delusion" (*kāzāḇ*- v. 9). They are pictured as going up in the balances, and as together being lighter than a breath (v. 9b). "Breath" (*heḇel*) can be used to refer to the transitory condition of people, as is the case in Ps 39:5.[26] Cox proposed that it is used in Ps 62:9 as a reference to "one's self-interest," although he did not provide arguments for this thesis.[27] "Delu-

[23] So e.g., Alexander, *The Psalms*, 267-269; Jacquet, *Les Psaumes*, 284; Dahood, *Psalms II*, 89; J. Perowne, *The Book of Psalms*, (Grand Rapids: Zondervan, 1966) 484. It should be noted, however, that *bĕnê-'āḏām* does not consistently designate the rich, nor does *bĕnê-'îš* consistently refer to the poor. See, e.g., the use of the former term in Pss 11:4; 12:2; 14:2; 45:3; 59:3 and the use of the latter in Gn 42:11,13.

[24] So, e.g., Beaucamp. *Le Psautier: Pss.1-72*, 258; Sabourin, *Le livre des Psaumes*, 288; Weiser, *The Psalms*, 451; J. Craghan, *The Psalms* (Wilmington: M. Glazier, 1985) 62; Anderson, *The Psalms*, 1:453; E. Kissane, *The Book of Psalms* (Westminster, MD.: Newman, 1953) 266; Westermann, *Living Psalms*, 151.

[25] So, e.g., Kraus, *Psalmen 2*, 598. In an interesting combination of the first and the third views, C. & E. Briggs, *The Book of Psalms*, 2:70, interpreted these words as referring to the common people and their leaders, both of whom are enemies of the psalmist.

[26] M. Tate, *Psalms 51-100* (WBC, 20; Dallas, TX: Word, 1990) 122, Weiser, *The Psalms*, 451, Anderson, *The Psalms*, 1:453, and Westermann, *Living Psalms*, 155, interpret the breath image in v. 9a in this way.

[27] D. Cox, *The Psalms*, 93. G. Ravasi, *Il libro dei Salmi* (Bologna: Dehoniane, 1983) 248-249, 251-252, 256, 258, claimed that v. 9 refers to people who trust in riches, violence and idols as written about in v. 10. He wrote that just as v. 7 says

sion"[28] (*kāzāḇ*) can also mean "a lie, a falsehood or a deceptive thing."[29]

The words "breath" (*heḇel*) and "delusion" (*kāzāḇ*) are used by the psalmist to allude to the means by which the enemies are attempting to harm the psalmist and to indicate the futility of such attempts. This futility is conveyed by showing how unsubstantial are the enemies in relation to God. Some scholars note that "delusion" (*kāzāḇ*) is used both in verse 9 and in verse 4. What has so far not been appreciated is the fact that the word "breath" (*heḇel*) in verse 9 also links up to the description of the enemies in verses 3-4 along with the significance of these connections for the understanding of verse 9.

It is by falsehood (*kāzāḇ*-v. 4) that the enemies are trying to harm the psalmist (v. 3). "Breath" (*heḇel*) is used twice in verse 9, the first time in conjunction with "delusion" (*kāzāḇ*) in verse 9a: "those of low estate are but a breath (*heḇel*); those of high estate are a delusion (*kāzāḇ*)." "Breath" (*heḇel*) and "delusion" (*kāzāḇ*) figure in the balance imagery of verse 9b; they explain how light people are in the balances. The reason why the psalmist uses this type of "light" imagery, instead of other light imagery[30] such as chaff, is to allude to the verbal means by which the enemies are pressing the attack on the psalmist ("They take pleasure in falsehood [*kāzāḇ*]./ They bless with their mouths, but inwardly they curse"-

that God is a refuge and v. 8 claims that on this basis people should trust in God, so too v. 9 says that people are only a breath and delusion and v. 10 says to not trust in riches. In order for this pattern to hold, however, v. 10 would have to be an exhortation to not trust in people. This is not what Ravasi claims v. 10 is saying, and indeed v. 10 does not seem to express this idea.

[28] The translation offered by the NRSV, RSV, NAB and JB.

[29] *BDB*, 469; W. Baumgartner, *Hebräisches und Aramaisches Lexikon zum Alten Testament* (Leiden: Brill, 1974) 2:446.

[30] Note for example that in Isa 40:15 the nations are placed in the balances (*mō'zĕnayim* used both in Isa 40:15 and in Ps 62:9) and they are considered to be only dust (*šahaq*). Further, in Isa 40:15-17 the images of "drop from a bucket" (*mar middĕlî*), nothingness (*'ayin*), "emptiness" (*tōhû*) and "less than nothingness" (*mē'epes*) are used in conjunction with the balances imagery to describe the nations. The psalmist of Psalm 62 chose none of these "light" images to describe people in the balances.

v. 5bcd). Both "breath" (*heḇel*) and "delusion" (*kāzāḇ*) in verse 9 suggest this verbal violence.

"Breath" (*heḇel*) and "delusion" (*kāzāḇ*) in verse 9 also convey the idea of insubstantiality in order to show the futility of the enemies's attempts. In verse 9 "breath" (*heḇel*) is used in conjunction with the image of balances in order to show how insubstantial people are: "in the balances they go up; together they are lighter than a breath (*heḇel*)". What is on the other side of the balance causing people to go up? The answer is God, as solid, heavy rock, fortress, refuge. The psalmist has been presenting God by means of these substantial images six times in verses 1-2, 5-7 as a response to the enemies' attempts to "batter" him (vv. 3-4). In verse 8 the psalmist continues to use the image of "refuge" (*maḥseh*) for God. When we read in verse 9 that people are only a "breath" (*heḇel*) and a "delusion" (*kāzāḇ*), with the result that they go up in the balance, we have been prepared to view this light imagery in the context of the heavy imagery for God found in the earlier part of the psalm.[31]

Paul Dion has noted the following means of testing proposed correlations between words or patterns that are found in different sections of a poem. They must be compatible with the structure of the individual sections of which they are a part, and there must be "some sort of affinity or comparability between the contexts involved."[32] The preceding observations show that this interpretation of verse 9 meets Dion's criteria. Both verses 8 and 9 treat the need for God's help: in verse 8 this is implied by the words "God is a refuge for us," and it has been proposed in this chapter that verse 9 is a reference to the enemies' violence. Thus, the interpre-

---

[31] Thus, although it is common to interpret *heḇel* in this verse as referring to people's transitoriness on the basis of some other uses of *heḇel*, it is best to interpret both *heḇel* and *kāzāḇ* in v. 9 as referring to people's insubstantiality. As S. Croft noted, one must look not only at how a word is used throughout Hebrew poetry in order to determine its meaning, but also at how it is used in its immediate context. S. Croft, *The Identity of the Individual in the Psalms* (Sheffield: JSOT, 1987) 48.

[32] P. Dion, "The Structure of Isaiah 42:10-17 as Approached Through Versification and Distribution of Poetic Devices," *JSOT* 49 (1991) 113-124, 116.

tation of verse 9 offered in this chapter is compatible with verse 8. On the other hand, the traditional views that the people of verse 9 are meant to be either the rich and the poor or all people leaves verse 9 unmoored from verse 8.

My proposal also meets Dion's second criterion, that there be an affinity between the contexts of different sections of the poem. Both verse 8 and verse 9 continue the opposition between God and the enemies found in the first part of the psalm. Further, the specific type of light imagery used in verse 10 correlates both with how the enemies are attempting to harm the psalmist (vv. 4-5) and with the heavy imagery for God found in verses 2-3, 6-8.

The words (*heḇel...kāzāḇ*- v. 9a) by which the enemies are attempting to cast down the psalmist don't matter because God is with the psalmist so that the enemies' words are as unsubstantial as is a breath on one side of the balance with a rock, a fortress, and a refuge on the other side (v. 9b). Thus, verse 9 alludes to the enemies and to how inconsequential is their verbal violence given God's relationship with the psalmist.[33] This is not a delimiting of God's power; the psalmist asserts that "power belongs to God" (v. 11). It is bringing God's power to bear on the psalmist's situation vis-à-vis his enemies. This interpretation of verse 9 helps to explain the difficult verses (vv. 10-12) with which this psalm concludes.

Verse 10 reads: "Put no confidence in extortion, set no vain hope on robbery;/ if riches increase, set not your heart on them." Some have claimed that in verse 10 the psalmist is speaking to his

[33] This is not to quarrel with the view, expressed for example by A. Weiser, *The Psalms*, 451, and M. Tate, *Psalms 51-100*, 122, that in this verse the psalmist has in mind all people and not only the enemies. My point, however, is that it is the enemies who are the primary referents of this verse.

There are problems with the view that v. 9 not only treats the weakness of people but also is an exhortation not to trust in them. See, e.g., H. Gunkel, *Die Psalmen* (Göttingen: Vandenhoeck & Ruprecht, 1968) 265; P. Boylan *The Psalms* (Dublin: M. H.. Gill, 1936) 227-28; M. Mannati, *Les Psaumes*, 2:231-32; C. Westermann, *Living Psalms*, 155. (Although sounding similar, Ravasi's view [supra, pp. 210-211, n. 27] is the different one that v. 9 inveighs against trusting in riches.) In v.9 the psalmist does not decry trusting in people; rather, the psalmist encourages people not to worry about verbal attacks from others.

enemies and telling them not to rely on their wealth and their power.[34] The proposal presented here is that in verse 10 the psalmist provides the community with warnings for when they find themselves in a situation of verbal violence. This verse links up both to verse 8 and to verse 9. The linkage with verse 8 is provided by the verb "to trust" (*bāṭaḥ*) and by the words for "heart" (*lēḇ, lēḇāḇ*); these words are found both in verse 8 and in verse 10. Recall that in verse 8 the psalmist moved from the form of self-reflection and self-exhortation (vv. 1-7) to the form of encouragement for his community to trust (*bāṭaḥ*) in the Lord. The verb "to trust" (*bāṭaḥ*) is found at the beginning of verses 8 and 10: "Trust (*biṭḥû*) in him at all times, O people..."(v. 8) – "Do not trust (*'al tiḇṭĕḥû*) in extortion..." (v. 10).

The Hebrew word in verse 10 which is translated as "set no vain hope" (*tehbālû*) links up through the process of alliteration with the two uses of the Hebrew word for "breath" (*heḇel*) in verse 9.[35] As we saw, the *heḇel* imagery in v. 9 alludes to the verbal violence of the enemies.

A. Anderson has said that verse 10 is "the negative aspect of the exhortation given in verse 8."[36] On the basis of the connections between verse 10 and verses 8 and 9 we may be even more specific about the function of verse 10. In this poem the images of the verse function to encourage people not to trust (*'al tiḇṭĕḥû* – v. 10) in, nor set their heart (*lēḇ* – v. 10) on, wealth or power in times of verbal violence. That the psalmist says this with an eye to such situations is shown both by the proximity of verse 9 and by the connection between "breath" (*heḇel*, v. 9) and "set no vain hope" (*tehbālû*, v. 10). The aspect of not trusting in wealth comes through clearly in the NRSV translation of verse 10: "Put no confidence in extortion, set no vain hope on robbery;/ if riches increase, do not set your heart on them." The aspect of not trusting in power is also present in this verse because the word which is translated as

[34] C. Westermann, *Living Psalms*, 156; H. J. Kraus, *Psalmen 2*, 598-99.
[35] So, too, L. Sabourin, *Le livre des Psaumes*, 289.
[36] A. Anderson, *The Book of Psalms*, 1.454.

"extortion" (*'ōšeq*), also means "oppression" and the word which is translated as "riches" (*ḥayil*) also means "strength, efficiency or army."[37] The alternative disposition which the psalmist proposes is for people to trust (*biṭḥû*- v. 8) in, and pour out their hearts (*lēḇāḇ*- v. 8) to, God.

In verse 10 the psalmist is treating the human inclination to grab on to anything when you feel that you are sinking. The psalmist is saying that you should fight this tendency and trust in God in situations when you are verbally persecuted.

Verses 11 and 12 read: "Once God has spoken; twice have I heard this:/ that power belongs to God; and that to you, Lord, belongs steadfast love./ For You repay to all, according to their work." These verses have sometimes been regarded as later insertions.[38] This is especially the case with verse 12 because there is an abrupt shift to the second person singular ("you") to refer to God in this verse. Otherwise God is spoken about, not to, in this psalm.[39] Both verse 11 and verse 12 fit in well with the other verses of this psalm. Verse 11 functions particularly well in a psalm in which the psalmist is considering the power-plays of the enemies against him.

Verses 1-11 juxtapose passages on the power of the enemies and of God. The psalmist presents a struggle for the one whom he, and all of us, will recognize as the determinative power in our lives during times of verbal violence: the enemies or God. The use of *'ak* ("surely, only") in these verses are signs of the struggle for power that is occurring.[40] Recall that *'ak* is used in verses 1, 2, 5

[37] *BDB*, 298, 799; *HAL*, 102-103, 286.
[38] E.g., Beaucamp, *Le Psautier: Pss.1-72*, 259, wrote that v. 11 has no reason to be in the psalm, and C. Westermann, *Living Psalms*, 156, wrote that v. 12 is a later insertion.
[39] A. Aejmelaeus, *The Traditional Prayer in the Psalms* (Berlin/New York: De Gruyter, 1986) 50, claimed that Psalm 62 is mostly addressed to the enemy. In response, it may be said that only two (vv. 3-4) out of twelve verses are addressed to the enemy. The bulk of the psalm is directed to the psalmist (vv. 1-2, 5-7 and possibly v. 11), to the people (vv. 8-10 and possibly v. 11) and to God (v. 12).
[40] *'ak* stands at the beginning of each line in which it appears in this psalm. This "pride of place" emphasizes its importance.

and 6 to express trust in God, whereas in verse 4 it expresses the intent of the enemies to destroy the psalmist. The enemies are concentrated (*'ak*) in their attempt to shatter the psalmist, and the psalmist responds with an equally focused and concentrated (*'ak*) action. In verse 9 the result of the psalmist's concentration on God results in his being able to say that the enemies are "surely/only (*'ak*) a breath (*hebel*)." Concentration on the destruction of the psalmist has met concentration on God, and concentration on God has prevailed. The cry of victory is found in verse 11: "Once God has spoken, twice have I heard this:/ that power belongs to God."[41]

The shift to addressing God directly in verse 12 moves one from a reflection on the basis for a quiet trust in God (i.e., God's power over the enemies– vv. 1-11) to an actual relation with God. The enemies' words endanger the relation with the God who is lord of history. The hostile words of the enemies threaten to make one operate as if the enemies control one's history. The reflection on God's power vis-à-vis the enemies in verses 1-11 establishes God as the lord of the history of the person who is being subjected to verbal violence. God's lordship is affirmed in this specific situation; God's royal banner waves in this particular territory. God is reenthroned as God, in the mind of the one who is under verbal attack.[42]

In verse 12 there is the move to the renewal of the personal relation with the God whose identity has been reaffirmed in verses

A. Anderson, *The Book of Psalms*, 1:451, wrote that the use of *'ak* in this psalm may suggest that only God will prevail, whereas when people are opposed to God they are nothing.

[41] It has been noted that in v. 10 the psalmist warns people against seeking refuge from verbal violence in wealth or in power. (See supra, pp. 213-215.) In v.11 the psalmist presents power as God's possession. This metaphor undergirds the metaphors of God as rock, fortress, salvation and refuge, all of which are expressions of power.

[42] Ps 62:1-11 is an interior monologue guided by and strengthening faith. This reflection enables the renewal of the interpersonal conversation with God (v. 12). In Ps 62:1-11 we are afforded a glimpse both of the psalmist's psychomachy ("battle for the soul") and of the theotherapeutic perspectives which enable the paean in v. 11 and the trustful prayer in v. 12.

1-11. Thus, we have the shift to addressing God directly in verse 12: God is now a "You." Moreover, God is no longer addressed as "God" (*'ĕlōhîm*), as is the case seven other times in verses 1, 5, 7 (twice), 8, 11a and 11b. God is now "my Lord" (*'ădōnāy*). The shift in tone from the end of verse 11 to the beginning of verse 12 is especially pronounced.

> 11 that power belongs to God;
> 12 and to You, my Lord, belongs steadfast love.

The move from writing about the power of the third person "God" (v. 11) to the direct address by means of the second person "You" when writing about the Lord's steadfast love (v. 12a) is striking.

Verses 1-11 build to a rising crescendo in extolling God's power, and these verses culminate in the formal announcement (in the form of a numerical proverb): "Once God has spoken; twice have I heard this:/ that power belongs to God." God has been reenthroned in the mind and the life of the one exposed to verbal violence. Verse 12 moves to a long-awaited personal relation: "and to you, my Lord, belongs steadfast love./ For you repay to all, according to their work." The cry of the recognition of God's victorious reign in a person's life (v. 11) leads to the close relation (v. 12) in which one can focus on God's "steadfast love" and on one's response (*ma'ăśēh* – v. 12b) as all that matters.[43]

[43] Some have claimed that Psalm 62 is an individual lament. See, e.g., H. Kraus, *Psalmen I*, 57; E. Gerstenberger, *Der bittende Mensch*, 118, n. 27. The lack, however, of a petition to God for help argues against this categorization. See, e.g., A. Aejmelaeus, *The Traditional Prayer in the Psalms*, 51. Others have said that it is a song of trust. B. Anderson, *Out of the Depths* (Philadelphia: Westminster, 1974) 175; A. Anderson, *The Book of Psalms*, 1.450.

There are other songs of trust in which the psalmist moves from speaking about God to speaking to God. Thus, in Psalm 23 we move from the third person (vv. 1-3) to the second person (vv. 4-5) and then back to the third person (v. 6). What is intriguing about Psalm 62, however, is that the direct address to God (v. 12) is held until the very end, after all of the speaking about God and to the enemies and to the people has been completed. Perhaps the withholding of the direct address to God until the final verse indicates that in Psalm 62 this genre has been modified from a song of trust to a song leading to trust. This proposal does not imply a view on when the psalmist was exposed to verbal abuse (before or during the writing of this psalm) nor an opinion as to the psalmist's internal state (peace based on trust

Psalm 62 and Symbol Systems

Dennis Mumby,[44] a communications scholar, writes about the "interpretive" or "organizational culture" approach to analyzing organizations. This approach focuses on organizational symbols (e.g., "myths, stories, legends, jokes, rites, logos") as the means by which members create "a sense of organizational reality."[45] Communication in an organization provides meanings "which, when habitualized over time, provide the background of common experience that gives organization members a context for organizing their behavior."[46] Different types of metaphors will structure an organization in different ways. Thus, an organization's use of military metaphors will cause the organization to be structured in a rigid, formal way whereas family metaphors encourage a more flexible structuring.[47]

Communication has many different social functions (e.g., it may be a means to disseminate information). One way in which communication may function is as a means of domination. Mumby's study focused on the relationship between "communication, meaning and power as domination."[48]

One way in which power is perpetuated is by getting one's view of the organization to be accepted, and this is done through communication. Groups in power can co-opt the symbol system of an organization, and thus, certain groups within an organization can manipulate symbols to support their interests. Usually there are a number of groups in an organization who vie for the acceptance of

or agitation changing to peace) during the psalm's composition. What is being treated is a literary modification based on an unusual feature in the psalm; no historical reconstruction is implied.

[44] D. Mumby, *Communication and Power in Organizations: Discourse, Ideology and Domination* (Norwood, NJ: Ablex, 1988).

[45] Ibid., 3,10-12. See also L. Pondy, G. Morgan, P. Frost & T. Dandridge, *Organizational Symbolism* (Greenwich, CT: JAI, 1983).

[46] D. Mumby, *Communication and Power*, 14.

[47] Ibid., 18, 21, 93, 95, 97, 102, 158. So too S. Deetz, "Metaphors and the Discursive Production and Reproduction of Organization," in L. Thayer, ed., *Organization-Communication: Emerging Perspectives* (Norwood, NJ: Ablex, 1986) 168-182.

[48] *Communication and Power*, 6.

their symbol system. When a group's interests become accepted by the larger organization this group has a role in creating the way in which members look at life. In this sense this group and their symbol system exert a certain "domination of consciousness." This type of domination occurs because the accepted symbolic construction conditions the members of an organization to respond in a certain way. Thus, the interests of a certain group become a part of the fabric of the organization's life.[49]

The accepted symbol system reinforces certain ideologies and values. Paradoxically, in making these views explicit it also exposes them to criticism and to contradiction.[50] Once a symbol system is formulated, one is free to accept or to reject it. Thus, it is not the case that an organization's accepted symbol system is free from the possibility of criticism and reform.

What people in the "organizational culture" approach are dealing with is the power of words in constructing social reality. A community's myth, the response an organization has to information or events, structures the life of the group. People recognize implicitly the power of the interpretation of themselves or of their activities to which the group has given assent; that is why people are so concerned about the types of interpretations of themselves that are being proposed to the community. It is also why they attempt in numerous ways to influence the community's members, by their words and their actions, to accept a certain interpretation of themselves over other possible interpretations. People know the power of the accepted interpretation for influencing a community's structure.[51]

[49] Ibid., 3, 5, 67, 69, 72, 73, 92, 98.

[50] T. Dandridge, I. Mitroff & W. Joyce, "Organizational Symbolism: A Topic to Expand Organizational Analysis," *Academy of Management Review* 5 (1980) 77.

This is similar to M. Douglas' ideas on "purity" and "dirt." "Purity" is the structuring of the world, and "dirt" is the rejection of this structure. See M. Douglas, *Purity and Danger* (London: Routledge & Kegan Paul, 1966) 33-37; B. Malina, *Christian Origins and Cultural Anthropology* (Atlanta: John Knox, 1986) 37-41.

[51] See the following description of the power of slander to separate one from others, given by Don Basilio in Act 1, Scene 2 of Rossini's opera *The Barber of Seville*, C. Sterbini, libretto.

The psalmist's enemies are verbally creating a symbol system that they hope will result in harm to the psalmist. The metaphors of casting down the psalmist and of shattering him, linked up as they are to what the enemies are saying about the psalmist (vv. 3, 4), show that the psalmist perceives an attempt by his enemies to orchestrate communal opinion and to construct organizational reality in a manner that will result in his downfall. Once a response is formulated one is free to accept or to reject it. By making explicit his enemies' response, the psalmist has the chance to reject it. This is what he does.

The psalmist has exposed the enemies' symbolism to criticism and modification. He has deconstructed the enemies' discourse, and he has constructed a new frame of reference. The psalmist creates his own alternative symbol-system of God as rock, fortress, refuge.[52] He exhorts himself (vv. 1-7) to be quiet in the face of the enemies' symbolic construction, and to be at ease in his own symbol-system which is at odds with that of the enemies. He also exhorts others (vv. 8-12) to have this type of quiet trust in God when they are in a similar situation.

What is important for the psalmist is that the consciousness of anyone who is in this situation should not be dominated by the symbolic construction of enemies. This happens when the enemies' words have caused an unsettling effect: when they cause a

> A few, gentle rumors, a rake and a libertine – in four days he'll be hounded out... my system never fails... Slander is a little breeze – gentle, imperceptible – lightly, softly it starts to whisper. Quietly – close to the ground – under the breath – hissing – flowing widely, fiercely burning, reaching people's ears and brains, magnifying and distorting. Gradually the din increases, first in one place, then another, thunder rumbles in the distance, coming nearer it explodes, like the firing of a canon – violent earthquake, lightning, tempest, general tumult then resound. And the victim of the slander, now disgraced and trampled on, leaves the town for good and all.

See J. Cox, producer, *Rossini's The Barber of Seville*. (New York: National Video, 1982). See also P. Beaumarchais' description of calumny in Act 2 of his play *Le barbier de Seville* (NCL; Paris: Larousse, 1970).

[52] The psalmist has "reframed" his experience of verbal violence.

quiet trust in God's salvation not to be present.[53] The psalmist is convinced that it is God and not the dominant group ideology that constitutes social reality. ("On God rests my honor and my deliverance" [v. 7a] – "power belongs to God" [v. 11b]). Thus, he denies the power of the group's interpretation to be the determinative force in his life. In effect, he has rejected the idea that the group's interpretation of him, and their consequent action towards him, holds power over him; he has asserted that God's word is the determinative constructor of existence and not the accepted word of a group. "Once God has spoken; twice have I heard this:/ that power belongs to God" (v. 11).

The psalmist has come to the realization that it is the response to God's word, and not the response to the word of the group that should be the focus of people's concern ("and that to you, Lord, belongs steadfast love./ For you repay to all according to their work"[v. 12]). By so doing, the psalmist has broken down the gates to the citadel of concern for other people's symbolic constructions, and he has existentially asserted the presence of God's reign through God's word in what seems to be a realm controlled by people through their words. He has done so by exposing and juxtaposing in his symbolic construction what Beaucamp has called "the myth of the power of man and the restful and sure force."[54]

The Effects of Hostile Symbol Systems and the Theotherapy of Psalm 62

Both we and our children tend to become very upset when we learn that we have been slandered. This is verbal terrorism. There is virtually nothing that we can do to stop it, and we have no idea about what will be said about us and how it can hurt us. Often, we

[53] The theology of Psalm 62 liberates the heart from fear and unease in a situation of verbal violence.

[54] E. Beaucamp, *Le Psautier: Pss.1-72*, 260. The original French is "*le mythe de la puissance de l'homme et la force reposante et sûre*."

attempt to defend ourselves by means of retaliatory verbal assaults and/or by excessive self-concern. The result is either the spreading of the verbal violence or an insulation from others.

Psalm 62 is a great help for us to counter these effects of hostile symbol systems. We have seen how it helps us to have a quiet, trusting relation with God in these situations. The psalmist can remain silent in the midst of damaging things being said about him: silent because he trusts in the God of refuge! The image of remaining silent when potentially harmful things are being said about him is a striking one which shows the great security which God's presence evokes. (The psalmist is not advocating such a course of action; he is using this image to express the effects of God's presence.) The security is so great that it does not matter what the slanderers say about the psalmist (v. 4) because they are "but a breath" (v. 9a): "they are together lighter than a breath" (v. 9b). Though they say evil words, they are not even as substantial as a light breath (v. 9) because "power belongs to God" (v. 11) who is our rock, fortress, refuge and salvation (vv. 1, 2, 5-8). In such ways Psalm 62 can help parents and children remain committed to relationships when the stinging words of others make withdrawal and isolation so appealing.

The Scriptures reflect our souls; they show us the current status of our relation with God. If it is the God of Psalm 62 in whom we believe, then there are certain implications for the way we feel and the way we act. Excessive concern about, and unease over, what is being said about us is reason to question whether we truly believe in the God whom we read about in Psalm 62.

CHAPTER 9

PSALM 133: GOD AS THE UNIFYING FORCE

The process of beginning a relationship can be stressful. Will we be rebuffed? Will we have many shared interests? Can we discover them? Will we have the types of personalities that mesh? Will the relationship start well, only to end with one getting hurt? Attempting to sustain a relationship can also be stressful. No two individuals mesh perfectly. Will we make sacrifices for the other at those points where the connection is less than optimal?

These are some of the reasons why many, including children, are tentative about beginning and attempting to maintain relationships. We need, however, a variety of relationships for our intellectual[1] and emotional health. The value of healthy relationships far surpasses the stresses attendant upon making and nurturing them. If both we and our children are to participate in healthy relationships, we must have effective ways of dealing with the stressors that accompany them. Psalm 133 may be a great resource in such a situation. This psalm focuses attention both on how good are relationships and on how they are the medium of a special blessing. By so doing, Psalm 133 gives us the motivation for starting and sustaining healthy relationships. It also provides us with the perspective needed in order not to focus on the attendant stresses, and by so doing exacerbate their effects and strain the relationship.

After treating difficulties which both we and children face in starting and sustaining relationships, an interpretation of Psalm 133 is offered. It is proposed that Psalm 133 provides us with encouragement and incentive for living with others.

[1] As the proverb goes, "Iron sharpens iron, and one person sharpens the wits of another" (Prov 27:17).

The Difficulties in Starting and Sustaining Relationships

There are at least three major types of obstacles to relationships which confront us. First, vices such as pride, selfishness, jealousy and greed separate us from each other. The degree to which they exert a guiding force in our lives should not be minimized. The mass media bombards us with images of how wonderful it is both to be head and shoulders above others and to possess what only a few can afford. By so doing, the very vices that separate us from others are reinforced.

Second, the pervasive exaltation of individualism is a cultural factor that works against relationships. In American culture this aspect has been documented by a number of scholars. Robert Bellah and his colleagues have studied the effects of individualism on the private and public lives of white middle class Americans.[2] The authors are concerned with how one can "preserve or create a morally coherent life" in the midst of the pervasive, radical, American exaltation of individualism. In other words, how can one live ethically by maintaining personal relationships and by living a responsible public life, when one lives in a culture which espouses personal fulfillment and self-autonomy. The authors argue that, while these tendencies were found in the American past, today they are intensified. This has produced a sense of isolation and an erosion of citizenship. They find that people express this individualism in work by means of a pursuit of their interest and advantage, and in family and community by means of a cultivation of "personal lifestyles." As a result, marriage and family life "suffer the eroding impact of such an individualistic orientation."

[2] R. Bellah, R. Madsen, W. Sullivan, A. Swidler & S. Tipton, *Habits of the Heart: Individualism and Commitment in American Life* (Berkeley: University of California, 1985). It should be noted that their study deals only with one part of American society. Both the number of researchers involved in this project and budgetary considerations necessitated a limitation in the scope of the project.

These scholars note that religious communities have languages of commitment which can correct this primary language of American culture. There has been, however, a tendency – and a counter-tendency – to privatize religion in America.[3] The biblical tradition and republicanism were the languages by which we understood ourselves as a people.[4] These primary languages have become secondary languages; they have been replaced by the language of individualism as the primary means by which we understand ourselves. This is a limiting language. "There is in the desire for intense relationships with others, an attempt to move beyond the isolated self, even though the language of individualism makes that sometimes hard to articulate."

Suzanne Keller finds this individualism exacerbated by the mobility and heterogeneity of American society. The extremely mobile society that we have become makes community difficult. This has been a factor working against community from the colonial days when we began our expansion: our pushing back the frontier. It is a factor today when people often have to pull up roots and relocate because of their jobs. The heterogeneous character of our society has also often hindered us from establishing community in our society. Our history includes acts and policies of racial injustice and oppression, as well as the myths which we created to undergird them. Keller summarizes her study by saying "Community lost, found, built anew only to founder on the shoals of individualism, is a perennial cultural theme."[5]

Finally, the fear of being rejected is a powerful inhibitor to the attempt to enter into relationships. We are putting ourselves on the line when we try to form a relationship, and all of us know the fear that the other will not want to make the effort to get to know us.

[3] Ibid., 222-225.

[4] By the term "languages," the authors are referring to "modes of moral discourse that include distinct vocabularies and characteristic patterns of moral reasoning." By the term "republicanism" they mean that tradition "that originated in the cities of classical Greece and Rome" and that "views public participation as a form of moral education and sees its purposes as the attainment of *justice* and the *public good*." See Bellah et al., *Habits of the Heart*, 334, 335.

[5] S. Keller, "The American Dream of Community: An Unfinished Agenda," *Sociological Forum* 3 (1988) 167-183, pp.167, 168, 173, 178, 180.

Some people become socially paralyzed by this type of fear, and do not go out to others; most of us retreat from rejections for a time, gather ourselves, and try again.

The example which parents give will exert a strong influence on how much time children spend cultivating relationships, and how much time they spend retreating from them. The authors of *Habits of the Heart* say that we need to make our biblical and republican traditions our primary languages once again. We need both to "reappropriate tradition" and to apply it in creative ways.

> Indeed, we would argue that if we are ever to enter that new world that has so far been powerless to be born, it will be through reversing modernity's tendency to obliterate all previous culture. We need to learn again from the cultural riches of the human species and to reappropriate and revitalize those riches so that they can speak to our condition today.[6]

Psalm 133 is a part of our biblical tradition that can be a great inspiration to parents to initiate and sustain relations with others, and by so doing inspire their children to do the same.

Psalm 133: The Trust That Encourages and Undergirds Relationships

The Reading

A Song of Ascents

1 How very good and pleasant it is
  when kindred dwell in unity!
2 It is like the precious oil upon the head
  running down upon the beard,
upon the beard of Aaron,
  running down over the collar of his robes!
3 It is like the dew of Hermon which falls down
  on the mountains of Zion.
For there the Lord has ordained the blessing,
  life forevermore.

[6] R. Bellah et al., *Habits of the Heart*, 282, 283, 290-292.

The Thesis

Psalm 133 presents a literary portrait of a completely united people in such a way as to encourage fellowship. In the sections below, the psalm's artistry will be explored and its inspirational portrait will be studied.

Psalm 133 is about unity. Much of the discussion about this psalm has dealt with the question of who are the unified parties. Just what constitutes the focal point of Psalm 133 is the crux around which this discussion revolves. Little has been done on what the psalmist is actually saying about the unity itself. Hereinafter follows a brief presentation of the different theories on who are the united people, and an assessment of which is most probable. There follows an exposition of how the images found in verses 2 and 3 are used by the psalmist to vision unity. Two new theses on the meaning and function of verses 2 and 3 help to explain both what is the focal point of the psalm and the profundity of peace which is the leitmotif of Psalm 133.

The Good Oil, The Copious Dew and People Completely United: The Interpretation of Psalm 133

Those who have seen verse 1 as the main point of Psalm 133 have been inclined to opt for one of four proposals. First, the psalm is about fellowship between people.[7] Second, it is specifically about fellowship within the family.[8] Third, and still more specifically, it concerns the unity of brothers dwelling together in an extended family.[9] Fourth, this psalm expresses the hope that the

[7] E. Power, "*Ṣion* or *Si'on* in Psalm 133," *Bib* 3 (1922) 346-49.

[8] R. B. Y. Scott, *The Way of Wisdom in the Old Testament* (New York: Macmillan, 1971) 194; J. Kuntz, "The Canonical Wisdom Psalms of Ancient Israel," *Rhetorical Criticism: Essays in Honor of James Muilenberg*, ed. J. Jackson & M. Kessler (Pittsburgh: Pickwick, 1974) 215; W. Holladay, *The Psalms through Three Thousand Years*, 34.

[9] A. Weiser, *The Psalms*, 783; H. J. Kraus, *Psalmen 2* (BKAT; Neukirchen-Vluyn: Neukirchener, 1978) 1068; W. M. L. de Wette, *Commentar über die Psalmen* (Heidelberg: Mohr, 1856) 600; W. Oesterley, *The Psalms* (London: SPCK, 1959) 534, 535; Similarly, C. Stuhlmueller, *Psalms 2* (OTM; Wilmington, DE: Glazier, 1983) 178, 179.

southern kingdom and the remnant in the north will live in peace with Jerusalem as the "central location for communal unity."[10]

Little evidence is given to support these views. Those who propose that the unity refers to brothers living together point to Deut 25:5.

> If brothers dwell together, and one of them dies and has no son, the wife of the dead shall not be married outside the family to a stranger; her husband's brother shall go in to her, and take her as his wife, and perform the duty of a husband's brother to her.

Norrin and Berlin have provided arguments in support of the view that this psalm treats the unity of the northern and southern kingdoms. Norrin has noted that the psalmist mentions Hermon in the north and Zion in the south.[11] Berlin argued that "dwell in unity" (*yšḇ yḥḏ*), found in verse 1, is a "technical expression meaning 'living together on undivided land holdings'- a kind of joint tenancy." She adduces Gen 13:6; 36:7 in support of this assertion. This is not enough evidence for her proposal. Berlin said that these words are "a metaphor for an undivided kingdom."[12] Even if "dwell in unity" (*yšḇ yḥḏ*) is a technical expression for a "joint tenancy" – and there is very little evidence in support of this view – Berlin does not supply any arguments why it should be interpreted as an allusion to an undivided kingdom.

Those who have proposed that the main point of the psalm is expressed in verse 3 tend to view the unity of verse 1 as referring to communal worship in Jerusalem.[13] This may be indicated by

[10] S. Norrin, "Ps.133. Zusammenhang und Datierung," *ASTI* 11 (1977/1978) 93, 94. Similarly, A. Berlin, "On the Interpretation of Psalm 133," in *Directions in Biblical Hebrew Poetry*, ed. E. R. Follis (JSOTSS, 40; Sheffield: JSOT, 1987) 142.

[11] Norrin proposed that the *Sitz im Leben* was Hezekiah's calling all of Israel, including the tribes of Ephraim and Manasseh, to celebrate the Passover at the temple in Jerusalem (2 Chr 30:1). See Norrin, "Zusammenhang und Datierung," 94.

[12] Berlin, "On the Interpretation of Psalm 133," 142.

[13] O. Keel, *The Symbolism of the Biblical World* (New York: Crossroad, 1985) 138, 335; Idem, "Kultische Brüderlichkeit– Psalm 133," *FZTP* 23 (1976) 68; P. Auffret, "Essai sur la structure littéraire du Psaume 133," *BN* 27 (1985) 22-34; M. Mannati, *Les Psaumes* (vol.4; Brussels: Desclée de Brouwer, 1968) 191-94;

several features in this psalm. First, in verse 2 we read about the oil running down the beard of Aaron. Second, the first words of the second line in verse 3 (*kî šām* – "For there") link up to the last word of the first line in this verse (*Ṣîyyôn* – "Zion") by means of their proximity to indicate that God has commanded the blessing in Jerusalem: "For there (*kî šām*) the Lord has commanded the blessing, life for evermore." Even if the words "For there" (*kî šām*) in verse 3 point to the blessing being given where brothers dwell in unity (v. 1), rather than to Zion, the proximity of the word "Zion" to the reference to the Lord's blessing may be adduced in support of the communal worship thesis. Finally, this psalm is one of the psalms of ascents (Pss 120-134), and this shows that at one time it was viewed in reference to gathering together in Jerusalem for the major feasts.[14]

Although there is more evidence for the communal worship thesis than for the alternatives, the people about whom the psalmist is writing may elude us. (It may be that the psalmist is not concerned with such a specification.) We may, however, come to a better understanding of the psalmist's perception of unity by a close reading of this psalm: such a reading would exhibit both a rhetorical critical concern for the configuration of the psalm and a sensitivity to the way in which meaning develops in biblical poetry.

Are verses 2 and 3 metaphorical elaborations of verse 1: "How good (*ṭôḇ*) and pleasant (*nāʿîm*) it is when brothers dwell in com-

L. Jacquet, *Les Psaumes et le coeur de l'homme* (Brussels: Duculot, 1975) 3:542; J. Alexander, *The Psalms* (repr. Grand Rapids: Baker, 1975) 527; A. Anderson, *The Book of Psalms*, 2:885. A. Deissler, *Die Psalmen* (Dusseldorf: Patmos, 1964) 520; J. H. Eaton, *The Psalms* (London: SCM, 1967) 294; L. Allen, *Psalms 101-150* (Waco, TX: Word, 1983) 212; P. W. Skehan *Studies in Israelite Poetry and Wisdom* (CBQMS, 1; Washington, DC: CBA, 1971) 63; R. Kittel, *Die Psalmen* (Leipzig: A. Deichert, 1914) 458; J. M'Swinney, *Psalms and Canticles* (London: Sands, 1901) 562.

[14] In conjunction with this observation, it should be noted that the blessing of the Lord is written about both in Ps 133:3 and in Ps 134:3. Further, in Psalm 134 the call is to worship God in Zion (Ps 134:1, 2). It also should be pointed out, however, that this is not the only position among the psalms in which Psalm 133 is found. In both IIQPsa and IIQPsb Psalm 133 is placed between Pss 141 and 144.

plete unity?"[15] Beaucamp and Berlin have proposed that the *k* particles at the beginning of verses 2 and 3 link these verses up to each other rather than to verse 1. According to Berlin, this means that verses 2 and 3 are not explications of the unity written about in verse 1; rather, they are an anthropomorphic presentation of the land. Berlin translated verse 2 and the first line of verse 3 in the following way.

> Like the fragrant oil on the head,
> Flowing down on the beard, Aaron's beard,
> That flows down over the collar of his robe;
>
> So the dew of Hermon
> That flows down on the mountains of Zion.

The country is presented as a priest being anointed with holy oil so that the whole country – from Hermon to Zion – is presented as holy.[16]

There are problems with this view. As we have seen, Berlin said that verse 1 expresses the hope of a reunification of the kingdom. Yet her interpretation of verse 2 and the first line of v. 3 leaves this hope unrelated to the rest of the psalm; she does not explain how verse 1 relates to these lines. According to her, the *k* ("like") prefix in verse 2 is related to the same prefix in verse 3 which she translates as "so." For virtually every other commentator on this verse, each *k* particle is translated as "like," and is viewed as linking up to and elucidating the brotherly unity found in verse 1. Berlin's proposal leaves verse 1 standing apart from the other two verses of the psalm.

Berlin's thesis does not take into account the complicated gapping found in this psalm. Gapping is the literary procedure in which certain words necessary to the meaning of a half-line or line are not found there but rather occur in an earlier section of the poem. Gapping occurs usually between half-lines. An example is

[15] I have added the word "complete" to the NRSV translation because the emphasizing particle *gam* is used before *yāḥaḏ* in order to convey the meaning of complete unity.
[16] Berlin, "On the Interpretation of Psalm 133," 144-46.

found in Isa 14:8: "The cypresses rejoice over you, the cedars of Lebanon." Both the verb "rejoice" (*śāmaḥ*) and the word meaning "over you" (*lĕkā*) are found in the first half-line, but they are also implied in the second ("the cedars of Lebanon [rejoice over you]").[17]

Gapping is an important literary device in Psalm 133. The words "upon the beard of Aaron, running down upon the collar of his robes" refer to the good oil (*šemen haṭṭôḇ*) written about in verse 2a. There is another instance of gapping in this psalm and it shows the interconnection of verse 1 through the first line of verse 3.

Auffret has noted that the "good" (*ṭôḇ*) of verse 1 is picked up in verse 2a ("It is like the good [*ṭôḇ*] oil upon the head..."), and that the word "pleasant" (*nāʿîm*) in verse 1 is explained by the image of the dew in verse 3a.[18] When people dwell in complete unity, it is as good as the good oil (v. 2) and it is as pleasant as "the dew of Hermon which falls on the mountains of Zion" (the first line of v. 3). Thus, the images of oil and dew are metaphorical expansions of the ideas expressed in verse 1. Berlin's interpretation of them fails to take into account the connections which the psalmist has made between these verses and verse 1.

The following questions need to be explored. What do verse 2 and the first line of verse 3 say about fellowship? How does the second line in verse 3 ("For there God has commanded the blessing, life forevermore") fit into this psalm? Is it a continuation of the previous images, or is it a summary verse, or perhaps the focal point, of the psalm?

First, then, what are the images of fellowship to be found in verse 2 and the first part of verse 3? Verse 2 describes the rela-

[17] For some further examples and types of gapping, which is found frequently in biblical poetry, see, e.g., M. O'Connor, *Hebrew Verse Structure*, 122-129, 401-407; E. Greenstein, "How Does Parallelism Mean?," 50-52; D. Petersen & K. Richards, *Interpreting Hebrew Poetry*, 51. Greenstein (p. 50, n. 26) calls the pattern created by gapping "syntactic parallelism," and sees this as explaining many passages which have been considered examples of Lowth's third category, i.e., synthetic parallelism.
[18] P. Auffret, "Essai sur la structure littéraire du Psaume 133," 30.

tionship with others in terms of an anointing with oil. Scholars have wondered what oil is being written about: the oil used in ordinary life or the sacred oil?[19] I propose that the words "It is like the precious oil upon the head, running down upon the beard" refer to the festive oil, and that the next line ("upon the beard of Aaron, running down upon the collar of his robes") refers to the consecrating oil.

P. Raabe has dealt with instances of deliberate ambiguity in the Psalter, classifying them as examples of lexical, phonetic or grammatical ambiguity.[20] He notes James Barr's caution against assuming that the full range of meanings of terms must be found in each use of these terms;[21] Raabe says, however, that the determination of whether or not the context supports such ambiguity serves both as a control against such an error, and as evidence that there is deliberate ambiguity in the text. The following contextual evidence shows that there is deliberate ambiguity in Ps 133:2.

When the reader reads the first line of verse 2, he or she thinks of festive oil, the oil of joy, because he/she has just read in verse 1 about how good and pleasant it is when people dwell together in complete unity. This is a joyous, communal image. At festive gatherings oil was used for anointing.[22] By way of contrast, the anointing of Aaron took place in a very private setting.

The reference to "precious (*ṭôḇ* – ʿgood', v. 2) oil" in verse 2a need not imply the holy, anointing oil. These words (*šemen haṭṭôḇ*) are also used in Isa 39:2 and in Eccl 7:1. In these verses they do not denote the oil of anointing. Thus, the oil referred to in the words "It is like the precious oil upon the head, running down upon the beard" (v. 2a) is the oil of joy.

[19] E.g., Anderson, *The Book of Psalms*, 886, and F. Delitzsch, *Biblical Commentary on the Psalms*, (Edinburgh: T. & T. Clark, 1871) 3:317) wrote that v. 2 refers to the holy anointing oil whereas Kraus, *Psalmen 2*, 1068, wrote that it refers to oil used to soften and to soothe one, and H. Gunkel, *Die Psalmen* (Göttingen: Vandenhoeck & Ruprecht, 1926) 570, that it referred to the festive oil.

[20] Raabe, "Deliberate Ambiguity in the Psalter," *JBL* 110 (1991) 213-227.

[21] J. Barr, *The Semantics of Biblical Language* (Oxford: Oxford University Press, 1961). Barr calls this "illegitimate totality transfer."

[22] See Mic 6:15; Ps 45:8; Eccl 9:7-9; Amos 6:4-7; Ps 104:15.

The reference to oil running down Aaron (the second line of verse 2) clearly points to a holy oil; Aaron was the first high priest. There are priestly traditions about an anointing of Aaron and his sons. In Exod 30:22-25 we read that a mixture of sweet myrrh, cinnamon, aromatic cane, cassia and olive oil, the whole of which is called "a sacred anointing oil," is to be used for this anointing. This is the special oil which sanctifies whatever it touches: "you shall consecrate them that they may be most holy; whatever touches them will become holy" (Exod 30:29). This is the holy oil which is used to consecrate the most holy meeting place between God and people: the tent of meeting (Exod 30:26-29). No other "oil" like it in composition should be made, and no one but the high priest may be anointed with it (Exod 30:32,33: Lev 21:10). Further, this "sacred anointing oil" may not be upon the high priest when he leaves the tent of meeting: "Do not go out from the door of the tent of meeting, lest you die; for the anointing oil of the Lord is upon you" (Lev 10:7).[23] This oil is the Lord's oil: "the consecration of the anointing oil of his God is upon him" (Lev 21:12). Thus, this anointing oil (*šemen mišḥaṯ*) is a special oil used only by the Aaronic high priest, and only when he is in the meeting place with God: the tent of meeting is also consecrated with this oil.[24]

[23] See also Lev 21:12.

[24] In Exod 30:30; Lev 10:6,7 we read that Aaron and his sons are to be anointed with this oil; in Lev 21:10, however, we read that it is "The priest who is chief among his brethren, upon whose head the anointing oil is poured, and who has been consecrated to wear the garments..." This seems to imply that only the high priest was to be anointed. In Lev 8 we read that the anointing oil is sprinkled upon the clothes of both Aaron and his sons (8:30), but only Aaron's head is anointed with such oil (Lev 8:12).

Dahood, *Psalms III; 101-150* (AB, 17A; Garden City, NY: Doubleday, 1970) 251, wrote that the use of the participles *yōrēḏ* and *šeyyōrēḏ* indicates that only the anointing of Aaron is being referred to and not the anointing of any high priest. This is difficult to determine. The participle conveys the idea of continuous action, and thus, the use of the participle may be for the purpose of drawing the reader into the experience of the downward flow of the movement of the oil. The participle *šeyyōrēḏ* is used in v. 3a to describe the falling of the dew, and surely it is not one particular instance of dew that the psalmist is writing about.

Another caution against assuming that only the anointing of Aaron is written about in the second line of v. 2 is based on the observation of G.A. Mikre-

We cannot be certain if the psalmist was aware of these traditions, let alone if he was familiar with these texts in Exodus and Leviticus which may not have assumed a written form at the time of the psalm's composition. It should be remembered, however, that both the psalms and the priestly traditions of the Pentateuch were nurtured in the cult of Israel. In any case, the reference to oil running down Aaron (Ps 133:2), the first high priest, is clearly a reference to a holy oil used on one who comes into an especially close relationship with the divine.

Thus, it is not the case that the oil in verse 2 is either oil of joy or a sacred oil. It is both: the oil of joy in the first line of verse 2 and a holy oil in the second line of verse 2.[25] This is an example of how meaning develops in biblical poetry. There is an addition in meaning as we move from the first to the second line of verse 2.

More specifically, we can say that this "what's moreness" is achieved in Ps 133:2 by means of "deliberate ambiguity" of the type termed "syntactic ambiguity" by Walsh and "sustained ambiguity" by Raabe. Walsh defines "syntactic ambiguity"as the means by which the text allows itself to be read in two ways. Certain passages do not force us to choose between meanings; rather they invite us to hear both meanings. The text encourages us with one meaning, only to encourage us with another one later.[26] In Psalm 133 we are required to make imaginative leaps: from the oil of joy to a sacred oil (v. 2) and from the dew of Hermon to its accumulation on Mount Zion (v. 3).[27]

Selassie, "Metonymy in the Psalms, *BT* 44 (1993) 421, that in the Old Testament an ancestor frequently represents his or her descendants.

[25] A. Berlin, "On the Interpretation of Psalm 133," 144, also thinks that both meanings may be present in v. 2, although she does not provide arguments for this view.

[26] J. Walsh, "Poetic Style and Structure in Isaiah 41," SBL-AAR Mid-Atlantic Region Meeting, 1990. Walsh also uses the words "textual doublecross" to describe this literary feature.

P. Raabe, "Deliberate Ambiguity in the Psalter," 224-226, calls this "sustained ambiguity," which he classifies a a type of grammatical ambiguity in contrast to lexical and phonetic ambiguity.

[27] For attempts to solve the difficulty of the image of the dew of Hermon falling down on distant Zion, see, e.g., J. H. Eaton, *Psalms*, 294, 295; L. Allen, *Psalms 101-150*, 212, 213; A. Weiser, *The Psalms*, 784; L. Sabourin, *The Psalms* (New York: Alba House, 1970) 386. E. Power, "*Ṣion* or *Si'on* in Psalm 133," 346, 347.

Now let us return to looking specifically at the second line of verse 2. The image in this line is striking. The unity of people is like the experience of the holy oil upon Aaron. This moves the holy and very distinct into the realm of the secular and the common as a way of showing the value of this secular experience. This brings what is sacrosanct into the everyday world. What was experienced by Aaron can now be experienced when people are completely united.

In verse 2b we continue to read about the downward flow of the oil. The oil that was placed on the head (v. 2a) and which ran down to the beard has now run upon "the collar of his robes" (*pî middôṯāw*).[28] The masculine noun *maḏ* means "garment," but *middôṯāw* is the feminine plural of *midāh* with the third person, singular, possessive pronoun. Since *midāh* means "measure, stature, size," the plural form in verse 2 could refer to the entire body of the psalmist. Although the feminine noun *midāh* is used, scholars have usually translated *middôṯāw* in verse 2 as "robes" because of the presence of the construct form of the word *peh* before it.

Peh usually means "mouth."[29] For this reason some see it in 133:2b as referring to the opening in the tunic through which

Ṣiyyôn ("Zion") could also allude to *ṣayôn* ("dry place"). Although Jerusalem gets about thirty-five inches of rain a year, June through September especially tend to be very dry. Thus, *Ṣiyyôn* could call to mind *ṣayôn*; as the oil moistens the dry skin (v. 2) so the dew moistens the dry place. See H. J. Kraus, *Psalmen 2*, 1067 who emends Zion to "dry place" on the grounds of the topographical impossibility of the dew of Hermon falling on Zion.

[28] It is debated as to whether it is the oil or the beard which is flowing over the *pî middôṯāw*. The following are among those who think that v. 2b refers to the oil flowing over the *pî middôṯāw*. J. Alexander, *The Psalms*, 527; D. Tsumura, "Sorites in Psalm 133,2-3a," *Bib* 61 (1980) 416-417; M. Kissane, *The Book of Psalms* (Dublin: Richview, 1954) 2:275; M. Dahood, *Psalms III: 101-150*, 252. On the other hand, L. Allen, *Psalms 101-150*, 212, and W. Watson, "The Hidden Simile in Psalm 133," *Bib* 60 (1979) 108-109, are among those who think that it is the beard which is said to be flowing down over the *pî middôṯāw*. I think that the oil is referred to as flowing over the *pî middôṯāw*. Dahood is persuasive when in support of oil as the referent in this part of v. 2 he writes "the two bases of comparison are the 'oil' and the 'dew; the 'flowing beard' is not to the point." See *Psalms III: 101-150*, 252. This does not preclude the beard as also running down over the collar of the robes; it does support the thesis that the oil is flowing over the *pî middôṯāw*.

[29] For definitions of *midāh*, *maḏ* and *peh* see, e.g., *BDB*, 752,753; *HAL*, 2.519, 520; 3.864-866.

one's head was placed ("the mouth of his robes"), as is the case in Exod 39:23 which also describes the robe of Aaron. If this is the meaning of *peh* in 133:2b then the image is of the oil running down onto Aaron's torso. On the other hand, though rarely used to mean "collar," *peh* does have this meaning in Job 30:18. Further, the preposition *ʿal* is used with the construct *pî middôṯāw* in Ps 133:2b and *ʿal* usually means "upon."[30] This lends support to the interpretation of *peh* in verse 2b as meaning "collar" because oil can run upon a "collar" but not upon an "opening."

Finally, Keel has proposed that *middôṯāw* refers to the body, and that the words *ʿal-pî* which precede it, mean "according to."[31] This is a possible meaning of *ʿal-pî*[32] so we could read "according to his measure" in 133:2b. Thus, the phrase *ʿal-pî middôṯāw* in verse 2b can be translated: (1) "upon the collar of his robes," (2) "over the opening of his robes," or (3) "according to his measure." The one constant in all of these translational possibilities is that the image is of the oil working its way down one's body.

The image is of joy and holiness spreading over one because the oil in the first line of verse 2 is the oil of joy and the oil in the second line of this verse is a sacred oil. At a celebration it was generally just the head which was anointed with oil, probably because of the expense of the oil. In verse 2 we read about a liberal use of oil so that it runs down from the head to the beard, and down one's body spreading joy and holiness. This is how good (*ṭôḇ* – vv. 1-2) it is when people dwell in complete unity.

Verse 3a begins with "It is like the dew of Hermon, which falls on the mountains of Zion!" This line tells how "pleasant" (*nāʿîm*– v. 1) it is when people dwell in complete unity. As the oil runs down (*yōrēḏ* [v. 2], *šeyyōrēḏ* [v. 2]) the body (v. 2), so dew falls down (*šeyyōrēḏ* [v. 3]) from Hermon to Jerusalem.[33] The dew moistens the earth as the oil moistens the body.

[30] Rarely, *ʿal* is used to mean "over."

[31] O. Keel, "Kultische Brüderlichkeit – Psalm 133," 71, 72, 74, 75. L. Allen, *Psalms 101-150*, 212, agrees with Keel.

[32] See *BDB*, 805.

[33] Hermon is a 9,232 ft. mountain north of Palestine in the anti-Lebanon range. The elevation of Jerusalem is circa 2,500ft.

Verse 3 continues, "For there the Lord has commanded the blessing, life forevermore."[34] As far as I can determine, no one has yet suggested the possibility that this line is an extension of the similes found earlier in verses 2 and 3. The most probable reason for not thinking along these lines is because the image of the dew seems to be dropped at this point. As noted earlier, verse 2 and the first line of verse 3 constitute two similes which explain the goodness and pleasantness of brotherly unity in terms of festive oil, consecrating oil and dew respectively. The last line in verse 3 does not seem to continue this image.

There is a formal characteristic which links the concluding line of the psalm to the preceding figures of speech. The inseparable preposition *k* begins each simile and the word *kî* begins the last line of verse 3. This similarity of sound at the commencement of these parts of the psalm at least leaves open the possibility that the final words of the psalm are part of the similes which illustrate verse 1.

This indeed appears to be the case. The word "beard" (*zāqān*) is the last word of the first image (the oil of joy) and the first word of the second image (the holy oil). In both cases the oil is flowing down the beard. Similarly, the image of Zion as that on which the dew falls (the first line in v. 3) concludes the third image in the psalm and it begins the last line of verse 3 as the place on which God's blessing comes, or in which it is given;[35] the word "Zion" (*ṣîyôn*) is found at the end of the first line of verse 3, and the word "there" (*šām*), referring to Zion, is found at the beginning of the last line of verse 3.[36] Both in verse 2 and in verse 3 there is a

[34] Most exegetes agree that the words "life forevermore" do not refer to eternal life. See, e.g., Anderson, *The Book of Psalms*, 2:887; Jacquet, *Les Psaumes*, 3:458; Oesterley, *The Psalms*, 536; C. & E. Briggs, *The Book of Psalms*, 1.475. The phrase may refer to a quality of life. This is supported by 11 QPs (col.23) where *šālôm ʿal yiśrāʾēl* ("peace upon Israel") is substituted for *ḥayyim* ("life").

[35] The clause, "For there the Lord has ordained the blessing," is ambiguous. It could refer either to God's blessing being given to Jerusalem or to it being given in Jerusalem.

[36] Some have noted that the psalmist has formed an alliteration with *ṣiwwāh* (he commanded- v. 3b) and *ṣiyôn* ("Zion"- v. 3). This would be another way of referring, at the beginning of the second line of v. 3, to Zion.

movement from that which causes human pleasure (oil of joy [v. 2], dew [v. 3]) to the bestowing of God's favor (a holy oil, [v. 2], God's blessing [v. 3]).

In such a way the last line of verse 3 continues the image of how good and pleasant it is when people are completely united.[37] It is as good as if both the oil of joy and a holy oil flowed down (*yōrēd, šeyyōrēd* – v. 2) one's body. It is as pleasant as dew and God's blessing falling down (*šeyyōrēd*) upon Zion. Each couplet is about the spread of both joy and grace.

To sum up, I have argued that Ps 133:2-3 contain four images which are designed to explain "How good and how pleasant it is when people dwell in unity" (v. 1). They are not primarily linked to each other rather than to verse 1, as Beaucamp and Berlin have claimed; they are metaphorical elaborations of verse 1. Various contextual considerations show that the use of *šemen* in verse 2 is a case of "deliberate ambiguity" designed to refer both to the festive oil and to a holy oil. Furthermore, the structure of verses 2-3 favors viewing the second line of verse 3 as a continuation of the images for unity found earlier in verses 2-3, rather than as a summary verse or as the focal point;[38] verse 1 is the focal point of this psalm. Finally, verses 2 and 3 not only explain how good (v. 2) and how pleasant (v. 3) is unity, as Auffret pointed out, but each verse treats this goodness or pleasantness respectively by images expressive both of joy and of grace. To live with others in unity is to live in the sphere of joy and in the sphere of the blessing.

[37] In this connection the observation of O. Keel, "Kultische Brüderlichkeit," 76, that *kî* at the beginning of the last line of v. 3 is emphatic ("for") rather than causal ("because") should be noted.

[38] The last line of v. 3 continues the elaboration of "how good and how pleasant it is when brothers dwell in unity" (v. 1). It links up directly to v. 1 by means of an *inclusio* of sound: *'aḥîm* ("brothers–" v. 1) and *ḥayyîm* ("life–" v. 3). "Moreover, each line ends with a superlative expression and contains a pair of positive terms, *ṭôḇ* 'good' and *nā'îm* 'pleasant', *bĕrākāh* 'blessing' and *ḥayyîm*." L. Allen, *Psalms 101-150*, 214, 215.

God as the Unitive Force and the Encouragement of Psalm 133

Psalm 133 can inspire parents, and in such a way also children, to live in fellowship with others by showing us how good and how pleasant is this type of life. [39] It is as good as the oil which moisturizes and soothes dry skin, moving us from the workaday world into the world of relaxation and joy.[40] To live with others is as good as a holy oil which signifies God's special presence. It is as good as having one's whole self washed with the oil of joy and holiness (v. 2). The good oil (v. 2) depicts both public joy and private communion with God to show how good is unity with others.

Fellowship with others is as pleasant as the dew of Hermon falling on the mountains of Zion (v. 3). It is as pleasant as living in the sphere of God's blessing (v. 3). As the dew falls from Hermon to Zion (the first line of v. 3), the blessing descends from God to Zion (the second line of v. 3) to show how pleasant unity is. To live with others in unity is to live where the blessing descends.

There will be times when in good conscience we must disagree with, and stand in opposition to, the views and practices of others; we should never let this cause us to abandon, however, the attempt to live justly with them.

[39] H. Gunkel, *Einleitung in die Psalmen* (Göttingen: Vandenhoeck & Ruprecht, 1933) 384, 385, J. K. Kuntz, "The Canonical Wisdom Psalms," 190, 191, 210, and R. B. Y. Scott, *The Way of Wisdom*, 197, 198, have noted the wisdom elements found in this psalm (e.g., the use of the third person). This may suggest that Psalm 133 is an exhortation to live in unity.

[40] Previous observations must be repeated for a short time in order to show how Ps 133 can help us with both the intrahuman and the interhuman obstacles to community which have just been treated. C. Broyles' comments in *The Conflict of Faith and Experience in the Psalms*, 32, 33, are apropos:

> "Because poetry does not convey meaning additively–as a sum of individual items– but globally or integrally– as a network– the interpretive process cannot proceed simply in a linear, step-by-step fashion. Research must be a repeated process of analysis and synthesis, a repeated engagement of wholes and parts. It cannot simply move along a line, but must try to move along an upward spiral, returning and returning to the same facets of a text but each time, after reflection upon the other features, at a higher level of understanding."

CHAPTER 10

CONCLUSION

This book correlates the poetry of seven psalms and the stress experienced by many parents. It is not a haphazard connection; the type of theotherapy that composes people is integrally present in the Psalms.

A work such as this one inevitably opens itself up to numerous methodological questions. I have attempted to do justice both to the poetry of seven psalms and to the contemporary experience of many parents and children. Poetic and rhetorical criticisms were employed to understand the former, and modern literature, psychological, sociological and communication theories to highlight the latter. Only seven psalms were treated so as not to overreach, but rather to ground observations regarding parenting thoroughly in psalmic poetics.

The results of this study are as follows. First, there is an integral connection between trust, a sense of security and the ability to enter into healthy relationships. Second, the poetry of the seven psalms which are treated in this book provides a solid foundation for parents to emotionally experience and provide for their children the trust that engenders a strong sense of security. Third, it is from this well-grounded assurance that healthy relationships begin, grow and continue despite difficulties.

APPENDIX: "MOSCOW NIGHTS"

As we have seen in chapter three ("Psalm 131 and a Secure Base for Children"), no matter how old one gets one needs an attachment figure. As more families experience divorce, more parents are placed in situations of need: situations which threaten their role as attachment figures to both young and adult children. This type of situation is portrayed in Marly Swick's short story, "Moscow Nights."

Swick writes about a young man, Jonathan, whose parents have divorced within "the last year or so." Jonathan himself has recently experienced a separation; his girl friend, Farrell, with whom "he had been in love ... most of his adult life," has terminated the relationship and moved out to an apartment of her own. Jonathan seeks to reestablish the relationship under the guise of remaining in touch as friends.

Both mother and son are in need, and so at times the mother feels compelled to invert the care giver-care receiver relationship with her son. She begins to confide in him "things he did not particularly want to hear. Intimate things. Private feelings. Details of her sex life." Early in the story we read that she calls her son up and informs him that she is going to have an abortion; she asks him to take her to Planned Parenthood.[1]

All of these disclosures make Jonathan very uncomfortable. He complains to his former girl friend. "I don't think she should tell me these things. I'm her *son*, for Christ's sake... It gives me the creeps." Farrell responds, "I think it's nice she's so open and that she trusts you. She's treating you like an adult." This does not satisfy Jonathan who counters, "I'm not an adult! I'm her kid. No matter how old I am, she's still my *mother*."[2]

[1] M. Swick, "Moscow Nights," *The Atlantic* (August, 1990) 59,60.
[2] Ibid., 60.

The situation with Farrell worsens. One night Jonathan goes to Farrell's apartment only to discover that she has probably found someone else. From there, he drives to his mother's house "surprised that the night was still young when he felt so old and tired. And at the same time young – a small, very old, very tired child in need of comfort." His mother comforts him with words and with touches.

> The barking next door had escalated into a frenzied, lovelorn howling. A canine aria of outraged loss. Jonathan leaped up, walked over to the open window, and yelled, 'Quiet'!
>
> For a moment there was a stunned silence. Then the dog started up again – a tentative whimper at first, then a yelp, then a full-fledged howl. Jonathan slammed the window shut and went back to bed.

There, he played canasta with his mother when "he suddenly had an odd sensation, as if he were a ventriloquist and that dog out there were his dummy, whimpering and howling in the night."[3]

Swick gives us an artist's sensitive insight into the need for an attachment figure throughout one's life and the difficulties that ensue when family divisions make it hard for the parent to be a secure attachment figure.

[3] Ibid., 67,68.

WORKS CITED

Aejmelaeus, A. *The Traditional Prayer in the Psalms*. BZAW, 167. Berlin: Walter De Gruyter, 1986.

Agee, J. "Knoxville: Summer 1915." In *The Modern Short Story*, pp.360-363. Ed. W. Shanahan. New York: Van Nostrand Reinhold, 1968.

Ainsworth, M., S. Bell, & D. Stayton. "Individual Differences in Strange Situation Behavior of One-Year-Olds." In *The Origins of Human Social Relations*, pp. 17-51. H. R. Schaffer, ed. London: Academic, 1971.

Ainsworth, M. et. al. *Patterns of Attachment: Assessed in the Strange Situation and at Home*. Hillsdale, NJ: Erlbaum, 1978.

Ainsworth, M. "Social Development in the First Year of Life: Maternal Influences on Infant-Mother Attachment." In *Developments in Psychiatric Research*. Ed. J. Tanner. London: Tavistock, 1977.

Albertz, R. *Weltschöpfung und Menschenschöpfung*. Stuttgart: Calwer, 1974.

—. *Personliche Frömmigkeit und offizielle Religion*. Stuttgart: Calwer, 1978.

Albright, W. "The Old Testament and Canaanite Language and Literature." *Catholic Biblical Quarterly*. 7 (1945): 5-31.

—. "The Amarna Letters." In *Ancient Near Eastern Texts*, ed. J. Pritchard. Princeton: Princeton University Press, 1950.

Alexander, J. *The Psalms*. Reprinted Grand Rapids: Baker, 1975.

Allen, L. *Psalms 101-150*. Waco,TX: Word, 1983.

Alter, R. *The Art of Biblical Poetry*. New York: Basic Books, 1985.

—. *The World of Biblical Literature*. New York: Basic, 1992.

Anderson, A. *The Book of Psalms*. NCB, 2 vols. London: Oliphants, 1972.

Anderson, B. *Out of the Depths: The Psalms Speak for Us Today*. Philadelphia: Westminster, 1974.

Arend, R., F. Gove & L. Stroufe. "Continuity of Individual Adaptations from Infancy to Kindergarten: A Predictive Study of Ego-resiliency and Curiosity in Preschoolers." *Child Development* 50 (1979): 950-59.

Atkins, S. *Johann Wolfgang von Goethe, Faust I and II*. Cambridge: Suhrkomp/Insel, 1984.

Auffret, P. "Essai sur la structure littéraire du Psaume 133." *Biblische Notizen* 27 (1985): 22-34.

Barr, J. *The Semantics of Biblical Language*. Oxford: Oxford University Press, 1961.
Baumgartner, W. "Ras Schamra und das Alte Testament." *Theologische Rundschau* 13 (1941): 3-31.
Bazak, J. "Numerical Devices in Biblical Poetry." *Vetus Testamentum* 38 (1988): 333-337.
Beaucamp, E. *Le Psautier: Pss.1-72*. Paris: J. Gabalda, 1976.
—. "Vers les pâturages de Yahweh." *Bible et Vie Chrétienne* 32 (1960): 47-57.
Beaumarchais, P. *Le barbier de Seville*. NCL: Paris: Larousse, 1970.
Bellah, R., R. Madsen, W. Sullivan, A. Swidler, & S. Tipton, *Habits of the Heart: Individualism and Commitment in American Life*. Berkeley: University of California Press, 1985.
Bellinger, W. *Psalmody and Prophecy*. JSOTSS, 27. Sheffield: JSOT, 1984.
—. *Psalms*. Peabody, MA: Hendrickson, 1990.
Belsky, J. & T. Nezworski. "Clinical Implications of Attachment." In *Clinical Implications of Attachment*, pp. 3-17. Eds. J. Belsky & T. Nezworski. Hillsdale, NJ: Erlbaum, 1988.
—. "Maternal, Infant, and Social-Contextual Determinants of Attachment Security." In *Clinical Implications of Attachment*, pp.41-94. Eds. J. Belsky & T. Nezworski.: Hillsdale, NJ: Erlbaum, 1988.
Benson, H. *The Mind/Body Effect*. New York: Simon & Schuster, 1979.
—. *The Relaxation Technique*. New York: Morrow, 1975.
Bergland, R. *The Fabric of Mind*. New York: Viking, 1986.
Berlin, A. "Grammatical Aspects of Biblical Parallelism." *Hebrew Union College Annual* 50 (1979): 17-43.
—. *The Dynamics of Biblical Parallelism*. Bloomington: Indiana U., 1985.
—. "On the Interpretation of Psalm 133." In *Directions in Biblical Hebrew Poetry*, pp.141-47. Ed. E. R. Follis. JSOTSS, 40. Sheffield: JSOT, 1987.
Beyerlin, W. *Die Rettung der Bedrängten in den Feind- psalmen der Einzelnen auf institutionelle Zussamenhänge untersucht*. FRLANT, 99. Göttingen: Vandenhoeck & Ruprecht, 1970.
—. *Werden und Wesen des 107 Psalms*, BZAW, 153. Berlin/New York: De Gruyter, 1979.
Blaiklock, E. *Commentary on the Psalms*. Philadelphia: Holmgren, 1971.
Booij, T. "The Hebrew Text of Psalm XCII, 11." *Vetus Testamentum* 38 (1988): 210-213.
Boylan, P. *The Psalms*. Dublin: M. H. Gill, 1936.
Bowlby, J. *Attachment*. New York: Basic, 1969.
—. *Loss, Sadness and Depression*. New York: Basic, 1980.

—. *A Secure Base*. New York: Basic, 1988.
—. *Separation*. New York: Basic, 1973.
Briggs, C.& E. *The Book of Psalms*. ICC, 2 vols. New York: Scribners', 1906.
Broyles, C. *The Conflict of Faith and Experience in the Psalms: A Form-Critical and Theological Study*. JSOTSS, 52. Sheffield: JSOT, 1989.
Brueggemann, W. "From Hurt to Joy, From Death to Life." *Interpretation* 28 (1974): 3-19.
—. "Psalms and the Life of Faith: A Suggested Typology of Function," *Journal for the Study of the Old Testament* 17 (1980): 3-32.
—. *Israel's Praise: Doxology Against Idolatry and Ideology*. Philadelphia: Fortress, 1988.
—. *Abiding Astonishment: Psalms, Modernity and the Making of History*. LCBI. Louisville: Westminster/ John Knox, 1991.
Buber, M. *Good and Evil: Two Interpretations*. New York: Scribners, 1953.
Buechner, F. *A Wizard's Tide*. San Francisco: Harper & Row, 1990.
Burch, J. R. & R. J. Hunter. "Pastoral Theology, Protestant." In *Dictionary of Pastoral Care and Counseling*, pp. 867-872. General Editor, R. J. Hunter. Nashville: Abingdon, 1989.
Cahill, M. "The Oracles Against the Nations: Synthesis and Analysis for Today." *Louvain Studies* 16 (1991): 121-136.
Caird, G. *The Gospel of St. Luke*. New York: Seabury, 1963.
Capps, D. *Biblical Approaches to Pastoral Counseling*. Philadelphia: Westminster, 1981.
—. "Bible: Pastoral Use and Interpretation of." In *Dictionary of Pastoral Care and Counseling*, pp. 82-85. General Editor, R. J. Hunter. Nashville: Abingdon, 1989.
—. *Reframing: A New Method in Pastoral Care*. Philadelphia: Fortress, 1990.
—. *The Poet's Gift: Toward the Renewal of Pastoral Care*. Philadelphia: Westminster/John Knox, 1993.
Carroll, L. *The Annotated Alice: Alice's Adventures in Wonderland and Through the Looking Glass*. Edited by M. Gardner. New York: Bramhall House, 1960.
Castelot, J. & A. Cody, O.S.B., "Religious Institutions of Israel," In *The New Jerome Biblical Commentary*, pp. 1253-83. Editors, R.E. Brown, S.S., J.A. Fitzmyer, S.J., R.E. Murphy, O.Carm. Englewood Cliffs, NJ: Prentice Hall, 1990.
Cather, W. *My Antonia*. Boston: Houghton Mifflin, 1977.
—. *The Professor's House*. New York: Random House, 1973.
Chatman, S. *A Theory of Meter*. The Hague: Mouton, 1965.

Clark-Lempers, D., J. Lempers & A. Netusil. "Family Financial Stress, Parental Support and Young Adolescents' Academic Achievement and Depressive Symptoms." *Journal of Early Adolescence* 10 (1990): 21-36.

Clarke-Stewart, K. & B. Bailey. "Adjusting to Divorce. Why Do Men Have It Easier?" *Journal of Divorce* 13 (1989): 75-94.

Cohen, L. "Measurement of Coping in Stress and Health." In *Issues in Research Methodology*, pp. 283-305. Eds. S. Kasl & C. Cooper. New York: J. Wiley, 1987.

Coleridge, S. T. *Biographia Literaria*. Ed. J. Shawcross. Oxford: Oxford University Press, 1954.

Collins, T. *Line Forms in Hebrew Poetry*. Rome: Pontifical Biblical Institute, 1978.

Conzelmann, H. *The Theology of St. Luke*. New York: Harper & Row, 1960.

Cousins, N. *Anatomy of an Illness*. New York: Norton, 1979.

—. *Head First: The Biology of Hope*. New York: Dutton, 1989.

—. *The Healing Heart*. New York: Norton, 1983.

Cox, D. *The Psalms in the Life of God's People*. St. Paul: Slough, 1984.

Cox, J., producer. *The Barber of Seville*. New York: National Video, 1982.

Craddock, F. *Luke*. Interpretation. Louisville: John Knox, 1990.

Craghan, J. *The Psalms*. Wilmington: Glazier, 1985.

Crawford, P. "Cedar." In P. Achtemeier, Gen. Ed., *Harper's Bible Commentary*. San Francisco: Harper & Row, 1985, 159.

Creed, J. *The Gospel According to St. Luke*. New York: St. Martin's Press, 1969.

Crittendon, P. "Relationships at Risk." In *Clinical Implications of Attachment*, pp. 136-174. Child Psychology. Hillsdale, NJ: Erlbaum, 1988.

Croft, S. *The Identity of the Individual in the Psalms*. JSOTSS, 44. Sheffield: JSOT, 1987.

Crusemann, F. *Studien zur Formgeschichte von Hymnus und Danklied in Israel*. Wissenschaftliche Monographien zum Alten und Neuen Testament, 32. Neukirchener: Neukirchener Verlag, 1969.

Custer, J. "The Poetics of Complaint at the Limits of Theology." S.T.D. diss., Pontificia Universitas Gregoriana, 1987.

Dahood, M. *Psalms I: 1-50*. AB, 16. Garden City, NY: Doubleday, 1966.

—. *Psalms II: 51-100*. AB, 17. Garden City, NY: Doubleday, 1968.

—. *Psalms III: 101-150*. AB, 17A. Garden City , NY: Doubleday, 1970.

—. "Stichometry and Destiny in Ps.23:4." *Biblica* 60 (1979): 417-19.

—. "Ugaritic-Hebrew Parallel Pairs." In *Ras Shamra Parallels*. Ed. L. Fisher. Vols. I, II, III. Rome: Pontifical Biblical Institute, 1972, 1975, 1979.

Danker, F. *Luke*. Proclamation Commentaries. Philadelphia: Fortress, 1987.
Davis, E. "Exploding the Limits: Form and Function of Psalm 22." *Journal for the Study of the Old Testament* 53 (1992): 93-105.
Deetz, S. "Metaphors and the Discursive Production and Reproduction of Organization." In *Organization- Communication: Emerging Perspectives*, pp. 168-182. Ed. L. Thayer. Norwood, NJ: Ablex, 1986.
Deissler, A. *Die Psalmen*. Dusseldorf: Patmos, 1964.
Delitzsch, F. *Biblical Commentary on the Psalms*. Two Vols. Edinburgh: T. & T. Clark, 1871.
Delozier, P. J. "Attachment Theory and Child Abuse." In *The Place of Attachment in Human Behavior*, pp. 95- 117. Eds. C. M. Parkes & J. Stevenson-Hinde. New York: Basic, 1982.
Dion, P. "The Structure of Isaiah 42.10-17 as Approached Through Versification and Distribution of Poetic Devices." *Journal for the Study of the Old Testament* 49 (1991): 113-124.
Donner, H. "Ugaritismen in der Psalmenforschung." *Zeitschrift für die alttestamentliche Wissenschaft* 79 (1967): 322-50.
Douglas, M. *Purity and Danger*. London: Routledge & Kegan Paul, 1966.
Eaton, J. H. *Kingship and the Psalms*. SBT, 32. Naperville, IL: Allenson, 1976.
—. *The Psalms*. London: SCM, 1967.
Ehrlich, A. *Die Psalmen*. Berlin: Poppelauer, 1905.
Eliot, R. *Stress and the Major Cardiovascular Disorders*. Mount Kisco, New York: Futura, 1979.
Elkind, D. *All Grown Up and No Place to Go: Teenagers in Crisis*. Reading, MA: Addison-Wesley, 1984.
—. *Miseducation: Preschoolers at Risk*. New York: Alfred Knopf, 1987.
—. *The Hurried Child: Growing Up Too Fast Too Soon*. rev. ed. Reading, MA: Addison-Wesley, 1988.
Ellis, E. *The Gospel of Luke*. Revised Edition. Greenwood: Attic, 1974.
Ember, A. "The Pluralis intensivus in Hebrew." *American Journal of Semitic Languages and Literatures* 21 (1905): 195.
Fisch, H. *Poetry with a Purpose: Biblical Literature and Interpretation*. Indiana Studies in Biblical Literature. Bloomington: Indiana University Press, 1990.
Fitzmyer, J. *Luke X-XXIV*. AB, 28A. Garden City, NY: Doubleday, 1985.
Flanagan, N. "The What and How of Salvation in Luke- Acts." In *Sin, Salvation and the Spirit*, pp. 203-13. Ed. D. Durkin. Collegeville, MN: Liturgical, 1979.
Freedman, D. *Pottery, Poetry and Prophecy: Studies in Early Hebrew Poetry*. Winona Lake, IN: Eisenbrauns, 1980.

—. "Acrostic Poems in the Hebrew Bible: Alphabetic and Otherwise." *Catholic Biblical Quarterly*. 48 (1986): 408-31.

Geller, S. *Parallelism in Early Biblical Poetry*. Decatur, GA: Scholars Press, 1979.

—. "Theory and Method in the Study of Biblical Poetry." *Jewish Quarterly Review* 73 (1982): 65-77.

George, C., N. Kaplan & M. Main. "The Attachment Inter- View for Adults." Unpublished manuscript. University of California, Berkeley.

Gerstenberger. E. *Der bittende Mensch: Bittritual und Klagelied des Einzelnen im Alten Testament*. WMANT, 51. Neukirchen-Vluyn: Neukirchener, 1980.

—. *Psalms: Part I*. FOTL, 14. Grand Rapids: Eerdmans, 1988.

Gesenius, W. *A Hebrew and English Lexicon of the Old Testament*. Edited by F. Brown, S. R. Driver & C. Briggs. Oxford: Clarendon, 1907.

Glueck, N. *Hesed in the Hebrew Bible*. Cincinnati: Hebrew Union, 1967.

Goldingay, J. "Repetition and Variation in the Psalms." *Jewish Quarterly Review* 68 (1978): 146-151.

Graham, W. *Beyond the Written Word: Oral Aspects of Scripture in the History of Religion*. New York: Cambridge University Press, 1987.

Grassi, J. *God Makes Me Laugh*. GNS, 17. Wilmington, DE: Glazier, 1986.

Green, E. & K. *Beyond Biofeedback*. New York: Delacorte, 1977.

Greenberg, M. & M. Speltz. "Attachment and the Ontogeny of Conduct Problems." In *Clinical Implications of Attachment*, pp. 177-209. Eds. J. Belsky & T. Nezworski. Hillsdale, NJ: Erlbaum, 1988.

Greenstein, E. "How Does Parallelism Mean?" In *A Sense of Text: The Art of Language in the Study of Biblical Literature*, pp. 41-79. Eds. S. Geller, E. Greenstein, A. Berlin. Winona Lake, IN.: Eisenbrauns, 1982.

Grieve, K. & J. Heminway. *In Search of Paradise*. New York: Granada Television International, 1991.

Grossberg, D. *Centripetal and Centrifugal Structures in Biblical Poetry*. Atlanta: Scholars Press, 1989.

Grossmann, K. E., K. Grossmann & A. Schwunn. "Capturing the Wider View of Attachment: A Reanalysis of Ainsworth's Strange Situation." In *Measuring Emotions in Infants and Children*. Eds. C. Izard & P. Read. New York: Cambridge University Press, 1986.

Gunkel, H. *Einleitung in die Psalmen*. Göttingen: Vandenhoeck & Ruprecht, 1933.

Hathaway, W. 7 K. Pargament. "The Religious Dimension of Coping: Implications for Prevention and Promotion." In *Religion and Pre-*

vention in Mental Health, pp. 65-92. Eds. K. Pargament & K. Maton. PHS, 9: New York: Haworth, 1991.

Hays, R. *The Faith of Jesus Christ*. SBLDS, 56. Atlanta: Scholars Press, 1983.

Hecht, A. *The Essential Herbert*. New York: Ecco, 1987.

Herder, J. G. *The Spirit of Hebrew Poetry*. Burlington, VT: Edward Smith, 1933.

Hess, R. "Hebrew Psalms and Amarna Correspondondence from Jerusalem: Some Comparisons and Implications." *Zeitschrift für die alttestamentliche Wissenschaft* 101 (1988): 249-65.

Hollady, W. *The Psalms through Three Thousand Years: Prayerbook of a Cloud of Witnesses*. Minneapolis: Fortress, 1993.

Jacquet, L. *Les Psaumes et le coeur de l'homme*. Three vols. Brussels: Duculot, 1975.

Jameson, F. *The Political Unconscious: Narrative as a Socially Symbolic Act*. Ithaca: Cornell University Press, 1981.

Johnson, A. *The Cult Prophet in Ancient Israel*. Cardiff: University of Wales, 1962.

—. *Sacral Kingship in Ancient Israel*. Cardiff: University of Wales, 1967.

Johnson, L. *The Writings of the New Testament: An Interpretation*. Philadelphia: Fortress, 1986.

Kaiser, W. *Das sprachliche Kunstwerk. Eine Einführung in die Literaturwissenschaft*. 8th ed. Berne: Francke, 1962.

Keel, O. "Kultische Brüderlichkeit– Psalm 133." *Freiburger Zeitschrift für Philosophie und Theologie* 23 (1976): 68-80.

—. *The Symbolism of the Biblical World*. New York: Crossroad, 1985.

Keller, S. "The American Dream of Community: An Unfinished Agenda." *Sociological Forum* 3 (1988): 167-183.

Kirkpatrick, A. F. *The Book of Psalms*. Cambridge: Cambridge U., 1912.

Kissane, M.*The Book of Psalms*. Dublin: Richview, 1954.

Kittel, R. *Die Psalmen*. Leipzig: Deichert, 1914.

Klein, R. *1 Samuel*. AB, 8. Garden City, NY: Doubleday, 1980.

Knierim, R. "Old Testament Form Criticism Reconsidered." *Interpretation* 27 (1973): 435-468.

Kobak, R. & A. Sceery. "Attachment in Late Adolescence." *Child Development* 59 (1988): 135-46.

Kohler, L. & W. Baumgartner. *Hebräisches und aramaisches Lexikon zum Alten Testament*. Vols. 1-3. Leiden: Brill, 1967-83.

Kohler, L. "Psalm 23." *Zeitschrift für die alttestamentliche Wissenschaft* 68 (1956): 227-234.

Kraus, H.J. *Psalmen*. BKAT, 2 vols. Neukirchen-Vluyn: Neukirchener, 1978.

—. *Theology of the Psalms*. Minneapolis: Augsburg, 1986.
—. *Psalms 1-59: A Commentary*. Minneapolis: Augsburg, 1988.
—. *Psalms 60-150: A Commentary*. Minneapolis: Augsburg, 1989.
Kroll, J. *Gott und Hölle: Der Mythus von Descensuskampf*. Leipzig: Teubner, 1932.
Kugel, J. *The Idea of Biblical Poetry*. New Haven: Yale University Press, 1981.
Kuntz, J. "The Canonical Wisdom Psalms of Ancient Israel." In *Rhetorical Criticism: Essays in Honor of James Muilenberg*, pp. 186-222. Eds. J. Jackson & M. Kessler. Pittsburgh: Pickwick, 1974.
Lagerkvist, P. *Barabbas*. New York: Random, 1989.
Lambourne, R. *Community, Church and Healing*. London: Darton, Longman & Todd, 1963.
Landy, P. "Poetics and Parallelism: Some Comments on James Kugel's *The Idea of Biblical Poetry*." *JSOT* 28 (1984): 61-87.
LaVerdiere, E. *Luke*. NTM, 5. Wilmington: Glazier, 1980.
Lawson, K. & R. Hays. "Self-Esteem and Stress as Factors in Abuse of Children." *Psychological Reports* 65 (1989): 1259-65.
Lazarus, R. & S. Folkman. *Stress, Appraisal and Coping*. New York: Springer, 1984.
Leaney, A.R.C. *A Commentary on the Gospel According to St. Luke*. 2nd edition. London: A. & C. Black, 1966.
Leslie, E. *The Psalms*. Nashville: Abingdon, 1949.
Levin, J. & H. Vanderpool. "Is Frequent Religious Attendance *Really* Conducive to Better Health?" *Social Science and Medicine* 24 (1987): 589-600.
—. "Is Religion Therapeutically Significant for Hypertension?" *Social Science and Medicine* 29 (1989): 69-78.
—. "Religious Factors in Physical Health and the Prevention of Illness." *Religion and Prevention in Mental Health: Conceptual and Empirical Foundations*, 40-56. Eds. K. Pargament & K. Maton. PHS, 9: New York: Haworth, 1991.
Loewenstamm, S. "Ballōtî bĕšāmān raʿănān." *Ugarit Forschungen* 10 (1978): 111-13.
—. "An Additional Remark upon Ps.92:11b." *Ugarit Forschungen* 13 (1981): 302.
Lohr, M. *Psalmenstudien*. BWAT, 3. Berlin: Kohlhammer, 1922.
Loretz, O. "Die Analyse der ugaritischen und hebräischen Poesie mittels Stichometrie und Konsonantenerzählung." *Ugarit Forschungen* 7 (1975): 265-69.
—. "Kolometrie ugaritischer und hebräischer Poesie: Grundlagen, informationstheoretische und literaturwissenschaftliche Aspekte." *Zeitschrift für die alttestamentliche Wissenschaft* 98 (1986): 249-266.

Lowth, R. *De Sacra poesi Hebraeorum*. Oxford: Clarendon, 1753.
Lundbom, J. "Psalm 23: Song of Passage." *Interpretation* 40 (1986): 5-16.
MacNeice, L. "Whitmonday." In *The Collected Poems of Louis MacNeice*. Ed. E.R. Dodds. London: Faber and Faber, 1979.
Magonet, J. "Some Concentric Structures in Psalms." *Heythrop Journal* 23 (1982): 365-76.
Main, M. & R. Goldwyn, "Adult Attachment Classification System." Unpublished Manuscript. University of California, Berkeley.
Main, M. & J. Stadtman. "Infant Response to Rejection of Physical Contact by Mother: Aggression, Avoidance and Conflict." *Journal of the American Academy of Child Psychiatry* 20 (1981): 292-307.
Main, M. & D. Weston. "Quality of Attachment to Mother and to Father Related to Conflict Behavior and the Readiness for Establishing New Relationships." *Child Development* 52 (1981): 932-40.
Main, M., N. Kaplan & J. Cassidy. "Security in Infancy, Childhood and Adulthood: A Move to the Level of Representation." In *Growing Points in Attachment: Theory and Research*, pp. 66-104. Eds. I. Bretherton & E. Waters. Chicago: University of Chicago, 1985.
Malina, B. *Christian Origins and Cultural Anthropology*. Atlanta: John Knox, 1986.
Mannati, M. *Les Psaumes*. Brussels: Desclée De Brouwer, 1966.
Marshall, I.H. *The Gospel of Luke*. NIGTC. Grand Rapids: Eerdmans, 1978.
McCarter, P.K. *1 Samuel*. AB, 8. Garden City, NY: Doubleday, 1980.
McCormick, R. "Discernment in Ethics: What Does It Mean?" A Paper Delivered at Marquette University, Milwaukee, WI., 29 November 1990.
Meichenbaum, D. & M. Jaremko. *Stress Reduction and Prevention*. New York: Plenum, 1983.
Mettinger, T. *In Search of God: The Meaning and Message of the Everlasting Names*. Philadelphia: Fortress, 1988.
Mikre-Selassie, G.A. "Metonymy in The Psalms." *Bible Translator* 44 (1993): 418-25.
Miller, P. *Interpreting the Psalms*. Philadelphia: Fortress, 1986.
Mittmann, S. "Aufbau und Einheit des Danklieds Psalm 23." *Zeitschrift für Theologie und Kirche* 77 (1980).
Morgenstern, J. "Psalm 23." *Journal of Biblical Literature* 65 (1946): 13-24.
Morris, D. "Attachment and Intimacy." In *Intimacy*, pp.305-23. Eds. G. Stricker & M. Fisher. New York: Plenum, 1983.
Mowinckel, S. *Psalmenstudien II*. Kristiana: Dybwad, 1921.
—. *The Psalms in Israel's Worship*. 2 Volumes. Nashville: Abingdon, 1962.

M'Swinney, J. *Psalms and Canticles*. London: Sands, 1901.
Mumby, D. *Communication and Power in Organizations: Discourse, Ideology and Domination*. PEO. Norwood, NJ: Ablex, 1988.
Newsom, C. *Songs of the Sabbath Sacrifice: A Critical Edition*. Atlanta: Scholars Press, 1985.
Nezworski, T., W. Tolan & J. Belsky. "Intervention in Insecure Infant Attachment." In *Clinical Implications of Attachment*, pp. 370-389. Eds. J.Belsky & T. Nezworski. Hillsdale, NJ: Erlbaum, 1988.
Norrin, S. "Ps.133. Zusammenhang und Datierung." *Annual Swedish Theological Institute* 11 (1977/1978): 90-95.
O'Connor, C. "The Structure of Psalm 23." *Louvain Studies* 10 (1985): 205-230.
O'Connor, M. *Hebrew Verse Structure*. Winona Lake, IN.: Eisenbrauns, 1980.
Oesterly, W. *The Psalms*. London: SPCK, 1959.
Olshausen, J. *Die Psalmen*. Leipzig: Hirzel, 1853.
Pardee, D. "The Preposition in Ugaritic." *Ugarit Forschungen* 8 (1976): 215-322.
—. "Ugaritic and Hebrew Metrics." In *Ugarit in Retrospect: Fifty Years of Ugarit and Ugaritic*, pp. 113-130. Ed. G. Young. Winona Lake, IN: Eisenbrauns, 1981.
—. "Un héritage poétique commun." *Le Monde de la Bible*. 48 (March-April, 1987): 45-46.
Payne, I., A. Bergin, K. Bielema, & P. Jenkins. "Review of Religion and Mental Health: Prevention and Enhancement of Psychosocial Functioning." In *Religion and Prevention in Mental Health*. Eds. K. Pargament & K. Maton. New York: Haworth, 1991.
Peguy, C. *God Speaks: Religious Poetry*. New York: Pantheon, 1965.
Pederson, J. *Israel, Its Life and Culture*. London: Oxford University Press, 1940.
Pelletier, K. *Mind as Healer, Mind as Slayer*. New York: Delacorte, 1977.
Perowne, J. *The Book of Psalms*. Grand Rapids: Zondervan, 1966.
Petersen, D. & Richards, K. *Interpreting Hebrew Poetry*. GBS. Philadelphia: Fortress, 1992.
Plantin, H. "Leviternas Veckodagspsalmer i templet." *Svensk Exegetisk Årsbok* 48 (1983): 48-76.
Plummer, A. *The Gospel According to Luke*. ICC. Edinburgh: T. & T. Clark, 1922.
Pondy, L., Morgan, G., Frost, P., & Dandridge, T. *Organizational Symbolism*. Greenwich, CT.: JAI, 1983.
Power, E. "The Shepherd's Two Rods in Modern Palestine and in Some Related Passages of the Old Testament." *Biblica* 9 (1928): 434-442.
—. "Ṣion or Si'on in Psalm 133." *Biblica* 3 (1922): 342-349.

Pritchard, J. *Ancient Near Eastern Texts Relating to the Old Testament.* Princeton: Princeton U., 1969.

Pym, B. *The Sweet Dove Died.* New York: Dalton, 1978.

Raabe, P. *Psalm Structures: A Study of Psalms with Refrains.* JSOTSS, 104. Sheffield: JSOT, 1990.

—. "Deliberate Ambiguity in the Psalter." *Journal of Biblical Literature* 110 (1991): 213-227.

Ravasi, G. *Il libro dei Salmi.* Bologna: Edizione Dehoniane, 1983.

Rich, A. "Double Monologue." In *The Norton Anthology of Poetry*, pp. 1177,1178. Ed. Arthur M. Eastman. New York: Norton, 1970.

Ricoeur, P. "Biblical Hermeneutics." *Semeia* 4 (1975): 75-88.

—. "Philosophy and Religious Language." *Journal of Religion* 54 (1974): 71-85.

Ridderbos, N.H. *Die Psalmen. Stilistische Verfahren und Aufbau mit besonderer Berücksichtigung von Ps 1-41.* BZAW, 117. Berlin/New York: De Gruyter, 1972.

Rieff, P. *The Triumph of the Therapeutic.* Chicago: University of Chicago, 1987.

Ringren, H. *King and Messiah.* Oxford: Oxford University Press, 1955.

Roff, M., S. Sells & M. Golden. *Social Adjustment and Personality Development in Children.* Minneapolis: University of Minnesota, 1972.

Ruether, R. *Mary: The Feminine Face of the Church.* Philadelphia: Westminster, 1977.

Sabourin, L. *Le livre des Psaumes.* RNS, no. 18. Montreal: Belarmin, 1988.

—. *The Psalms.* New York: Alba House, 1970.

Sakenfeld, K. D. *The Meaning of Hesed in the Hebrew Bible.* HSM, 17. Missoula, MT: Scholars Press, 1978.

—. *Faithfulness in Action: Loyalty in Biblical Perspective.* OBT. Philadelphia: Fortress, 1986.

Sarna, N. "The Psalm for the Sabbath Day (Ps 92)." *Journal of Biblical Literature* 81 (1962): 155-68.

Saroyan, W. "The Oranges." In *The Saroyan Special*, pp. 42-45. Ed. W. Saroyan. New York: Harcourt, Brace & Co., 1948.

Scott, B. *Hear Then the Parable.* Minneapolis: Fortress, 1990.

Scott, R. B. Y. *The Way of Wisdom in the Old Testament.* New York: Macmillan, 1971.

Seybold, K. *Das Gebet des Kranken im Alten Testament.* BWANT, 99. Stuttgart: Kohlhammer, 1973.

Shelley, P. B. "The Defence of Poetry." In *Shelley's Literary and Philosophical Criticism*, pp. 120-159. Ed. J. Shawcross. London: Humphrey Milford, 1932.

Skehan, P. W. *Studies in Israelite Poetry*. CBQMS, 1. Washington, DC: CBA, 1971.

Snaith, N. *Five Psalms*. London: Epworth, 1938.

Spengler, O. *Gedanken*. Munich: C.H. Beck'sche, 1941.

Stoebe, H. "Bedeutung und Geschichte des Begriffes häsäd." Munster: Unpublished Doctoral dissertation, 1951.

Stroufe, L. "Attachment-Classification from the Perspective of Infant-Caregiver Relationships and Infant Temperament." *Child Development* 56 (1985): 1-14.

—. "Patterns of Individual Adaptation from Infancy to Preschool: The Roots of Maladaptation and Competence." In *Minnesota Symposia on Child Psychology*, pp. 41-83. Ed. M. Perlmutter. Vol. 16; Hillsdale, NJ: Erlbaum, 1983.

—. "The Role of Infant-Caregiver Attachment in Development." In *Clinical Implications of Attach- ment*, pp. 18-40. Eds. J. Belsky & T. Nezworski. CP: Hillsdale, N.J.: L. Erlbaum, 1988.

Stuhlmueller, C. *Psalms I*. OTM, 21. Wilmington, DE: Glazier, 1983.

—. *Psalms II*. OTM, 22. Wilmington, DE: Glazier, 1983.

Swick, M. "Moscow Nights." *The Atlantic* 266 (1990): 59-68.

Sylva, D. "The Changing of Images in Ps 23,5. 6." *Zeitschrift für die alttestamentliche Wissenschaft* 102 (1990): 111-116.

Tannehill, R. *The Narrative Unity of Luke-Acts-Volume 1: The Gospel According to Luke*. Philadelphia: Fortress, 1986.

Tate, M. *Psalms 51-100*. WBC, 20. Dallas: Word, 1990.

Thomas, D. W. "ṣalmāweṯ in the Old Testament." *Journal of Semitic Studies* 7 (1962): 191-200.

Tromp, N. *Primitive Conceptions of Death and the Netherworld in the Old Testament*. Rome: Pontifical Biblical Institute, 1969.

Tsumura, D. "Sorites in Psalm 133,2-3a." *Biblica* 61 (1980): 416-417.

Tyrell, B. *Christotherapy*. New York: Seabury, 1975.

—. *Christotherapy II: The Fasting and Feasting Heart*. New York: Paulist, 1982.

Untermeyer, L. *Robert Frost*. Washington, DC: Reference Department of the Library of Congress, 1964.

Vogt, E. "The 'Place in Life' of Ps.23." *Biblica* 34 (1953): 194-211.

Walsh, J. "Poetic Style and Structure in Isaiah 41." SBL-AAR Mid-Atlantic Region Meeting, 1990.

Waltke, B. & M. O'Connor. *An Introduction to Biblical Hebrew Syntax*. Winona Lake, IN: Eisenbrauns, 1990.

Warren, R.P. "Star-Fall." In *Now and Then: Poems 1976-1978*. New York: Random House, 1978.

—. *A Place To Come To*. New York: Random House, 1977.

Watson, W. "The Hidden Simile in Psalm 133." *Biblica* 60 (1979): 108-109.

Watzlawick, P., J. Weakland & R. Fisch. *Change: Principles of Problem Formation and Problem Resolution*. New York: Norton, 1974.

Weingreen, J. *A Practical Grammar of Classical Hebrew*. 2nd ed. Oxford: Clarendon, 1959.

Weiser, A. *The Psalms*. OTL. Philadelphia: Westminster, 1962.

Westermann, C. *The Living Psalms*. Grand Rapids: Eerdmans, 1989.

—. *The Praise of God in the Psalms*. Richmond: John Knox, 1961.

—. *The Psalms: Structure, Context and Message*. Minneapolis: Augsburg, 1980.

Wette, W. M. L. De. *Commentar über die Psalmen*. Heidelberg: Mohr, 1856.

Wharton, E. *Hudson River Bracketed*. New York: Appleton, 1929.

—. *Summer*. New York: Macmillan, 1981.

—. *The Touchstone*. New York: Harper, 1991.

Wilder, A. N. *Grace Confounding: Poems*. Philadelphia: Fortress, 1972.

—. *Theopoetic*. Philadelphia: Fortress, 1976.

Work, W., G. Parker & E. Cowen. "The Impact of Life Stressors on Childhood Adjustment: Multiple Perspectives." *Journal of Community Psychology* 18 (1990): 73-78.

Yerushalmi, Y. H. *Zakhor: Jewish History and Jewish Memory*. Seattle: University of Washington, 1982.

Zahn-Waxler, C. & M. Radke-Yarrow & R. King. "Childrearing and Children's Prosocial Initiations Toward Victims of Distress." *Child Development* 50 (1979): 319-30.

INDEX OF SUBJECTS

INDEX OF AUTHORS

INDEX OF SCRIPTURAL REFERENCES

ORIENTALISTE, KLEIN DALENSTRAAT 42, B-3020 HERENT